Living Well

PRAYERFUL MEDITATIVE STREAMS
SCRIPTURE PRAYERS

PrayStill

TRILOGY CHRISTIAN PUBLISHERS
TUSTIN, CA

Trilogy Christian Publishers

A Wholly Owned Subsidary of Trinity Broadcasting Network

2442 Michelle Drive

Tustin, CA 92780

10 9 8 7 6 5 4 3 2 1

Library of Congress Cataloging-in-Publication Data is available.

ISBN 978-1-64088-347-5

ISBN 978-1-64088-348-2 (ebook)

t

All dedication for this book is the to the expressed WORD of God's Kingdom living in people's perspectives and especially in the encouragements that motivate and inspire persistence.

Preface

Scripture Prayers is a compilation of daily prayers posed as collects, poetry, prayers meditations. The method for receiving writings is done through Lectio Divina type process that allows for free expression of living in the WORD of God. Meditative and expressive creativity is inspired in the development of refining scriptures.

The scriptures are chosen from five different sources

1. Spirit driven selections

2. Tres Dias Weekend Scriptures

3. FDBD.org

4. You Version Bible daily scripture

5. Bible Gateway daily scriptures

PrayStill is the band's name. The prayer posts originated in my "PrayStill" Facebook page after encouragement from personal groups requesting and suggesting inspiration for publishing a collection.

Acknowledgements

Much gratitude and appreciation is due to those who have helped put the foundational components to be able to get to publish

Sarah Edwards Seelye Eighmy – Limerick instructor

George Wells Eighmy Jr - Morning Prayers

Arielle Katherine and Patricia – Family support

Tres Dias Community – Deep Dive scripture Perspective

Episcopal group - Lectio Divina

St Anthony Fairfield – Corporal meditation

PrayStill - Facebook followers

FDBD.org - Group encouragements

JRad4Jesus – Prayerful encouragement

LB – AWI Personal text encouragements

TBN, WIHS, WFIF, The Message, and every beautiful bold pastor

Introduction

Make the best moment of your day in quiet reflective meditation focusing on the joy of Scripture in the now. The year of this writing, 2018, the stars align and Ash Wednesday falls on Valentine's Day and Easter falls on April Fools. The Heavenly falls over the worldly. Hopefully this inspires time alone and together in the word of God.

Acronym Keys

TBTJC=Thanks Be To Jesus Christ

TBTG=Thanks Be To God

TBTHS=Thanks Be To Holy Spirit

TBTHT=Thanks Be To Holy Trinity

3N1=Three In One

JANUARY 1

PrayStill

Psalm 19:14
May the words of my mouth and the meditations of my heart be pleasing in Your sight, O Lord, my Rock and my Redeemer.

Scripture Prayer: Wisdom

Lord,
I listen in still silence for Your WORDs. Celebrate and rejoice!
Let my lips form praises in your breaths. Make my mouth proclaim your glories. My tongue is made to lift Your name on high and declare Your names to Heaven. My voice is set to vibrate music in a sweet sound.
Dismiss the unspoken in casting away the idle thoughts. Focus all my words to be the channeling reflection back to You! Autopilot my words from beginnings to endings to be the song sounding in sweetness surrounding.
Keep guard and watch over my words falling fresh in Your WORD. I pray to meditate your mediation on my heart. Discern my motive. Refrain my words thoughts and deeds from regret.
Fill my mouth with abundant blessing. Make my intention lift those to new heights. Let me encourage and inspire with calm soothing words of wisdom. Instruct my faithfulness!

Through Jesus Christ Lord and Savior

JANUARY 2

PrayStill

John 6:35-36
Jesus said to them, "I am the bread of life. Whoever comes to me will never be hungry, and whoever believes in me will never be thirsty. But I said to you that you have seen me and yet do not believe."

Scripture Prayer: Waking Word

Lord
WORD walking, alive from the beginning of time in numbered days. First WORD of the fresh scent of creation. Communion of imbibing that fills souls to joyous contentment. Soul nourishment of ages sufficing all needs.

Lord, you are all I need. You are the seed of life who springs shoots of content. You fill me with Your perfect WORD in thoughts and feelings spoken in parable to elevate me to your table. Your spiritual banquet feasts my heart to consume me. I want more of you.

Lord
My gaze lifts to feast on Your eyes.
My hunger and thirst are for You first; You fill me with grace content.
My way and belief, for you is relief, obedience my repent.
Wean me from my physical, to take me supernatural and rest my trust in thee.
TBTG

JANUARY 3

PrayStill

Proverbs 16:3
Commit to the Lord whatever you do, and he will establish your plans.

Scripture Prayer: Delightful Inheritance

God
Adoring treasures of Heaven pouring out abundance. Fulfilling prophecies and dictates and obedience in True loving compassion. Brilliance of crystalline golden silver in waterfalls of holy weaving. truth knowingly wills delicate splashes into time for the eager to see and know. Washing tides lap and cleanse to the receptive.

God
Today, as in all, I am yours. The more I surrender the more you render my path. Weaving words of glory raise up my soul. My content intent is in peaceful communion with you. My future is assured. My less of me is more of You. My little by little is your tidal wave in me.

God
Guard me from deception. Springs of prudent insight and wisdom guide dashing steps to delightful insistence. You hold my cheek, gazing into my understanding. You are the stipulation of my firm and stable rock foundation.
TWBD

JANUARY 4

PrayStill

John 14:13
I will do whatever you ask in my name, so that the Father may be gloried in the Son.

Scripture Prayer: Free Alignment

Spirit
Divine Counseling Advocate. Breadth and depth of breath of life. Heartbeat of the world in rhythm to the pulse of holy attractive persuasion. Crystal clear flowing and going to every end of the earth.

Spirit
Inescapable and always present. Your presence assures and insures my focus away from fear. Unknown pain looks in and cannot see. Peace calm and rolling pastures intoxicate my soul. You are my only idol beaming and streaming and making my gleaming all for You.

Spirit
Walk my steps in the sand. Hover and lift my soul from my quick mire. Take me in, fix my sin, in you is all I'm needing. I'm free to proclaim "Thy Will," makes me stand still, aligned to your word feeding. Your gait is straight and never late, in you I have my leading.
TBTJC

JANUARY 5

PrayStill

Psalm 2:13
Happy are they all who take refuge in him.

Scripture Prayer: All Blessings

Jesus
Precious and Holy in adoration. Throne in the manger of Heavens flowing pastures. Great arm of God holding worlds nations and generations of hearts. Divinely clothing and pouring out all of the highest Heaven to the humble. Heeding in flaring warn the waning desire and righteous retribution.

Jesus
Friend of the meek. Answer to the seek your hand holds my cheek in endearment. Surrounding is your robe encompassing in hope. Everywhere I go you're there. All knowledge is yours, your fortress the cure, you know the before and after.

Jesus
The Rock of foundation ringing and bringing centuries of new life. Your name and face eternally mark all the ages. light of rebuke you shine like a healer's light of salvation. You see all, know all and save all. In Your palace chambers' refuge robe is life abounding.
TBTJC daily new born bread of Heaven.

JANUARY 6

PrayStill

Matthew 2:2
and asked, "Where is the one who has been born king of the Jews? We saw his star when it rose and have come to worship him."

Scripture Prayer: Heavenly Signs

Heavenly Father
Celestial designer speaking in skies of dreams. Take forth the kings and prophets and magicians and light the nights of the sleepers. Pointing arrows from the sky reign in redemption. grace and mercy are right in the preordaining city of love marking for ages to know.

Holy Spirit
Divine ruler of celestial persuasions and essence of all that is solid liquid and gaseous. Surround me in every form. Raise up a Heavenly scent. Dance my tongue and nose and fill my air that goes through breath and blood and fill me.
Rest me x Selah.......   Drink deeply in me the fluid love abiding. Still me x 77.......
Warm presents in chariots, my heart to You illuminate, the anointing oils in ordinance. Awake me. Your gold in me refine, Your myrrh in me incline, Your sense in me define.
Fill me fill me fill me!

Jesus With Us
Babe of centuries we adore You. We worship and implore You. Prophets sing signs to following You. The blind in the valleys don't see You ... but want to remove You?
You are precious and beheld in endearing. Your deep silent sleep is appearing, Your will to awaken, to the joy of Your taking, is the power. Almighty! Ever caring.
Ever living power of ages, You are in me forever.
TBTHT 3N1

JANUARY 7

PrayStill

Matthew 5:6
Blessed are those who hunger and thirst for righteousness, for they will be filled.

Scripture Prayer: Longing Desire

Holy Father
King of all that is righteous. Master of all the law and the prophets. Beautiful enticement of all that is noble and true and Kingdom enhancing. Wellspring of abundance and banquets of delight. Sustenance of souls yearning to learn the right way.

Blessing Spirit
Waterfalls of grace loving mercy spray sprinkle and pour over the worship. The praise sparkles in the holy colors in bowing bows of reigning delight. Hover my soul and fill me to wanting more of Your righteousness in me. Make my small appetite ravenous for You. Quench and quell my unnatural earthly desires in wander. Fill me up with your extra special glorious banquet of communion

Teacher Jesus
You are my portion. You fill me up. You are my decision overflow my cup. The goodness comes in, the goodness comes out. I reap what I sow. Spill me throughout. Thirst me on water make me your wine, I thirst no more in your divine.
Show me in the wheat wine calling. Feast me with Heavenly WORD divining. Devour me in Your WORD unveiling, satisfies my soul for in craving. Fill me past overflowing. Take Your fields of good, good sowing.
TBTJC Beautiful Attitude

JANUARY 8

PrayStill

Isaiah 55:6-7
Seek the Lord while he may be found; call on him while he is near. Let the wicked forsake their ways and the unrighteous their thoughts. Let them turn to the Lord , and he will have mercy on them, and to our God, for he will freely pardon. (NIV)

Scripture Prayer: Exit us

Abba God
Grandest and utmost rock of reception. Foundation of beauty un moved by the anger and wrath of man. Receptor and reflector of the sins of the world. Mighty strong and true is the love that cleanses and washes all to new.

Holy Ghost
Don't depart from me. Let me not wander. Draw me nigh in the night. Let not my sin and fear and anger enter Your Holy Tabernacle. Take away the sin city in me. Forsake away the pain of my heart. Grant me refuge in your field. Lay me down and make me calm. Soak me in your pasture. Selah x 77

Lord Jesus
How much wrath in pain does the world have to offer? The whole of it captures away in Your Holiness. A grain of Your righteous sand wipes away the sins of centuries. Jesus, let me never mock, never forsake, never depart, never go familiar. Jesus, new and fresh, with us, in us, for us, Masterful merciful mighty maker. Lord above all Lords

TBTHS gatekeeper of sanctity

JANUARY 9

PrayStill

1 John 5:14
This is the confidence we have in approaching God: that if we ask anything according to his will, he hears us.

Scripture Prayer: Sign Deliver

God Almighty
Author of water and air. Master of transforming liquid gas and solid with pressure heat and time. Beautiful creator of creation worthy of all praise. Flowing eternal magnet to the repenting.

Holy Spirit
Have my hesitation. Take it away. It is now, yes or no. I have to let it go, there is no time to show, all the different outcomes. It is the time to ask, remove this fear I mask, put me to the task. Your truth is loud and clear. You do allay my fears, You plan my every year. Flow through me. Your river sets me free.

Jesus Redeemer
Precious blood of life in robes of flesh. Pure unending Savior. You know my name you hear my prayer you know just what I need to hear. You lift me up and make me strong in you I find my worship on. You give me faith and I believe to God through you can I receive.
TBTHT 3IN1

JANUARY 10

PrayStill

James 1:5
If any of you lacks wisdom, you should ask God who gives generously to all without finding fault, and it will be given to you.

Scripture Prayer: Pure Holy

Abundant God
Abounding charity and chastity. Pure innocence pouring out for health longevity. Beautiful serene and holy in the chamber of sanctity. City of fortitude patience and restraint.

Maiden Spirit
You restrain my every thought and desire. You child me to know she waits. Her no is wise and bold and waves of love she creates. She knows the unwise know not to ask. The ignorance cannot hear nor mask. Her care is the importance of no. Hairs of snares braid quickly to delight.

Merciful Jesus
Wisdom weeps from your Son of Man's pores. This pure son of God cries out. Let me exhaust myself of me to come to Thee. Through the cross is Deity.

Give me all the pure I want, take away all the want that taunts. Hear my repent, recompense my lent. This forgiveness inheritance is the church bride.
TBTJC

JANUARY 11

PrayStill

Jeremiah 17:7
But blessed is the one who trusts in the Lord whose confidence is in him.

Scripture Prayer: Hope in

Blessing Father
Verdant pastures fruiting delicacies design to spark desire. Flavorful Lord of myriads of stimulation dancing taste smell and touch to the Heavenly produce from on high. Masterful maker of banquet tables of desire. Faith of ages.

Faithful Counselor,
Advocate of assurances. You are my emboldening. I fear not the parch. You lay me down in the field of strength and dreams where dry sands cannot go. Your fresh clear food fills me to blossom. My need to knead the nectar of sweetness fills my heir. Sitting in the knitting of your fabric design You grow me.

Knowing Jesus
Inescapable is your knowing me. Your counselor marks and confirms my every thought. My quench is brought to light. My quell is set to right. Your spirit comes to me increasing. You walk beside me bold, my life in Thee you hold, relentless is Your light in me unceasing. TBTHS truth alive!

JANUARY 12

PrayStill

Colossians 2:2
My goal is that they may be encouraged in heart and united in love, so that they may have the full riches of complete understanding, in order that they may know the mystery of God, namely, Christ.

Scripture Prayer: Ravenous

Indulging God
Circumspect Creator enveloping completeness. Pure delight in the right of righteousness. Patient delay in the receiving anticipation. Fulfilling and glorious communion union without restraining.

Spirit of Purity
Pure in desire for you. Nothing comes between. Strait and great without restraint I feel the calling call. Rooted in desiring love no law can stop at all. The love inside cannot deny the pride laws step aside.

Thankfully Jesus
Better a moment in your sight than any other. My vessel empties and my spirit is with you. Adorned in riches beyond compare, my life alone is in despair, with you is life I give in trust, to you my life is right and just.
TBTJC Pure love

JANUARY 13

PrayStill

Romans 10:17
So then faith cometh by hearing, and hearing by the word of God.

Scripture Prayer: Ear-sight

God communicator,
Input device of the Lord of lords calling. Receptive wave of senses opened. King of kings of the True WORD seeping open fissures of sponge absorption. God of gods tracking to hearts throbbing.

Holy Spirit
Come fall fresh on me. Open my soul to Thee. Wash my winged foot messenger feet to proclaim the beat of holy righteousness. May the path that I step and the message that I carry be acceptable in thy sight oh Lord my light and my persuasion.

Jesus WORD
Expression of angels flows through your face. In your eyes is forgiveness and love with glimmers of mercy and hope. Faith's brow raises the bows sending trust and hope. Beautiful is your gaze upon me.
Jesus be the way, the hope, the faith, the crave.
In thee I cannot stray. The WORD alive in Thee.
Wash my hands and feet, Walk me to the beat.
Quaking rhythm streets, the Path is always Thee.
Make the listen learn, understanding in the earn,
Take my every turn, intent is forth from Thee.
TBTW, WORD or the World

JANUARY 14

PrayStill

Lamentations 3:22-23
It is of the Lord's mercies that we are not consumed, because his compassions fail not. They are new every morning: great is thy faithfulness.

Scripture Prayer: Sustaining love

ABBA God
Merciful kind and true. Always welcome here. Fresh like the dew. light of the sunrise, heart of hope. Eraser of iniquities and assurance of redemption.

Merciful Spirit
My tears grieve away the dust of my skin. My other cheek blushes my hands shake, and I cannot look up. I am made with crooked in me. I am ignorant. I believe my crooked is straight. I am in the corner dead end and am trapped. Help! I am dying.

Lord Jesus
You watch me to my end and pick me up. My Savior, my Redeemer, my Rock, and my Salvation. My truth, my Justice, my Hope, my Life. My mercy seat, Advocate, Counselor, Protector. My gorgeous instructing life-giver. My loving brother lavishing love all over my renewal. Just one glimmering glimpse of Your name in my soul saves me. You love love LOVE me to reborn renewing restore.
TBTJC Renewing Redeemer

JANUARY 15

PrayStill

Matthew 11:15
He that hath ears to hear, let him hear.

Scripture Prayer: Here Hair

Prophetic Father
Delivering the futures of tomorrow today. Insight to the weaving of grace mercy love and forlightening. Sweet sound of embracing arms of Heavens gait walking through time.

Holy Spirit
Wind weaving wrestling waves of God word food to ears open, eyes perceiving, hands talking, mouths gaping, and noses finding. Let the contemptuous contempt, the derides deride, the naysayers say.
Let those who love, love. Those who believe live, those who receive give, and those who know show how awesome is your precept law and forbearance. You reign supreme we gain and glean.

Rabouni Jesus
I sense you advocate presence. You stand before you stand beside the blazing path that cannot hide. You are above you are below you whisper how and where to go. You have my flank you have my back this schooling kiss is vessel smack.
TBTHT 3in1 set in the future

JANUARY 16

PrayStill

Matthew 16:24
Then Jesus said to his disciples, "Whoever wants to be my disciple must deny themselves and take up their cross and follow me."

Scripture Prayer: Cross Keys

Father God
Creator maker of perishing flesh. Creator maker of self-wills, souls, and thoughts. Beautiful solution to perishing in the hope and belief of the Savior Jesus. Leader of life eternal through the valley cross-land.

Spirit lover
You are my life my hope my desire my key to eternity. My choice is You. I call out Your name. I cry out reclaiming, Take me back and never let me go. You lead me by voice command me by name, You transform my heart I am never the same.

Jesus Salvation
You give and love everything. You live and love everyone. My belief is in You. You plant me a tree to grow into a cross. I carve and I lift it my flesh is a loss. In You there is life You pay for my cost. New life new hope I desire most. Try me, deny me. The flesh pays the cost. Lead me feed me, the Host at the Cross.
TBTJC Saving Salve Solution

JANUARY 17

PrayStill

James 1:17
Every good and perfect gift is from above, coming down from the Father of the Heavenly lights, who does not change like shifting shadows.

Scripture Prayer: Immutable

ABBA God
Ceiling of Heavenly stars. Halo of earth holding seas of glory rising and setting in the shadow of the moon. Brilliant endearing enduring and constant ray of showering delight. Completely finishing reign joy showering love

Good Spirit
Scatter away the hiding darkness. Cast away often fears. Shatter the dark to dust and make the light right. Burn the searing marks of glory into abiding angel force. Let light manna from above send warm sensations basking.

Jesus Christ,
Light, truth and Way of the world. In you, Lord Jesus, the darkness cannot go. You are the perfection injection healing selection of God. Beautiful redeeming savior not tainted. Relentless keeper of babes in winged arms. Angelic host of Heaven.
Jesus my rock and redeemer, my soul light retriever. My obsession possession progression.
TBTG

JANUARY 18

PrayStill

Matthew 7:24.
Therefore everyone who hears these words of mine and puts them into practice is like a wise man who built his house on the rock.

Scripture Prayer: Rock Builders

Lord God
Diamond of the skies and reignbows. Buloke cross of eternity placed in graphene of the earth. Dashable cleavable lustre streaking foundations of universes perpetually present in here and now. Azure emerald golden amber, teal embers Heavens pleasure.

Spirit of truth
Speak to me and through me. Let my words thoughts, deeds and intentions fall upon the fallow rock of redemption. Let not my sword words fall upon ears. Hear my prayer for succulent sweet effervescent adorning words to fall upon fresh ears. Make my mouth muse marvelous mysteries of your mighty magnificence

Jesus Brother
Turn my stone to You to speak. In you this life resides complete. For You I find my life is meek, humbled by the WORDs You speak. Shatter rocks reroll the scrolls your WORD in me is here to seek. Heaven's rock and holy roll; your life in me now owns my soul.

TBTG

JANUARY 19

PrayStill

Colossians 2:7
Let your roots grow down into him, and let your lives be built on him. Then your faith will grow strong in the truth you were taught, and you will overflow with thankfulness.

Scripture Prayer: Vine Grip

Abiding Father
Patient parent filling gratitude boxes galore. Root of Jesse hundreds of times cast in verdant fallow spirit. True Lebanon Cedar strengthened in the wind and rains. Cast and shaken out in abundance dances. Lord of love designing.

Jesus Root
My connection to God. Font of holiness firmly rooted around the crystal Rock of Heaven. How deep and wide surpassing understanding. Folds of joy engulf lasting seeds and roots of assurance. You love me first before my birth you set my confidence in You

Spirit Growing
The dew worships the tangle of sunrise. Deep and dark colors blossom to rainbows delighting in the truth of the days raise capture. Together attraction pulls the cohesion adherence to thy breath of life. WORD fills mountains to capacities overflowing. Gratitude remains imbibing. You love me first last and always.
TBT Abba Mamma Creator 3in1 459 831 143 411.

JANUARY 20

PrayStill

Genesis 1:27
So God created mankind in his own image, in the image of God he created them; male and female he created them.

Scripture Prayer: Imagine Nation

Jesus Alpha
First flesh of creation. Second to end in everyone. Last lasting and beautiful. Millions and millions of variety overflowing into extraordinary feats and gorgeousness. The righteous reflection of beauty is very, very awesome, very, very good.

Life Spirit
Hovering between breath and speaking. First day morning eve, dark and light vaulted sky. Land and seas planted seed kinds according. Sacred Heaven sun and stars vaulting moons in time. Bird and fish expanding dish. Wild stock all for arc. This day, your day is very good. Very, very good.

God in Creation
Evident in unrelenting. You dip and soak in conquering. Breath of life and skin without sin The Son of man imagining. Beautiful mirror reflects without fear beautifully Thy Kingdom come. Sunday to sabbath, the days we trespass us You lay us in pastures to bath us.
TBTHT 3N1

JANUARY 21

PrayStill

John 15:2
He cuts off every branch in me that bears no fruit, while every branch that does bear fruit he prunes so that it will be even more fruitful.

Scripture Prayer: truth Progress

Joyful God
Creator of the elements that renew. Wind and rain bless the land. Cold and ice bless the land. Fire and gravity bless the land. Lord of creation bless the land. Land and sea of fertile dew. Verdant pastures in fallow lands.

Jesus Gardner
Take away my sinful branches. Break me in two to be more like you. Envy and lust fall into the fire. Greed and selfish no longer desire. Blossom in truth the virtues are clean, they grow in your dark rich firmament green. Roots of pure love shake off prideful anger fear.

Divine Spirit
Raise me to rays of praise. Draw me to the light. Let me grow in right and blossom to, the way the truth the life. Clean away the bad and fill it up with good. Flourish me to flower flow, bloom me in your food.
Beautiful is rejoicing. Fruited stems drip in blossom dew smooth in scent. Slippery sweet nectar grows your ivory tower pomegranate cheeks. Honey birds buzz and multiply. The Word grows in the world more than one hundred times.
TBTHT flourishing three.

JANUARY 22

PrayStill

Hebrews 10:24
And let us consider one another to provoke unto love and to good works.

Scripture Prayer: Forgiving Remembrances

God Communion
Cajoling spirit of beauty inspiring. Master weaver of encounters and circumstance. Creator of each precious moment together lifted up high in praise to your glorious name. Chief encouraging officer of Spirit filled angelic realms.

Spirit Between
In with around in the surround You call the words. Let them be fresh effervescence floating around the chambers of our hearts. You lift me up I take your cup and fill to all this overflow. I give it up and pass the cup and share you are the way to go.

Jesus Champion
How gorgeously you sustain the love of others. Bold bright beautiful healing fills our souls to brimming. Open my senses to your beauty to know and love and share Your precious ways. Forgiving, loving, a kind word here. A soft response a silent smile there. Reveal and heal and seal my heart. I kneel to real and feel Your start.
TBTHT 3N1 persuading persistence

JANUARY 23

PrayStill

Ecclesiastes 4:9-10
Two are better than one, because they have a good return for their labor: If either of them falls down, one can help the other up. But pity anyone who falls and has no one to help them up.

Scripture Prayer: Stranded Weaving

Lord God
Worshipful intercessor. Interceptor of evil from every bulwark. Mighty strong and powerful hailing gale force of love. Protector of all. Selector of all. Injector of all the goodness and graciousness there is. In you is always impending victories.

Lord Spirit
You weave your word in my life's relationships. I am never stranded standing alone stranded with the King of kings glory. Walking a closer stride in thee I am never alone. Watch over and protect my aloneness. Guide me to your fertile relations entwined in the WORD of loves first companion.

Lord Jesus
Embrace me from wander. Tie me to the weaving sails of your abundant overflowing ocean. Drag my net of life to the banquet table of fruitful relation. Humble my steps to be kind loving and compassionate with and to the friends you will have me engage. My loving trusting uplifting protecting friend Jesus.

TBTHT 3N1

JANUARY 24

PrayStill

Galatians 5:22
But the fruit of the Spirit is love, joy, peace, forbearance, kindness, goodness, faithfulness, gentleness and self-control. Against such things there is no law.

Scripture Prayer: Truly Unruly

Righteous God
Creator sole planter and harvester of all that is good. Holy true and infinite. Overflowing truth reigning on the joyful fruited positioning of love guaranteeing happy contentment acceptance beyond any human knowledge.

Jesus Provider
In you is the peace fuel. The ignition of love. Flames fawning over kindle beauty enrapturing Heaven on earth. Your kingdom keys open doors to palace castles of everything that is beautiful. Let me see the beauty in everything. Let me not hold back your uncontainable unstoppable completely desirable love. Free me to be in Your virtue.

Holy Spirit
Fall fresh with the inheritance of virtues. Open me to the flowing. Receive my flesh exchange for Spirit renewing. Take away my inclinations of disobedience. Incline me to your pastures protecting in rods and staffs of truths, harmonies and justices. Guard the temple within to keep the love without restraint. Feed my soul food desire to follow You.
In Christ alone.
TBTJC Savior Smiling

JANUARY 25

PrayStill

Hebrews 4:16
Let us then with confidence draw near to the throne of grace, that we may receive mercy and find grace to help in time of need.

Scripture Prayer: Faith Seeds

God King
Love right here and now. Enriching territories reflecting all. Daily faith the size of a mustard seed sprouting. Right where planted is the nutritious faith food delicacies. Open invitations of blossom sprout and grow.

Spirit Lord
Satiate me in your showering love, mercy, grace and comfort. Open my receptors of light sound taste scent and touch. Feel and sense me to surrender in assurance to Your beautiful design for glorious living in your lining. Flow freely in me and protect me from me if I wander from your presence. Let my woes and pains be fuel for Kingdom growth. Draw me back first always to You my Master.

Lord Jesus
Calm me to the voice of your calling. Let me notice hear and discern your powerful WORD direction. Convict me to step in awareness rightly to your cadence of love. Settle and tune my soul to your understanding let my rest in you be genuine and true. Lord of full circles beginnings and ends be everything in between in my presence mercy seat.
TBTG In Attractive Growth

JANUARY 26

PrayStill

Matthew 18:22
Jesus answered, "I tell you, not seven times, but seventy-seven times."

Scripture Prayer: Heavenly Divine

ABBA Father
Ruling judge and maker of all things. Merciful creator of redemption. Purveyor of peace passing through all beyond comprehension. Placid still calm of the world needing to submit to forgive.

Lord Jesus
Continual grace that melts away my fleshly unforgiveness. All my prideful anger fear and disappointment unacceptable I hurl at you. You take and forgive my inequities in a split second before I even ask. You forgive me I forgive you. Help me to forgive me and forgive others. You cleanse my soul.

Holy Spirit
In you is peaceful fountains and calm river oceans. Every attempt to quench or quell your mercy fails. Basking in the sunshine of your freedom absolves me. You forgive me to let me forgive myself and others. Let us all give and receive reprieve.
TBTG

JANUARY 27

PrayStill

Isaiah 11:6
The wolf will live with the lamb, the leopard will lie down with the goat, the calf and the lion and the yearling together; and a little child will lead them.

Scripture Prayer: One Den

Righteous Father
Heavenly calm. Peaceable after storm. Atmosphere pink clouded wind speed ceilings. Harmonious gentle childlike innocence rules the Heavenly palaces of praising worship silence. Victorious is the Lord of all things.

Gentle Spirit
Holy victor of newness abiding. Wipe away all to good tiding. Risen conquering son presiding. Welcome presence always inviting. Pure Eden holiness ruling again. Faith in the ruler and king of the den. Childhood trust reigns true in the end. All the king's horses all the king's friends.

Victorious Jesus
Fierce fiery friend defender to last. Devour the enemy hour to cast. Away eternal bliss is come, to thy eternal kingdom throne. Strength in calm the strongest balm overcomer in the realm.
TBTFG Reigning ruler

JANUARY 28

PrayStill

Philippians 2:12
Therefore, my dear friends, as you have always obeyed—not only in my presence, but now much more in my absence—continue to work out your salvation with fear and trembling.

Scripture Prayer: Unshakable mercy

Heavenly Father
Righteous revealing masterful maker. Judge of all things, redeemer of all contrite. Fulsome Father of all intimate in each abiding in every. Lord of the soul keys of nations uniting. Merciful mighty creator.

Lord Jesus
You see right through me. You know my motive before I act or speak. Yet you still adorn mercy on me. I shake in remorse I tremble in guilt and I repent. I am cracked and broken and cannot contain you fully. My pride eases you aside and I ride to deride. Help me surrender and give up to Heaven. Let me renew to you and stay true.

Lord Spirit
Search me seek me know me reach me, take me to your pasture. Know me grow me always show me, never let me wander past Thee. Shake me, break me, don't forsake me. Abide me next to Thee. Hold me boldly, don't let go of me, keep me in Your Peace.
TBTHT Precious Savior

JANUARY 29

PrayStill

Mark 9:35
Sitting down, Jesus called the Twelve and said, "Anyone who wants to be first must be the very last, and the servant of all."

Scripture Prayer: First in Last

Humble Father
Solution to the ailing pride that tries and fails to rule the world. Answer to all woes through servanthood. Master power in humility reigning throughout eons of eternities. Tender remedy to the ego esteem.

Jesus Savior
Weak and meek are exalted in your name. Lowly are lifted in esteem. You are the Way, the truth and the Life in light. Humble in mercy lifting up. Beautiful power of peace surpassing.

Chastening Spirit
Cleansing suppressing pride fear and anger. Fill me with your will to serve, bring me to your best reserve, teach me what I need to learn. Let me think of me less often let my heart for Thee be soften. In the living water well, let me come with Thee to dwell.

JANUARY 30

PrayStill

Psalm 119:66
Teach me discernment and knowledge, for I have believed in your commandments.

Scripture Prayer: Yes and No

God Almighty
Plateaus in Heaven pour out gold silver and platinum rivers of insight and knowledge. Celestial perspectives reign over and over and over again. Steps to the high and narrow pathways to righteousness enlighten.

Holy Counselor
You are silent partner extraordinaire. You speak to me beyond my consciousness, right to my heart and soul. You convict me to the aligning truth. Yes, no, or wait, I listen in prayer for you. You smile Your face upon me always in all ways. Teach me to discern Your way.

Shepherd Jesus
Retrieve and guide me to your path. Keep protection from the wrath. Direct and guide my days your ways. Hold me from my words and deeds that take me from your rooted seed. Call, incline my ear to hear, let me know that You are near.
TBTJC Rightful Director

JANUARY 31

PrayStill

Psalm 86:5
You, Lord, are forgiving and good, abounding in love to all who call to you.

Scripture Prayer: Powerful Provider

Good God
Attentive Creator Master, trusting and merciful offering of choice. The beginning to the end of exhaustion. Redemption and rock of desperation. Sole provider unchallengeable.

Lord of lords
You are. You are strong. You are strong powerful and mighty to save. Hear my cry and give supply take me from my folly. Take this pain, the foe is slain, let me in You remain. Pick me up and fill my cup lay me in your plain.

Jesus God
You are gentle sweet and easy. You hear and answer calls. You shame the enemies with trusted faithfulness and embrace the contrite hearts. Powerfully meek and awesome is Your Way, truth and Life.
TBTHT 3N1

FEBRUARY 1

PrayStill

Colossians 3:23-24
Whatever you do, work at it with all your heart, as working for the Lord not for human masters, since you know that you will receive an inheritance from the Lord as a reward. It is the Lord Christ you are serving.

Scripture Prayer: Brick and mortal

Lord God
Eternal father of creation making Heaven available on earth. Resident holiness resuming in souls aligning to Holy ways in every day. Master of more and plenty. True, true God of all. The gift and the lift from above.

Christ Jesus
My employment each day begins in your say, you guide me, direct me to knowing. It's you who is ruler, the finest of jewelers, you bring out the gem in us each. You take us to plateaus and teach us to reach you, my Master I apprentice to you true The Magnificent relationship builder.

Holy Spirit
Come fill this place. You tell me to love and forgive others like they are my brothers I love them as myself. The master enlister to love all my sisters and bring out the best I can give them. Respect my parents and raise up the children our family is centered upon You.
TBTCJ Master employer

FEBRUARY 2

PrayStill

February 2
John 15:5
"I am the vine; you are the branches. If you remain in me and I in you, you will bear much fruit; apart from me you can do nothing."

Scripture Prayer: Wine Vine

GOD love
Everywhere and present true Gardner. Planter and cultivator and curator. Conservator and guardian dwelling and enduring with in and through. Allegiant caretaker providing all needs awesomely.

SPIRIT Word
Lord You feed me Your WORD. I thirst no more I hunger no more. My cup overflows wine flowing. A masterful measure pressed down together pouring font from all the edge around. Pour out Your "all blessings flowing" in one hundred-fold, in you the answers are found.

JESUS Friend
With me to the end. From the beginning you send forth a new way to live abundantly. In you I am roots connecting and shooting and growing with rampant desire. You guide me and grow me always to show me the dwelling in You that is higher.
TBTG Great grape provider

FEBRUARY 3

PrayStill

Philipians 4:8
Finally, brothers and sisters, whatever is true, whatever is noble, whatever is right, whatever is pure, whatever is lovely, whatever is admirable—if anything is excellent or praiseworthy—think about such things.

Scripture Prayer: Dwelling Wellness

Lord God
Thought creator and invader. Energy of the mind amazing. Suddenly realization author of thought. Beautiful waves of pleasant presence wash over receptive minds eager to think and do good. Around and about unseen and always thought of.

Lord Spirit
You are goodness falling fresh. You are sweet sound rising. You are preciousness alive. You are pure noble right truth manifest. Effervescent tastes and sounds fill us up. So much goodness abounds.

Lord Jesus
I think about your humble beauty. Overwhelming is your admirable excellence. You are praiseworthy all the days long. I dwell in the lovely of adorning Your Holy Sacred name raising in praise, Jesus.
TBTHT 3N1

FEBRUARY 4

PrayStill

1Peter 1:22
Now that you have purified yourselves by obeying the truth so that you have sincere love for each other, love one another deeply, from a pure heart.

Scripture Prayer: Core Obedience

Eternal God
Loving Imperishable father planting eternal seeds of holiness throughout nations and ages. Loving and redeeming God of glory. love unstoppable beyond comprehension glorifying all to Heaven.

Jesus King
Lover of souls. Keeper of Heaven's keys. You pour out life. You are love eternal dripping breath of life. Your love is greatest of all other forms. Precious blood and water cleansing the palates of nations.

Holy Spirit
Convictor of obedience to the law of truth. Deep abiding truth is the plate of your salvation. love so deep you come to reap your conviction is alluring. You love us home and turn our stone to cups of gold and sterling.
TBTHT 3N1

FEBRUARY 5

PrayStill

Isaiah 43:19
See, I am doing a new thing! Now it springs up; do you not perceive it? I am making a way in the wilderness and streams in the wasteland.

Scripture Prayer: New Song

ABBA God
Father of all, maker of all, redeemer of all. Always new always present, always comforting. Shield in the fire, air in the flood, path to the pasture. Beautiful creator protector and provider.

Spirit Ruach
Oxygen for fire and water. Wind for breath and song. You surround me and enfold my life breath in the breadth of your breast. I am entombed in the womb of your newness. You carry me across the divide

Yashua Jesus
New wine, new blood, new name, eternal savior. Preciousness in flesh redeemer of nations. My footprints lead to You anew and wash away. Forever let me stay in the arms of Your Holiness.
TBTJC renewing redeemer

FEBRUARY 6

PrayStill

Hebrews 11:6
And without faith it is impossible to please God because anyone who comes to him must believe that he exists and that he rewards those who earnestly seek him.

Scripture Prayer: Axiom At-last

Great God
Focus of the vertical and horizontal, the atlas and axis, the X and the Y of the Cross. Lord of the intersection of real truth. Priceless procurer and purchaser of souls. Reckless redeemer reeling in the angst of the world's woes.

Super Spirit
On my own I am alone I cannot find the answers. With you at my side, the way You provide I finally find the cure.
Little is done from my power within. You provide from my state of without. Let the credit be given to the glory of living in Your grace and mercy abounding.

Jewel Jesus
Take me away from me. Unset my stone head rock from its pride clasps and free me to the surrender of your clarity. The color is true that the carat for you is cut from Heaven's adorning. Take me shake me break me make me I surrender all to you.
TBTG Possibility Possessor

FEBRUARY 7

PrayStill

Psalm 143:10
Teach me to do your will, for you are my God; may your good Spirit lead me on level ground.

Scripture Prayer: Flat Land

Lord God
Vast and spread out forever infinity. Dimensions of infinite planes of light beams pass through darkness. Brilliance in spectacular is your eminence emanating from everywhere. Heaven's surround abounds.

Wind Spirit
Your gentle breeze inclines me to your direction. You guide and protect my path. The way is clear when I feel and hear and know you are guiding my pathway. Sense me to Your divine.

Rabouni Jesus
To You oh Lord is easy. I do not need to slow. I do not need to speed. You lace my pace to you; I find it straight to you. More and more I see you are right beside me.
TBTG

FEBRUARY 8

PrayStill

Matthew 7:7
"Ask and it will be given to you; seek and you will find; knock and the door will be opened to you."

Scripture Prayer: Treasure Hunt

Giving God
Lord of every gift authored from above. The offering of every good lost and searched for desire. Open giver of beautiful bountiful inheritance.

Indulging Spirit
Finder and keeper in the soul food seekers. Divulging in the bulge of riches. Treasure beyond measure for any now pleasure, forever eternal the reward. Open for me and plainly to see the kingdom of Heaven on earth.

Welcoming Jesus
Guard me from deceptive evildoers. Keep me from stray wander. With you, at Heaven's door, You show presence galore. I revel in the presentation. My senses overwhelm. You are captain at the helm. Welcome is the invitation.
TBTJC Guiding Guardian

FEBRUARY 9

PrayStill

Philippians 4:6
Do not be anxious about anything, but in every situation, by prayer and petition, with thanksgiving, present your requests to God.

Scripture Prayer: Easy Side (TALCS pronounced TALKS)

Holy God
Collector of collects that praise and adorn Holiness Highness and humbleness. Worthy of adorning worship and praise overflowing. Thankfulness with hearing and being heard. The great communicator creator of all creation.

Holy Spiritess
You long for my attention. I lavish you in TALCS talk
T Thanksgiving
A Adoration
L Listen
C Confession
S Supplication
Let me hear your word alive inside. You are the powerful source of grace. I am not perfect or worthy and merely ask in mercy.

Lord Jesus
Thank you, Savior, beautiful Savior inclining my ear to hearing. I have fallen from worthy into the earthly; please save me from me with your steering. Thy rod and thy staff the comfort at last the guideposts are always preceding.
TBTHS Creator Communicator

FEBRUARY 10

PrayStill

Luke 13:18

Scripture Prayer: Perseverance

Lord God
Sustainer of all things. Giver of courage and strength. Comforter and assurance assuaging all ways to you. More of you is less of the world. Less of the world is more of Heaven. Verdant plateau streams grow forests of faith.

Growing Spirit
Let me give more of me away to get more of You. Only in Your strength can I sustain. You remain my beholden fortress Rock. I am weak and needy and only you know my comfort. You persist and insist I follow you. You are my life abundant growing in me.

King Jesus God
You grow on me you glow in me you take and make me yours. You know me and show me and bring me to these tears. You flow in me and go through me a channel for my ears. Forever with me. endeavor in me to praise and worship near. Draw me in.
TBTJC
What if all the amount of faith I have now is the size of a mustard seed.? Invite Christ Jesus always.

FEBRUARY 11

PrayStill

Luke 1:3-4
I too decided, after investigating everything carefully from the very first, to write an orderly account for you, most excellent Theophilus, so that you may know the truth concerning the things about which you have been instructed.

Scripture Prayer: Supplication

Lord Jesus Christ
Lover of my soul, Igniter of realization conviction and revelation to my life in You. You write in our moments together Your love on my heart. You teach me in new perspectives daily to write and record in diary, song, conversation, Prayer: and meditation all the epiphanies of blessings. Reveal in me the truth of light in pathway with You. Lord fill the story of Your saving graces so bountifully as to overflow to others.

Amen
TBTG

FEBRUARY 12

PrayStill

Luke 1:59-60 *On the eighth day they came to circumcise the child, and they were going to name him Zechariah after his father. But his mother said, "No; he is to be called John."*

Scripture Prayer:. Name Immutable

Lord Jesus
Let my faith be silent. Speak to me in assured conviction. Liven me to hear your voice incline to my disbelief. Wrestle me to the understanding of your beautiful revealing.

Lord
Look into the eyes of the God Child in everyone we meet. See and acknowledge the gift of being a child of God created with a purpose. We love to hear our names spoken called and sung. Lord, You especially are the Good Lord when You know and call our name and we hear it. God's servants always hear, sometimes listens and understand. Lord, we know your voice and follow Your direction. You whisper our name and we are loved loved LOVED!!!

TBTG

FEBRUARY 13

PrayStill

2 Timothy 1:7
For God hath not given us the spirit of fear; but of power, and of love, and of a sound mind.

Scripture Prayer: Who's am I?

Lord Jesus Christ

Be born in me daily. This is a special day of celebration before the wilderness of Lent. It is written, it is written, it is written, reminds me all temptation is dismissed behind me when Your sword of words lives in me. Your word is power over the wilderness of the shadowed valley. Prepare the way for Your strength and glory in conquering.

All day today You have written on my heart "Let everything that has breath praise the Lord...." and "At the name of Jesus every knee will bow and every tongue confess in Heaven and on earth and underneath the earth" and "Trees in the fields lift their arms to you..." All this presence of Your word in song brings me to ask, what name shall you be called today? At his hour? At this moment?

Anything from Alpha to Omega and everything in between and beyond. Every adjective and verb is filled with Your presence mighty counselor, teacher, comforter, lover of my soul and life. Jehovah...Adonai, Immanuel, Elohim, and yes...I AM. You are...for certain, Lord of all.

May every word that pours from my lips adorn Your infinite name drawing me to know You more. From every perspective, You are glorified. Continually adjusting me towards your great grace mercy and embracing love. How grateful I AM cannot be described or contained. Your flood of loving infinite flavors reveals the spice of Your variety.

What do You call me, Lord? Beloved friend? Beloved servant and follower? Please call me Yours and make me a grateful giver of multiplying gifts.

Amen TBTJC

FEBRUARY 14

PrayStill

Hosea 2:15 *I'll give her bouquets of roses. I'll turn Heartbreak Valley into Acres of Hope. She'll respond like she did as a young girl, those days when she was fresh out of Egypt.*

Scripture Prayer: Ashen Roses (Ash Wednesday)

Lord
Loved before birth and loved through death. The BIBLE is the book of love in love story. Yes, it's the book for me. Written on the hearts and pedals of love who live it is the greatest living love story personally and divinely crafted to come alive in our spirit. Stirring and convincing and speaking alive in me... surrounded in the armor of holy protection care and direction.
Let me write all over you and grow and learn and be taught the words of the author of salvation. My lover Jesus, I crave, long, and desire to be with You. Into me You see.
Amen

BIBLE
Beautifully
Inspired
Booking
Loving
Eternally

FEBRUARY 15 (LENTEN JOURNEY)

PrayStill

Luke 3:16b
I am not worthy to untie the thong of his sandals. He will baptize you with the Holy Spirit and fire.

Scripture Prayer: Soul Path

Lord
Release me of me and fill me with You. Blaze Your Spirit upon me to ignite your flaming will within me.
Prepare ye the way of the Lord
I sometimes sense the Lord is near and imminent for meditative presence. A grateful expecting feeling of the meditative moment with Christ Jesus. Just the anticipation of the moment triggers inward invitation of His presence. Lord, You prepare the way and come right in every time. Bring my wanderings and wonderings back right with you
We watch out for each other we lift each other up.
Jesus says, Come to me all you who are heavy laden, and I will give you rest.
Take Jesus and learn this gentle humble soul rest. Jesus' yoke is easy and His burdens light. Walk in yoke step with Jesus. Imitate and mirror the Lord. Much is done in seeming effortlessness to amplify abundant Christ living.
I want it all back. All my misgivings to be reversed. Do not look back. All things are possible through the strengthening Christ straightening the path.
Lord
As you are a lover of my soul let me freely imitate You and be a lover and yolk of souls. Your servant is listening
Amen

FEBRUARY 16

PrayStill

Luke 3:23-24, 38
Jesus was about thirty years old when he began his work. He was the son (as was thought) of Joseph son of Heli, son of Matthat, son of Levi, son of Melchi, son of Jannai, son of Joseph...son of Enos, son of Seth, son of Adam, son of God.

Scripture Prayer: Divine Inheritance

Lord
The daughters You God blessed me with to be their earthly father call me many names in endearment. Zaza. Dad dada dady.
Our Heavenly Father calls us many names. My grandfathers had names like Daddo and Boppie. What a gift in intimacy.
DNA IS GOD MADE
I have some and so does everyone else. It is written in DNA to grow and blossom and be revealed daily to this rejoicing in communion with the Creator Jesus. Fill this place and grow these God Deoxyribose Nucleic Acid ladders and markers in ancestry designed and grown for increasing spiritual communion. Sons and daughters begetting by design. ^^+++^^

FEBRUARY 17

PrayStill

Luke 4:13
When the devil had finished every test, he departed from him until an opportune time.

Scripture Prayer Holy Freedom

The enemy is already defeated. No need to test this. Jesus, take the wheel. You, Lord, put aside the enemy. The enemy has nothing to say. The Word Alive dismisses and puts behind the temptation of the chained enemy. Get behind me lower power!
With Jesus, the Word is the solution to every temptation and FEAR.
Face
Everything
And
Rise
Turn my fear into awesome excitement.
With Jesus, Word. It IS written X 3. Nothing separates from the love of God. Come fill this place, Jesus, so lower power has...
No sting.
No victory.
No presence in this vessel.
Absent from the body is present with the Lord Jesus Christ the Author of Salvation.
Being filled with Jesus in Trinity leaves no other room.
Amen

FEBRUARY 18 (I LOVE ISAIAH)

PrayStill

Luke 4:18-19 *The Spirit of the Lord is upon me because he has anointed me to bring good news to the poor. He has sent me to proclaim release to the captives and recovery of sight to the blind, to let the oppressed go free, to proclaim the year of the Lord's favor.*

Scripture Prayer: Savior Inside

God loved me first and all along the way. His messengers shower me with the Good News perspective to this world.

God You have the key to me. You deliver my life needs in timeless love and tenderness.

I tested my poor free will to the boundary of Your awesome grace and mercy.

You revive me. You illuminate my motive in this life and change my self-perspective to your loving Good News. Release me from captivity and shine Your freeing light. Free me from my transgressions that quench and quell communion in Holy Spirit. Make my motive love through Your Spirit.

Oh, Divine Lectionary. Reside, abide, and ride inside me.

FEBRUARY 19

PrayStill

Luke 5:6
When they had done this, they caught so many fish that their nets were beginning to break.

Scripture Prayer: Bountiful Bounty

Flip the ship and ride the wave! The boat is tipping full.
A sk
S eek
K nock
Out with complacency and in with change. Think outside the boat. Jesus, You said so. So it is yes.
With the limitless God is unlimited bounty. Hear direction and trim the sails to the Spirit's beckon. There is plenty to have and even more to give.
In expectation with God there is no fear. Hope abounds to tip the scales.
TBTG

PrayStill

Luke 5:18-19
Just then some men came, carrying a paralyzed man on a bed. They were trying to bring him in and lay him before Jesus; but finding no way to bring him in because of the crowd, they went up on the roof and let him down with his bed through the tiles into the middle of the crowd in front of Jesus.

Scripture Prayer: Healing in Kneeling

Lord Jesus
Bestow in me Your grace in faith in fishing. Mind me in my business to only use words if necessary. Let Your humble voice and love speak through actions.
Seal my lips in the underlying still water current of life. Present each moment for your great commissioning to be revealed and acknowledged as Your divine moment to witness and tend overflowingly to the infirmed.
Lord
Many carried me in your loving net to welcomed healing and restoration introduction to you. Let your drawing near of souls plant the contagious sight in faith to You.
Give us radical outside the boat creativity to carry those that hunger and thirst. Reveal and seal the place in your open arms presence where the old mat of security disappears.
In Your precious Name, Lord Jesus

FEBRUARY 21

PrayStill

Luke 6:20b, 24
Blessed are you who are poor, for yours is the kingdom of God. But woe to you who are rich, for you have received your consolation.

Scripture Prayer: Heaven's Haven

I needed to be stripped of everything. Pride, esteem, money and purpose to be gracefully broken in place with Jesus. Enough free will to come crawling back to Abba Father and grace-filled Mother for redemption. There is joy in the morning. There are blessings from ashes.
All things do work together for our good through God in His time.
Mammon is neither good nor evil. It is what I do with it as a tool. Am I loving its gain or fearing its loss? Is it a plate for me to offer into God's purpose in Kingdom? Is it a bag for me to accumulate selfish desire?
Lord Jesus Christ. You are first. You are beyond and above any precious jewel in coin in wanton desire and value. Limitless and indescribably beyond my meager understanding. Your price and value well beyond my finite needs and desires.
I pray for Your holy presence in my desires and actions so as to give freely and cheerfully all for this Great Kingdom on earth as it is in Heaven.
Amen

FEBRUARY 22

PrayStill

Luke 6:31-32

Do to others as you would have them do to you. If you love those who love you, what credit is that to you? For even sinners love those who love them

Scripture Prayer: Given Forgiveness

Lord Jesus

I know I must forgive others, myself, and strangely enough, even You, Lord.

I am willing to forgive.

I am praying to forgive.

I wait on Your presence in meditation.

You, Lord, grant the forgiveness in your moment. The pride of unforgiveness is crucified.

+++ Humbly washed to the justice of Your mighty kingdom for Your reconciling.

Complete forgiveness is your precious peace. Waiting to be claimed redeemed and processed.

Let me forgive before its needed. Place me in still waters, not stirred; and green pastures in rest and release.

Lord, make me part your forgiving wholeness. Retrieve me from the hole of self-pity and selfishness.

With You, God, we can. You put back the pieces into peace. So awesomely moved.

In a good way, I am loved loved loved enough to be forgiven and to forgive. I am worthy in Your communion to love and be loved through Your mighty power.

Amen

FEBRUARY 23

PrayStill

Luke 7:33-35 *For John the Baptist has come eating no bread and drinking no wine, and you say, "He has a demon"; the Son of Man has come eating and drinking, and you say, "Look, a glutton and a drunkard, a friend of tax collectors and sinners!"*

Scripture Prayer: Throwing Word Stones

Am I casting stones at those I envy? Am I belittling those I perceive to be less than me? How easy is it for me to judge others and believe evil and cast away good? Sometimes unknowingly it's a habit. It shows up in character assassination of others and misdirected thoughts and doubts like, "That's not God. How could God do that? Where is God in all this circumstance?"

Fear fear fear... Get behind me! HELP ME, LORD. Deliver me from the corner I walked into. Deliver from this, in assurance I pray. Replace this iniquity with pure love unconditional.

Jesus, you wait in the corner and dead end my judgment of others. You wait for me to place this sin in judgment with You at the altar for altering so I can relate in love instead. Your welcoming embrace transfers my judgment and envy of others into lifting love and wholesome encouragement.

Draw near to my soul, Lord, and expand my finite understanding of Your loving Kingdom. Radically break all my limitations I place between us—known and not known. Continue increasing Your blessings and revelations to the glory of Your name.

Through Jesus Christ our Lord

FEBRUARY 24 (LENTEN JOURNEY)

PrayStill

Luke 7:38
She stood behind him at his feet, weeping, and began to bathe his feet with her tears and to dry them with her hair. Then she continued kissing his feet and anointing them with the ointment.

Scripture Prayer: Tear Oils

Spiritual laws and axioms are always true from every perspective. The greater the sin the greater the love the greater the forgiveness.

Catharsis from the heart reaches the heart of Jesus. Jesus Healer heals with patience for his patients. GOD'S transforming love overcomes and overwhelms all ways. All are called, all are welcome.

With Jesus' cleansing, grieving tears of salt and water dry and transform in perfect outpouring of sweet oils. Rejoice with strong alabaster columns of anointing perfume!

Mightily expansive consuming Son of man and God You evaporate away the flesh and with mercy and forgiveness the tears of the sin of the world. We rejoice and adorn You. You are Unending lover!! ^^+++^^¡¡

In your time, Lord, turn and transform and exchange my tears of repentance into oils of lavishing adornment offered up in praise and worship.

You complete me, Lord Jesus.

Lectio Divina!

TBTJC

FEBRUARY 25

PrayStill

Luke 8:1-3
Soon afterwards He went on through cities and villages, proclaiming and bringing the good news of the kingdom of God. The twelve were with him, as well as some women who had been cured of evil spirits and infirmities: Mary, called Magdalene, from whom seven demons had gone out, and Joanna, the wife of Herod's steward Chuza, and Susanna, and many others, who provided for them out of their resources.

Scripture Prayer: Maternal Healing

We watch out and tend for each other! Blessings are women found in strong firm faith. So much maternal Heavenly love calming the noise of the world.

I Starve and crave for the essence and substance and beauty and wonder of moms, sisters, daughters, aunts, cousins, and friends in this world. Each provide and deliver lessons and learnings in life. The power and love in the world reveal in their convicting perspectives. This feminine uniqueness makes completeness. The mother nurture and nature provide necessary aspects.

Peaceful Holy Spirit watch over us. Blessed are we to receive this gift of multitude.

In the calm provided one Voice can be heard. Awaken with a knock

Lord Spirit Holy Spirit God Spirit

Train and tune my faith hearing to the channeling of Jesus' shepherding calling. The voice of love and conviction. The clear bright voice above all voices Jesus.

The salve of ointment clears silence into hearing and ringing into silence. May Your voice Lord be a sweet, sweet sound.

Amen PrayStill

FEBRUARY 26

PrayStill

Luke 8:44
She came up behind him and touched the fringe of his clothes, and immediately her hemorrhage stopped.

Scripture Prayer: FAITH

Lord Jesus Christ, pure Son of God and Man. You reign, You heal, You love love love. I am weak and needy. I come up behind You, Jesus, as I follow in desiring and anticipation.

I hear You heal, I believe what they say. My belief fuels this momentum. In the anticipation, alone, I feel the healing.

There are physical, mental, social, emotional, and spiritual healings occurring in drawing nearer. Remove from me all obstacles to Your hem and cloak.

Lord. You know I touch the cloak. I am healed! Before "suddenly" can be said, it is finished. You want me to touch and heal. I need what you give. I am in flowing graces and mercies because you welcome me touching you in tears of desperation. I am safe and loved and alive anew.

Lord you invite and welcome. You heal and mend. Surround me in this cloak hem of FAITH.

Father
Always
In
Thy
Hands

FEBRUARY 27

PrayStill

Luke 9:17
And all ate and were filled. What was left over was gathered up, twelve baskets of broken pieces.

Scripture Prayer: Spiritual Food

Lord Sufficing,
Satisfy to fully satiate. Fill me up please may I have some more, please. Oops. I ate too much. I have too much I can't give it away. I throw it away. I plan for next week, buy for the month and hoard and store up. My cabinets are full. I eat my plate clean usually just to tidy up...and not be wasteful. How inconsistent tidying up and throwing away. As a child, I save the best on the plate for last.

This sustenance material soothes a need and desire physically and sometimes emotionally. Come and be welcome at God's banquet table.

Jesus, my abiding best communion sustenance is fuel and nutrition for the soul. At the fields of communion is healthy spiritual feasting. Delightful physical tasting, renewed emotional palate cleansing, sustaining spiritual fulfillment. Oh, so overwhelmingly pleasant and present.
Lord Jesus
Your table, Your presence, Your gift, Your love. Teach me to give this in Your name. Allow this life sustaining essence and sustenance to cast and flow freely. There is peace. Feast me on this peace like there is no tomorrow.
Selah Lubdub Lubdub Lubdub
Wow x 7+++++++

5000 people, groups of 50, 5 loaves, 2 fishes. Everyone partakes and there are broken pieces made whole in leftovers shared in eternity.

I believe I am filled over and over and over. It is such awesomely flavorful preciousness. May I have a taste and see? I am full here in the Lord Jesus' place.

TBTLJC

FEBRUARY 28

PrayStill

Luke 9:28-29
Now about eight days after these sayings Jesus took with him Peter and John and James, and went up on the mountain to pray. And while he was praying, the appearance of his face changed, and his clothes became dazzling white.

Scripture Prayer: Lectio Divina

Jesus
You are Kingdom of God and You are Kingdom come. YOU ARE HEAVEN HERE ON EARTH.

Your Mighty Word cuts through and defeats evil and raises succulent living.
At your table is translucence. You come alive and spark the flames of desire. Transcribe my heart. Transmute my will to Yours. Illumine my transparencies in Your fields of communion. Let me see the trees transfigure into people and trans mutate into newnames. Transpire your will into this place.

You are mighty, holy and transforming. Emblazon pathways to Your will. Transcend my weak barriers. Your mighty fortress of light translates into substance of bright life into You. Only light remains. Unending in Your continued relentless pursuit of souls. Here I am Lord. There is no other. Take and make me Yours.

Selah WAY
Amen

FEBRUARY 29

PrayStill

Joshua 10:12 12
On the day the LORD gave the Amorites over to Israel, Joshua said to the LORD in the presence of Israel: "Sun, stand still over Gibeon, and you, moon, over the Valley of Aijalon."

Scripture Prayer: Season Solstice

Lord of light
Universal force of stellar gravities. Rotational God of the skies and the movements. Creator of time and Space. Masterful maker of miracles only explained in the deity of the Heavens adorning your name. Celestial father and starlit mother of creation in time and space surpassing knowledge from the inside. Creator of the enduring Earth. Indivisible by man.

Jesus Planter
Almanac of the centuries and millenniums. You know the days from the creation of time. You place them in eternity and make them shout to the lord the precious intricacies of the world. In you there is no mystery. Sense is made of the way the planets move. You let us know your ways are beautifully and majesty filled in design. You set the shadows back ten degrees. The darkness trembles.

Holy Spirt
You take away the moment in time. With you there is no reference. Only abiding presence of the lamb of creation made fresh in kairos moments. You tell us when to reap and sow you show us how the harvest goes you make the sun to set and rise your design on earth is no surprise.
TBTJC our Lord and universal Creator of linear and circular 365.247

MARCH 1

PrayStill

Luke 10:3-4
Go on your way. See, I am sending you out like lambs into the midst of wolves. Carry no purse, no bag, no sandals; and greet no one on the road.

Scripture Prayer: Lenten Journeys

Thank you thank you Jesus.

I was wandering wolf like in the field. Enjoying my own will and desire. In relentless pursuit of me you, sent out after me a messenger with an eternity key to carry guide and entice me to You. Precious lifting directing angel of commissioning, Written on my soul. The eternity key unlocks the wandering in the field into harvesting in the field.

Your will and WORD grow like wildflowers in me. All of me, just as I am, ready to do your will. Taken from the scorching sun of the field to the tall cedars beside your gentle river refreshing. Dipped and cleansed.

I refine to nothing from this world. Loose garment, socks knocked off, doing your desired inspiring. Carry not the world with you! Pure communion and commissioning in Your yoke of love, Delighting in Your ways. I am saved into You to messenger in the field.

Direct and deliberate, suddenly is seen Your power of Your overwhelming scene. Harvested and Commissioned and in your book of love. Received and doing Your Bible will.

God's Divine lectionary lives...

TBTG always in all ways

MARCH 2

PrayStill

Luke 10:33
But a Samaritan while traveling came near him; and when he saw him, he was moved with pity.

Scripture Prayer: Healing Journey

Lord, help me. Your compassion is so great. You are Holy Spirit sanctifier, come to make holy. Counsel and Comfort to instill in me Your courage and fortitude. Make my life point to You. Your Power conforms me in Divining Spirit I am fallen in the pit and I cannot save myself. I thought I could and me saving myself has slipped away.
Where am I? How did I get here? Who told me...? The others give no relief. You are my advocate Samaritan rescuer. In reverence, I offer You my fear.
Selah
In your awesome wisdom and understanding Lord Spirit Jesus, counsel me in might and knowledge. Let me delight and excite in the fear of You changing me Lord!!!
Place me in Your inn. Indwell Your SON-ship in me. Fill me to dripping saturation. Judge NOT by Your eyes and ears.
Welcome and heal this guilt in doing wrong and shame in being broken. Shame off me!!! Guilt behind me!!!
Holy Spirit lift Your essence of grace in my soul. Let your mercy raise this sense of incense rising to your home.
Assurance in Your presence this new place with you remains. Take the glory and make it Yours...
TBTHS

MARCH 3

PrayStill

Luke 11:2-4
[Jesus] said to them, "When you pray, say: Father, hallowed be your name. Your kingdom come. Give us each day our daily bread. And forgive us our sins, for we ourselves forgive everyone indebted to us. And do not bring us to the time of trial."

Scripture Prayer: Lectio Divina

Lord Jesus You make me smile. You taught me to +++ always say Your prayer with a smile on my face. You are simple and true. I love You with all my heart mind soul and strength. I am forever placed in Your words with Abba Father You, and Counselor Mighty Holy Spirit. Our Place... at The Cross of Communion
Selah x 7
At Your feet, holding on, hand in hand, arms wrapped around (Y)our cross. You forgive me. I am forgiven, I forgive.
Laying face down, in the hume of this earth, holding on, arms wrapped around the foot of the cross of pure love, I lay it down. Let it go. Cast my cares, release my woes. You receive. You are mighty and strong. Have my weakness.
Take my life and give me Your eternal peace in You. This is where I belong. Strip me of this world of sin that can't pass through. love is whole, love is one. We are one.
Selah
Still silence, warming peace. Even Heaven leavened here on earth, I offer, hands up to You. Find saving and birth in Your loving arms. True life is in You, beautiful Lord Savior. Word's Breath and breadth of life. Pure desire is Yours.
Amen
TBTG TBTJC TBTHS

MARCH 4

PrayStill

Luke 11:24-26

When the unclean spirit has gone out of a person, it wanders through waterless regions looking for a resting place, but not finding any, it says, "I will return to my house from which I came." When it comes, it finds it swept and put in order. Then it goes and brings seven other spirits more evil than itself, and they enter and live there; and the last state of that person is worse than the first.

Scripture Prayer: Imploring

I Gather with You, Jesus. You guide protect and expel the sin. You place virtue within. Cleanse me from inside. Set aside my pride.

Build in me keen reflexes of spiritual intuition. Alert me to any enemy advances. Keep my persistence in You, Lord Jesus. Let the principalities of Your great virtues reign in me.

With great gratitude and acceptance let me welcome Your vessel cleansing spirits.......

Kindness

Patience

Generosity

Diligence

Abstinence

Chastity

Humility

In with through around under above and because of Your cleansing virtues the sudden clashing principalities of your great mercy overcome and sustain.

Place the stones the serpents and the scorpions in the dry desert behind me. Set aside and wipe away the tempting power. Keep that lower power distant weak and chained away.

Selah

Wash me. Cleanse me fill me with your principalities. Certainly, I believe You can, Lord Jesus. I submit. You are Trinity alive inside keeping the annoying nuisance at bay. Shine light in the darkness. Enlighten me to You. Comfort my assurance of Your protection. TBTJC Abba God Holy Spirit

MARCH 5

PrayStill

Luke 12:6-7
Are not five sparrows sold for two pennies? Yet not one of them is forgotten in God's sight. But even the hairs of your head are all counted. Do not be afraid; you are of more value than many sparrows.

Scripture Prayer: Love x 3

Heavenly Father: mighty, strong, all knowing. Powerful God, You breathed life into me.
I am loved!
Jesus You are flesh of man
You intimate me You take away the sin of the world.
I am loved!
Holy Spirit you are in and all around me. You comfort and surround me.
I am loved!
Selah
Father God, Your eagles watch and lift. I am esteemed!
Jesus, Son of God, Your dove purifies and renews. I am worthy!
Counselor, Holy Spirit, Your owl draws wisdom. I am valuable!
Lord your whole creation sings praise and glory to You. Trees in the fields and all of the earth cries out to You.
I am a sparrow designed to carry word in mustard seeds. I am genuinely Yours. Camouflaged songbird, I am fast and agile and flocking. I am many as is Your great seed of love opening faith. I am calm and ready to receive.
Selah
I am loved, loved, loved. You loved me first before and after time began so I can love first too. You make me smile Lord. I love you right back.
Amen

MARCH 6

PrayStill

Luke 12:48b
From everyone to whom much has been given, much will be required; and from the one to whom much has been entrusted, even more will be demanded.

Scripture Prayer: Parallel

Lord Jesus, my strength and redeemer, make my prayers and meditations acceptable.
Word of God, spiritual law of truth. Your sword cuts through the indecision to make lean and true Your way. Rid me from doubt and fear. I am weak and needy yet in you is my strength.
Test this rope stranded with you. The seemed impossible is possible. You are my solution growth and change. My ability is derived from you. Your portion makes me whole. You strengthen and make all things possible.
Jesus, grow my soul! In you I am whole and complete.
You are my fortress, my shield and salvation. Pure faith in you removes the dross of fear.
My plate and cup are full and overflowing in Your good abundance. Your banquet table pasture is unending. In You is the Glory. In your court is rest.
Selah
Jesus, my strength in all things. You overcome the world You overcome me, You overcome the need.
Unlimited is your way. Your steps light and lighten possibility. My delight is found in You. My trust faith and hope are in you. You LORD, the rock-firm foundation.
Amen

MARCH 7

PrayStill

Luke 13:12
When Jesus saw her, he called her over and said, "Woman, you are set free from your ailment."

Scripture Prayer: Well

Jesus you say…. "Blessed is he who comes in the name of the Lord."
Lord, Let me listen and hear in tune for this call to heal grow and prosper. Silently calling powerful drawing, blessings installing grace and mercy. Your life spoken into me.
Call me over
Draw me near
Reveal more… Heal more.
Selah
This infirmity wants me alone and outcast. Separate different and comfortable in misery. It ails. Is there more than this? will I ever change. I long and pine for help. Help me to break free suddenly and ask for help to be in help.
My weakness is Your open door to me Lord. You are near me! I know you heal! I am worthy to come be led and healed… I'm next. You called my name. You want me!
Call me over my fear. Call me over me. Call me over this chasm and divide.
Distance is gone.
Your keys of faith flow and allow wholesome union. Two are healed. You revive me. We are healed.
TYLJ amen

MARCH 8

PrayStill

Luke 13:32
[Jesus] said to them, "Go and tell that fox for me, 'Listen, I am casting out demons and performing cures today and tomorrow, and on the third day I finish my work.'"

Scripture Prayer: Renew

Jesus attraction without distraction. This abiding spiritual law is spoken. "Blessed is he who comes in the name of the Lord." Sense this Hosanna praise rising.

Speak only good. Evil will not have breath. In living God's will through Jesus, doubt and fear are silenced. Behind me and defeated, unheard unknown unspoken.

Foxes, wolves, scorpions, stones and vipers eat themselves powerless. Crushed in their own devices. Weeping rivers in howling pain. Sparks from gnashing teeth. Behind and chained away.

The hens and sheep are in comfort and protection peacefully grazing.

Praises spoken in every exhale. Faith received in every inhale. Hail to Lord Jesus, ruler of hope, faith and confidence in love. Surrounded, protected and injected with Word alive inside. Sustaining peace unending.

Sustained relief, continued belief, grants inner peace.

Pastures, alter tables, warm sunlight with gentle lapping waves, calm currents, beautiful colors and 12-part harmony. This is home on earth in loving open arms.

TBTG

MARCH 9

PrayStill

Luke 14:16-18a
Then Jesus said to him, "Someone gave a great dinner and invited many. At the time for the dinner he sent his slave to say to those who had been invited, 'Come; for everything is ready now.' But they all alike began to make excuses."

Scripture Prayer: Feast

Ready now? Yes, ready now. Is it ready now? It is ready here and now and the banquet hall is open and welcoming. Immediately gratified if not sooner. There is no greater than this welcomed loving invitation.

Open my heart and senses to Your invitation, Jesus. Make me know You in Your Heaven's Banquet Pasture reclining. Make me be worthy and esteemed for you. Make me strong to say yes Lord! Yes Lord! Yes Lord!

I drop my nets. I put Christ first and idols behind me.

Yes to You first and always, Lord Jesus Christ, my strength and my redeemer. Come reign freely in me.

When I humble myself to you and not the world, Lord, You, Lord, exalt me in Your kingdom. How awesome is this spiritual law continually revealed in drawing near to You.

Lord, fill me at Your feasting table to the overflowing brim to live and give freely in:

Kindness

Patience

Generosity

Diligence

Abstinence

Chastity

Humility
Especially where there is none in me or my neighbor.
I love You Lord. Let my yes to You be yes and my no to the world be no.
TBTJC

MARCH 10

PrayStill

Luke 14:26, 33
Whoever comes to me and does not hate father and mother, wife and children, brothers and sisters, yes, and even life itself, cannot be my disciple. So therefore, none of you can become my disciple if you do not give up all your possessions.

Scripture Prayer: Opine Meditation

40 years ago I asked the reverend, "Why are Scripture versus excluded and missing from the readings?" The reply was, "The church does not want the harsh evil of the Bible presented." What is skipped today? What possessed who to make certain "possession" removals be removed?
Wow. Start ripping out pages, make it more human and less divine. Scripture picking is manipulation of true WORD and non-god humanism has a hand in it.
Truth reigns and cannot be ignored. Turning the blind eye to sin propagates rather than alleviates sin. Reveal it all to know the evil that can be slayed with WORD.
Test me in this. Micah 3:10

Do not put the Lord to test. Luke 4:12
Without context, I can take either verse to have my own will supported by whichever tide adrift I am today. How much of the BIBLE is being used to support promote, validate, or justify a human desire?
Lord Jesus
Help put the whole contextual truth from Your holy inspired Word back into church Scripture teachings. Heal the aching human church trend to appease the masses. Shine light and speak truth and life. Slay sin where it lay.

LORD, truth, make Word in love be spoken.

Lord Jesus

I am weak and needy. You are my rock and salvation. Journey me from where I am to You. I'm together with you.

Jesus

I confess my sins. Fill this place. I take you, Jesus, my Lord and Savior. I pray my loved ones take you too.

Amen Amen Amen

MARCH 11

PrayStill

Luke 15:4

Which one of you, having a hundred sheep and losing one of them, does not leave the ninety-nine in the wilderness and go after the one that is lost until he finds it?

Scripture Prayer: Thankfulness

God has a way of finding me wherever I may be. In the middle of self-will and instinct. Even when I can't find me myself, He finds me. Even when I don't know I am lost He finds me. I wander away in adventure or distraction he knows where I am. Sometimes I run away. Other times I'm forgotten away. Sometimes even cast away or set aside. YOU find me Lord. and never let go. Ever.

God, You call out for me. You know my name. You ask me where I am.

Where are you?

Selah

You know where I am. You found me. I cannot hide I am not lost you fold and include me include me right back in. You love me back home. You did not forget me. You remembered me and came and found me. Even when left, forgotten and alone, You protected me and never let me go.

I insist to wander. When I ran from You, You let me run an picked me up and set me down in right direction. You designed me to run in circle right back to you by default. My GPS (God Positioning Service) is honed to your safe pasture. My forever key of faith is set to your gated Heavens pasture at the field in the sand at the altar in communion at the cross. Your door pathway is especially always open welcoming return.

When I least expect it you find me where I am when I least desire it, you got me. You revive renew and restore me. loved loved loved and never let go. You are so taking care of me. Your inescapable insistent relentless pursuit is uplifting me. I love you back always in all ways. TBTJC in union with God and Holy Spirit.

MARCH 12

PrayStill

Luke 15:20
So he set off and went to his father. But while he was still far off, his father saw him and was filled with compassion; he ran and put his arms around him and kissed him.

Scripture Prayer: Reflection.

When looking out the back door 40 calling for the furry dogs I always smile ear to ear to see them tear around the corner and bound up the stairs to get back inside. Its treat time big time. So exciting.... No reservation remorse or guilt. Pure desire to be back "in"
Whom shall I get to be today.?
The child friend coworker returning to be accepted and loved and taken in care?
The father friend coworker loving and welcoming the willing repentant unloved?
The judging jealous colleague friend coworker wondering why not me?
Lord help me to...
Crucify fear!!! Know that fear is the liar and burn it in the fire. love burns fear to ash.
Parent says... I'm afraid you would remain lost forever
Child says... I'm afraid you will not love me any more
Sibling says... I'm afraid I don't have as much or enough
God designs many returns home... Through assurance in expectations in caretakers. Esteem renewal in lost and desperate wanderers. Encouraging lifting up in resentful siblings
Pure faith... Pure esteem... Pure gratitude
Lord Jesus Teach me how to love unconditionally You, myself, and others.
Let me, Meet them where they are. accept them where they are. Leave them where they are, for YOU.
Let me, Attracted them to You Lord !

Let me share my hope and understanding of your awesome loving delivering. Make me a channeling instrument of your great glories expressing Your transforming work in me. Inhabit me.

Strong deep abiding faith...Dwell in me and make me sustain and endure in each role. Make me obey and be firm in your loving faith.

Through Jesus Christ Lord

Amen +++

MARCH 13

PrayStill

Luke 16:8-9

And his master commended the dishonest manager because he had acted shrewdly; for the children of this age are more shrewd in dealing with their own generation than are the children of light. And I tell you, make friends for yourselves by means of dishonest wealth so that when it is gone, they may welcome you into the eternal homes.

Scripture Prayer: Axiom

I reap I sow. Trust that spiritual truth.

I'm confused. Jesus help me understand Your spiritual economics. In selfishness, I took love and trust and peace and joy from others. Stole away feelings and memories and relationships. It happened all around. I reaped and sowed, and I sowed and reaped. A spiritual axiom truth both ways.

My time is short. In You, with You, because of You, I can pay back all I took from others tenfold.

I have an awesome repayment plan with You. I make installments daily. It's easy. Every day I have the opportunity to smile and help and be cheerful for your cleansing eternal gift. You magnify healing you mend the tapestry. You put another piece of the puzzle back in place. You let me pay it forward. Your interest rate is 7x77 and then some. My inheritance is with You Lord!!! The best loving employer I always in all ways ever have forever.

Selah

Jesus Christ my fulfilling life provider and I can repay. Everything plus some. I pay it forward with You Jesus. We are in the business of making broken pieces whole.

Lord Spend me lavishly on others. Let me pay them abundantly in...

Solid Gold... Liquid Myrrh... Gas Frankincense...

To grow Your business of love forgiveness truth and kindness. Free gifts given continually. The gifts needed for earthly journey.

God I need lots from your wealthy bank of Heaven here on this temporary earth.

More peace to give! More forgiveness to advance! More hope to lend!   More inspiration to deliver!

More happiness in credit to point towards You!!!

More of You less of me. Today Lord my God vault is brimming and open for business. I give it away to keep it. Turn it over, empty it out, let it go. You fill and fulfill me back up again before any of it is gone. Your wealth in richness never ends. Make me a channel of your great God economy of love.

Amen.

MARCH 14

PrayStill

Luke 16:24
He called out, "Father Abraham, have mercy on me, and send Lazarus to dip the tip of his finger in water and cool my tongue; for I am in agony in these flames."

Scripture Prayer: Regret

Grampa Daddo always said.
"I'm Okay! Are you Okay? "
I always said the same back. Then we would repeat it again in laughter. Im ok r u ok?
A friend asks me "Are you smiling today?" ... Then I am.
Lord Jesus Christ my savior. I repent of my sins. You are in my heart. I humbly request and take You my Lord and Savior! Amen x amen daily and forever..
I love and trust the Lord Jesus Spirit God. Thank God for God. Eternally
No more lake of fire. Thank God. No more burn. No more fear. No more agonizing here. The message is clear. I care. Respect the dignity of life. Lift up the souls and body of Christ that are in agony on earth. The least last soul is the body of Christ Jesus in lifting.

I hear and heed the Rich man's cry. The no to Gods banquet. The yes to looking back.. The fall of pride. Painful eternal loneliness burning?
No no no. Jesus is clear. Trust in God's guaranteed assurance in love ransomed and paid for through the blood of Jesus
Jesus says,
Believe in me for eternity in grace and mercy and light. Go be righteous. love me with all your heart soul mind and strength... and your neighbor.
John 3:16-17

God loves everything
God gives everything
God requires belief
God grants eternal Heaven
God is mercy and grace and Redeemer and truth and light of the world.
I love You Lord Jesus!!!
Amen x salvation

MARCH 15

PrayStill

Luke 17:1-2
Jesus said to his disciples, "Occasions for stumbling are bound to come, but woe to anyone by whom they come! It would be better for you if a millstone were hung around your neck and you were thrown in the sea than for you to cause one of these little ones to stumble."

Scripture Prayer: Comfort

Precious impressionable little one children. WOW x WOW
Jesus Lord Christ, most very powerful stern advocate for the flock of all your little one children 9 months to 90 years. You Are the compelling force of sovereign justice.
Jesus you have my back. I am so well protected. When someone stumbles on me, You gracefully, in personally designed revealing, unravel unpack and reflect it right back to their journey!!! I accept that you are Justifier omnipotent. You can have it all back from my plate. I surrender.
This reap and sow spiritual truth comes back at me hard full circle beginning and end. I get angry... I spawn anger... it comes right back!
I get greedy... lustful... slothful it circles back.
Millstone albatrosses drown me to rendered unconsciousness. Heal this compliant patient in Your lifeboat of Saving grace. I am so loved and protected in your Holy Spirit counsel and guidance. Surrounded in the womb of your nurture.
The good news is in you Lord. You intervene and break the chain. You make good effect.
All this grace and mercy you inspire in me to aspire towards comes right back tenfold. Lift and be lifted. Smile and be welcomed. Give kindness and be loved back continually. Amen x 7

Let the little one in me be oblivious of any onslaught. YOU PROTECT ME AWESOMELY. I am surrounded in shields of comfort, safety, loving kindness. Praise God these blessings flow.

let me love love love my neighbor and enemy by loosening the albatross millstone around my neck to cast it to your great receiving ocean of mercy. Before I speak or do anything. LORD... guard my lips and steps to navigate the waves of life with Eyes locked on your magnetic pull, Lord Jesus my eternal sustainer. You render me weightless in the gravity. TBTHS TBTG TBTJC

MARCH 16

PrayStill

Luke 17:31-33
On that day, anyone on the housetop who has belongings in the house must not come down to take them away; and likewise anyone in the field must not turn back. Remember Lot's wife. Those who try to make their life secure will lose it, but those who lose their life will keep it.

Scripture Prayer: Straight

Yoke in surrender with eyes on the prize. Drop everything immediately to submission. and then some.... Right now and continually now.
Incline and press forward for more. There is not time or merit or unmerit to look back for in hindsight. My sin is remembered no more. My victory is Yours Lord
Jesus
take the bad or the good. Focus my desire Locked in and rerouting always to You Lord. You are light that never slows... Son of man, Lamb of God sin crucified. You are love that conquers all... Son of God risen in light, man redeemed.
I miss that mark of being in full grace and miss the target and fall short in sin.
Lay sin down in the dusty mire and exchange it for the merciful cross that crucifies the sin and redeems replaces and overcomes with the defending and conquering virtue. Hate the sin.
No more sorrow no more pain. Given up its all for gain. Again and again this law holds true. There is less of me and more for You. Make faith my fuel. You in me and me in You
I love you LORD

MARCH 17

PrayStill

Luke 18:7-8
And will not God grant justice to his chosen ones who cry to him day and night? Will he delay long in helping them? I tell you, he will quickly grant justice to them. And yet, when the Son of Man comes, will he find faith on earth?

Scripture Prayer: Lectio Divina

I don't believe everything you are Jesus but I do believe as you would have me believe and follow your principles??? I don't completely believe in everything you are yet I believe in your justice??? Wait, hold on, stop the press. LORD, do you want all of me? All of my faithful belief. All of my unbelief. No more doubt, no more fear no more me giving up on me?
Ahhah just surrender to you. Your patient persistence insists my behavior. Why is answered in acceptance
I surrender, I surrender to you.
I surrender my unforgiveness to you. I am designed and created by You. You Lord make me to unknowingly and instinctively and instinctually acquiesce to Your Spiritual laws. Lord sometimes even knowingly. My footprints you carried for me when.... I could not.
I did not engage the sin, I walked away. Where did that come from how did that happen?
I loved my enemy enough to break the chain of hate. You Lord... authored that.... You filled me up with your Great Goodness and even let me take some credit for it. Before I could hurt my arm patting myself in the back you gently let me know it IS YOU all along that authors this sampling of this great love of my neighbor.
Peace is the choice you insist upon me to reveal your sweetness. I Breath out "what it is.. ' I breathe in what You Lord make it. Your fulfillment guaranteed beyond my knowing. Your

pure justice reigns on the just and unjust. All glory is yours. Mighty Powerful and Just. I SAY Yes to your invitation of...

Quick to listen Slow to speak Slow to anger

Quickly Quickly Quickly. Immediately if not sooner. I want to be forgiven in Your Justice leveling. LORD, Inspire me to pre-Forgive before it's even required. Everything that happens in the justice of Your Spiritual economy is used for Your exalted revealing Glory. What part of thy kingdom come am I taking credit for, not believing in, or trying to impose?

Jesus is persistence insistence. YOU LORD DESIGN THE OUTCOME

Take the bridge of forgiveness to the Leveling field of your all powerful justice.

Autopilot spiritual communion draws nearness to God. GPS GOD Positioning Service points to God. Automatic lane departure protects toward God. Emergency braking only if required.

Take the wheel Jesus +++ free me of me

MARCH 18

PrayStill

Luke 18:35-38
As [Jesus] approached Jericho, a blind man was sitting by the roadside begging. When he heard a crowd going by, he asked what was happening. They told him, "Jesus of Nazareth is passing by." Then he shouted, "Jesus Son of David, have mercy on me!"

Scripture Prayer: Desperation
Lectio Divina

Oh Lamb of God that takest away the sin of the world
Have mercy on us
Oh Lamb of God that takest away the sin of the world
Have mercy on us
Oh Lamb of God that takest away the sin of the world
Grant us thy peace
mercy, some say is me not getting what I deserve!
I do deserve mercy.
I see the other side of that implied negativity in shame guilt and remorse. mercy lives and conquers my humanness. Man designed with a solution to the flaws. Return to my creator to be repaired. I am under guaranteed warranty. TBTG! mercy is simply me accepting, getting, and receiving, MERCY. This key to freedom I do deserve. God said I need it. Holy spirit surrounds me with its shield. Jesus transformed my debt of sin to merciful forgiveness on the cross. TBTHS His Service Holy Spirit
Like grace is unmerited favor. mercy is unmerited forgiveness and redemption. I do deserve it since Jesus esteemed and cleaned me through Him to cover my imperfections. Lord I am imperfect. Lord Jesus make me whole in you. TBTJC

MERCY: Most Eternal Redeeming Creator Yearnings

GRACE: God's Riches At Christ's Expense

Plain and simple... I cannot fix myself or purify myself. What is impossible with all my exertion is handed off to Gods possibility and opportunity. The meaning of the lessons and the revealings is hidden from me until it is prepared and perfect in His will to be seen. Thank God for restraining the revealing. Perfect Kairos. Perfect love in awesome protection. You Lord build and prepare the way to be seen today for tomorrows merciful blessings

Lord be my eyes of faith. Make me see emotionally mentally physically and spiritually.

How light is my earthly travel bag with God Jesus removing the weight of my living. Less is more. Godspeed is Good.

MARCH 19

PrayStill

Luke 19:5-6 When Jesus came to the place, he looked up and said to him "Zacchaeus, hurry and come down; for I must stay at your house today." So he hurried down and was happy to welcome him

Scripture Prayer: Reflection

Zac is smart and very wealthy and very despised by envious folks. He is "short" in height and apparently in sharing wealth. Zac goes ahead to where he knows God Jesus will be. The massive sycamore is "the place" of climbing for sight and perspective, shade from the heat, and hiding from view.

Jesus sees and calls Zac and Zac is happy to come down and welcome Jesus joyfully. Zac gives the ill gotten tax collected money back and half of his own

Lord Jesus

I love you. You meet me where I am. You welcome me in love and you inspire your spirit in me.

Take all I have, inside and outside, and use it for your good. It is all Yours it was all Yours it will be all Yours.

I will love you first and not money.

I will not fear the loss of money as my idol.

Jesus You own me so my possessions of wealth do not.

YOU LORD make me good with little so I can be trusted with much.

I am paid enormously in...

Your great love awesomely

Your great grace continually

Your great mercy immediately

Your great Forgiveness surrounding me

Your great Comfort embracing me.

Your great Price and Cost delivering me, exchanging healing and cleansing me.

At your leveling spiritual money table Lord my soul is exchanged my soul is revealed.

Jesus you make me. You make me a cheerful giver. Live in me. Make me a cheerful giver of all of me.

Amen

MARCH 20

PrayStill

Luke 19:39-40
Some of the Pharisees in the crowd said to [Jesus], "Teacher, order your disciples to stop." He answered, "I tell you, if these were silent, the stones would shout out."

Scripture Prayer: Lectio Divina

This cannot be contained Lord! There is no hiding it. This momentum will not be quenched or quelled.

Make it stop lord make it go away. this must not change the status quo must remain. I can resist, I can hem and haw and squirm like a worm. This is casting dust on the inevitable exercised in futility and all for naught. Lord you convict me. You convince me. You make Your presence known. You prepare me, You position me. This is certainly assured in the comfort of the change. Excited in the waiting in patience.

Jesus

Jesus is

Jesus is winning

GOD always wins^^^

All things work together for God's good.

Lord you change me you make me yours. You have your way with me. I'm not my own. Forces beyond my control bring Your will to light. Uncontainable and unrefrainable, all the earth.

Sing Your praise!

Great are you Lord!

The stones are torn down, seen laid out flat. The noise is crackling, they sing out, they sing out. The waters are weeping and drops from within. Cold and rough its right here within.

Exchanged for warm and smooth, I feel it in my hand. Smell the dust is incense rising. Taste the texture in communion abiding. light and hope break stone heads and hearts. Life's love remains.

Thank you, Lord, in assuring me what will be. For showing and telling Your story on my heart. For breaking my rocks of defense and denial and stationary complacency.

Scorch and seer away this layer shed for Your glory.

Join me in concert with all the company of Heaven to rejoice in enjoyment. Great are you Lord. Holy is the lamb. Praises rising +++

Amen

MARCH 21

PrayStill

Luke 20:25-26
[Jesus] said to them, "Then give to the emperor the things that are the emperor's, and to God the things that are God's." And they were not able in the presence of the people to trap him by what he said; and being amazed by his answer, they became silent.

Scripture Prayer: Silence

Be still, God is not deceived. truth reigns. Trust that truth is always revealed.

Lord your ledger is true. My chronos time is finite. Your kairos moments endure through generations.

My child in me tests the boundary. If I lie just a little will you convict me just a little?

Lord, you know my heart. You reveal my motivation. You gently reveal your truth in me. I see what you want. You want me in peace with you. You take away my fog and make it crystal clear.

You are jealous for me and nothing comes between us.

Anything I place on the horizontal of the Cross falls. It is the world's dominion of non - spiritual matter that balances on Your level cross of justice.

Jesus, let me live freely. Take all that I place on the cross and point it upward. Your plumb vertical truth cuts through my waning horizontal comforts. You pay me in your vertical truths and laws and turn me away from the world.

I turn vertical to you Jesus to lose and slip the world and gain know your peace. The coin rolls off.

It is paid for. You, Lord, paid my cost. You took all I owe on earth and set me free to you. You let me let it go in comfort truth and peace. You overflowed and washed away what I thought was gold. Refined in the turning to see what your eyes see.

You are relentless in me for me to live free with you

The gravity of the world slips away. Your light shines straight down through it. Nothing comes between us. The great abiding truth. Material is dropped off and exchanged for spiritual truth.

MARCH 22

PrayStill

Luke 21:16-19
You will be betrayed by parents and brothers, by relatives and friends; and they will put some of you to death. You will be hated by all because of my name. But not a hair of your head will perish. By your endurance, you will gain your souls.

Scripture Prayer: Glory

Forgiveness wipes away the pain. The cure to heal every relationship. love grows faster than hate can climb. love sows and showers and shows triumph. Kindness kills the harsh word away. TBTHS
Eternal living WORD, light of flowing life, sparkle like a diamond. Roaring lightning, blinding thunder. Stars and planets in the skies. Bless the LORD! The whole world cries out. Jesus, your irresistible WORDS...Known before spoken, sharpened and persistently given. Confident now and breathed into life. Lived in the inhale shared in the exhale. Beautiful living words flowing finding favor. Favorite grace of Jesus many favorites found. TBTJC
Traveling with You in nowness, future places assured comfort surrounding in Your spirit. Fragrantly present the alluring and attractive channeled path to Your brilliant glory. Unto thee and will look up.
The seed, the placement, the soil, the air and waters and the growing are all Yours. The fields of harvest are eternally plentiful.
The Glory is yours.
TBTG

MARCH 23

PrayStill

Luke 22:3-4
Then Satan entered Judas called Iscariot, who was one of the twelve; he went away and conferred with the chief priests and officers of the temple police about how he might betray [Jesus] to them.

Scripture Prayer: Safety

Lord Jesus
Creator and defender of souls, protect me from the evil one! You never let me go away. The evil trinity is chained beaten and behind us. With You, Jesus, Abba Spirit, we are free in Your preordained victory. The victory o'er the battle won. No fear here. Any temptation is cut away by the sword of God's Scripture Word. Comfort in knowing the love of Jesus reigns o'er all others. Place the stones the serpents and the scorpions in the dry desert behind me. Set aside and wipe away the temptive power. Keep that lower power distant weak and chained away. Foxes, wolves, scorpions, stones and vipers eat themselves powerless. Crushed in their own devices. Weeping rivers in howling pain. Sparks from gnashing teeth. Behind and chained away.

Thank you so much Lord Jesus for Your so awesomely powerful Word of God, Jesus, written to inhale and speak to exhale and hail to expel all evil. Conquering risen son slays every evil in spiritual principality warfare. Rest in assurance knowing the victory won, Lord Jesus, Father won and overcomes. The crucifixion slayed evil eternally eternal to the lake pit fire forever.

God wins every time.

"Make no mistake about it."

How grateful am I Lord Jesus^^+++^^

That you love me, love me, LOVE me... so much You die for me to be saved. You Lord Jesus reign in me around me and surround my soul in comfort.
Thanks be to the Holy Trinity (TBTHT)
TBTG TBTHS TBTJC

Phil 2:10,11
So that at the name of Jesus every knee should bend, in Heaven and on earth and under the earth, and every tongue should confess that Jesus Christ is Lord to the glory of God the Father. - Philippians 2:10-11

MARCH 24

PrayStill

Luke 22:44-45
In his anguish [Jesus] prayed more earnestly, and his sweat became like great drops of blood falling down on the ground. When he got up from prayer, he came to the disciples and found them sleeping because of grief.

Scripture Prayer: Submission

Exultant faith proclaims His Glory. To and from exhaustion Lord you watch over me. I drift into sleep and You heal and restore. I awaken, and you guide. Flood me! Surround me and protect me.
A friend told me Jesus in Heaven prays continuously for my soul.
Jesus, you are so ardent, so intimate, so personal, so loving. This is, will be, shall be forever true.
Jesus, You tell me...
Get up and pray that I not fall into temptation.
Selah
Get up and pray that I not fall into temptation.
Beautiful Savior:
Fill me with Your fragrance. Flood me with your radiance.
Shine in me and transform me to persistently give to others. May Your glory pass through me in living without words.
Model in me reverences to be Your effective emphatic testimony.
Lord you are mighty and strong and humbly loving. Grant me strength and courage and protection to be always connected and protected in Your flowing showers in light. All for Your glory.
TBTJC

MARCH 25

PrayStill

Luke 22:52b-53
Have you come out with swords and clubs as if I were a bandit? When I was with you day after day in the temple, you did not lay hands on me. But this is your hour, and the power of darkness!

Scripture Prayer: Imploring

I'm a human with tendency to follow power. I'm just doing as I'm told, doing as instructed. Humans follow power. It's easy to conform and jump on the band wagon. Wait! Which wagon? Which cliff? Which bully pride pulpit? (You're not like me ... or us.)
Lord Jesus! Help me... Make me... Convict me...
To lift the innocence
To uphold the truth
To promote what is right
To speak the unspoken
To speak to the unspoken to
To embrace the least of these
To see where my force and power motivates from and in Your awesomeness in love.
Lord
Reveal and convict in me the truth in every step and word and thought. Make me always lift the truth. Point and direct me through the clutter and noise of the world. Grant me senses of pure love to see hear feel taste and smell in my spirit the veracity of Your conquering. Bring me together with the forces of goodness, light and renewal. I am weak and needy. Blind to my own ways. Poor in spirit and easily sent stray. Mark and guard my thoughts and words and actions always to Your great love, mercy and graceful forgiveness and peace. Saturated in You, Lord, all this is possible. You are the solution to what ails me. You solve

and resolve over again the human frailty in me. Draw me near to what is always there in your embrace

This I pray, knowing in conviction and assurance the power to do your will is always greatest.

TBTHS

Galatians 5:22

MARCH 26

PrayStill

Luke 23:10-11
The chief priests and the scribes stood by, vehemently accusing [Jesus]. Even Herod with his soldiers treated him with contempt and mocked him; then he put an elegant robe on him, and sent him back to Pilate.

Scripture Prayer: Sorrow

Lord, Your light never dies. You are the one thing that remains forever. Your Word alive is eternal.

How has it gotten to this? This cannot be. The weight of the sins of the world must be crucified at the Cross.

I cry. Sometimes in gratitude for God that loves so much and gives and comforts and watches out for and takes care of me.

I cry. Sometimes in sorrow for loss and grieving that rips my heart out.

I cry. Sometimes for others in their pain and suffering.

I tear up in shame that I as a human have the capacity to treat God and another human being with such disdain... disregard... disrespect...

My eyes burn in sympathy and empathy. In the physical spiritual mental and emotional abuse so freely given. My heart is moved and saddened and emotes.

Lord is this what needs to be done to make the world right?

Is this how much evil needs to be forgiven. How powerfully powerful and strong and loving to let this happen to cleanse the sins of the whole world from beginning to end of time to every soul. The weight of the world is grave. The whole of it is in need.

Mighty Preciousness, Mighty Compassion, Mighty Maker of Heaven and earth, You love, in love, with love so much beyond my understanding to walk through evil to conquer and clean and free from sin.

MARCH 27

PrayStill

Luke 23:26

As they led him away, they seized a man, Simon of Cyrene, who was coming from the country, and they laid the cross on him, and made him carry it behind Jesus.

Scripture Prayer: Invitation

Lord Jesus
Let your Holy Spirit so dwell in and through me that I become the living WORD walking as your hands and feet on this earth. Let me be the best Bible anyone would meet. Make my words thoughts and deeds be Yours. Let me lift and be lifted by others.
Lord
Doing right is not always easy;
Must I walk in this path?
You, Lord, offer healing for what ails me. My fear and denials rooted in envy, greed, gluttony, pride, anger, lust, and sloth.
I must do my part and carry these sinful root fears to the crucifixion. I must do my part for myself and for others. I can carry my acknowledged sin for redemption at Yourinross. I can help others collect and carry. I am worthy to be helped.
The place of surrender and laying it at the foot of the Cross is what I must do.
Lord, you are the transforming love that inspires and enthuses to allow the gathering and casting of sin to the cross. You assure the unknown in the keys of faith granted IN inheritance to surrender to your cleansing and freeing will.
Without Your Great mercy Lord Jesus Spirit incarnate I am bound to this dust of sin.
Lord you watch and protect! Even in the way to the cross.
!^^+++^^!

Forty days tempted in the desert.

A life of healing and redeeming in the most powerful love ministry, given freely.

Scourged and beaten to the cross of redemption, all to save all. And any who can abide. How awesome a love is this that conquers all sin and fear at your great name, Jesus.

SELAH

Let me watch and protect and be protected with your angels and Spirit, saving in grace and mercy. Let me channel and instrument Your will through me to your glory for Your glory. You designed it this way, Mighty Creator. I surrender.

TBTJC

MARCH 28

PrayStill

Luke 23:44-46
It was now about noon, and darkness came over the whole land until three in the afternoon, while the sun's light failed; and the curtain of the temple was torn in two. Then Jesus crying with a loud voice, said, "Father into your hands I commend my spirit." Having said this, he breathed his last.

Scripture Prayer: Reflection

Selah x 3 x 7 x 365 x eternity
Be still
　God is God...
　　　Peace...
　　　　Calm...
　　　　　Silent...
　　　　　　Stillness...
Selah x 7
It is finished. No more dying no more pain.
Oh, Lamb of God. You takest away the sins of the world. Have mercy on us. Grant us thy peace.
At the cross, at the cross sin is dust and Glory lives.
Lord you know me better than I know myself. You ransomed the world so I can live abundantly. Oh no you never let go... ever.
As a child I wondered what was so good about Good Friday since Jesus dies.
Pastor Matthew explained a while back how John the Baptist in his wildness brought the Gospel of Jesus out of the clean mikveh temple into the wilderness for whole world to receive. Baptize all.

Today is in full circle, the curtain is torn revealing God to all. Totally accessible, wild and uncontainable God. Everywhere all powerful all knowing, all giving.

My God, my strength, my redeemer, my savior. So intimate and abiding, so infinite in enduring eternity.

Today I know whose I am.

TBTJC

MARCH 29

PrayStill

Luke 24:4-5
While they were perplexed about this, suddenly two men in dazzling clothes stood beside them. The women were terrified and bowed their faces to the ground, but the men said to them, "Why do you look for the living among the dead? He is not here, but has risen."

Scripture Prayer: Revealing

Lord
Your sudden convictions are "light on." I get it now, ah ha convicted, understood, realized and digested. Suddenly it is in immediacy this I know. Gleaned discerned and thrashed to truth in the threshing floor. The chaff dust blows away in winnowing. Take away from me, Lord, what blocks me from You.
Lord, you tenderly reveal to me in a flash of light the understanding and realizations in your perfect moments.
Quickly and immediately the messenger speaks to understanding. Your servant is listening. I am healed from ignorance. Faith vision sees clearly. Opened faith eyes take in the God-incidences. Faith hearts and minds receive digest and own the suddenly
My distraction is redirected in the gentle hand and touch of the messengers drawing my attention. Angels open pathways to the light and hope of the LORD. Jesus's persistence and patience with me assures peace.
Convicted in the truth of the Holy Spirit, the path is revealed and known. Inspirations from the Creator of love reigns and deigns worthy what always was, what is, and what will be.
Suddenly, Lord Jesus, Your suddenly message is crystal clear reflecting the colors of creation brilliantly.
Amen x convincing

MARCH 30

PrayStill

Luke 24:13-14
Now on that same day two of them were going to a village called Emmaus, about seven miles from Jerusalem, and talking with each other about all these things that had happened.

Scripture Prayer: Comfort

Good Lord Spirit
Whenever two or three are gathered for you! Your prayer transcends time and space. It is already there.
When I surrendered and offered my life to Jesus, I went looking for the best way and place to worship only to find the spiritual key right inside. Along the journey, I search in knocking and seeking and asking, delighted to find the pieces of the spiritual puzzle fall right into place. They tie and bind the whole life mental and emotional together. The keys are right inside
I come to the table and the altar and the cross to renew cleanse and enjoy this beautiful savory savior carry me through the sands of life.
When I step into the world in autopilot the Lord is in around and surrounding. What I thought I authored was really guided by His Holy Spirit. The glory of the goodness the strengthening in the trials. In all the revealings and carrying and everywhere else... To Thine be the glory.
The more I love you, Jesus, the more you show the infinite love you first have for me, that is always there and always deepening.
TBTG TBTJC TBTHS

MARCH 31

PrayStill

Luke 24:40-42
And when [Jesus] had said this, he showed them his hands and his feet. While in their joy they were disbelieving and still wondering, he said to them, "Have you anything here to eat?" They gave him a piece of broiled fish.

Scripture Prayer: Understanding

Lord Jesus Christ,
You communicate with me in suddenlies. I am startled and terrified. My comprehension needs tending to in patience and kindness. In my suddenly moments with You, You claim my perspective. You illuminate away the darkness doubt fear and pride. You break down my disbelief into fertile genesis.
Lord Holy Spirit
As you are suddenly revealed, all my unfaith and disbelief and fear of Your truth is suddenly presented for transformation to faith belief loving assurance. You open my mind in understanding.
Lord Abba Father God
Even in all this transforming belief just one more confirm request to solidify this miracle of Resurrected Heavenly flesh standing before me.
Angels, spirits, and ghosts cannot eat earthly human food.
Could you forge faith even more in me by revealing your new Holy Heavenly Son of God humanness and imbibe and eat something?
Oh ... You did this without me even needing to ask. Joy and wonderment.
Selah

How revealing your suddenly speaks my faithful believing into life. Crystal clear in quick swiftness. Diamond reflecting spectrums reveal all-knowing in this moment for what you will reveal to me. I am filled to overflowing.

In Your abounding grace filled suddenly moment, assurance reigns.

May the words of my mouth and the meditations of my heart continually flow forth

Your praise and worship, In Your perfect consuming love, my strong rock and redeemer.

TBTG

APRIL 1

PrayStill

Ephesians 2:10
For we are God's handiwork, created in Christ Jesus to do good works, which God prepared in advance for us to do.

Scripture Prayer: All Ready

God Almighty, Maker of days, Maker of ways. Marker of miracles in every moment, alive in the realm of Holy on earth. Predestining destinies all over creation. Creator of here's and now's.

Author Spirit
Hovering creation over each soul blossoming. You make the artful design, create and align in humble sublime. You make us in Your image to imagine our gifts to You. You are our esteem presiding.

Christ Jesus
Walking me to tomorrows, You have my days. I feel it inside when I know it's right. You convict me to know Your will. Already created in confidence rated the Way, the truth and the life. light of the world forever unfurled before I am there You are with me.
TBTHS Ready Counselor

APRIL 2

PrayStill

Acts 3:16

By faith in the name of Jesus this man whom you see and know was made strong. It is Jesus' name and the faith that comes through him that has completely healed him, as you can all see.

Scripture Prayer: Heal Me

Lord God
The greatest name in Heaven every knee bows to and every tongue confesses. Holy Holy Holy is the name. Master, healer, protector, and rejuvenator making all things possible.

Healing Spirit
Take away my extremes. Take away my need to be perfect. Take away my desire to please all. Take away my desire to do everything. Let me strive for excellence in being a God fearing God pleasing God accomplishing channel of peace.

Jesus Healer
In you is life and health and wealth. Surrender my depraved paucity to your healing table. Lay me down in the curing pastures that anoint this healing vessel. You are overcomer of every cell. You heal me in the saving salve of your salvation.
TBTJC Savior Divine

APRIL 3

PrayStill

John 3:16
For God so loved the world that he gave his one and only Son, that whoever believes in him shall not perish but have eternal life.

Scripture Prayer: Kingdom Keys

Loving God
Such a caring and sacrificing giving of redemption to a world crying out. Powerful beyond compare and intimately abiding. Drawing near in conviction and love. Insistent Creator of beauty.

Heavenly Spirit
You love everyone. You give everything. You, God, require belief. You give and design everlasting life. With You, life is possible. Because of You, life is faithfully loving. Trust and assurance and conviction follow you daily.

Sacrificing Jesus
Such love, so costly in giving. The weight of the world, the power of the WORD, the cost is paid in forward. To lay down life for others to live, is the greatest love of all. Surely grace and mercy surround Thee eternally.
TBTJC Salvation Author

APRIL 4

PrayStill

Hebrews 11:6
And without faith it is impossible to please God because anyone who comes to him must believe that he exists and that he rewards those who earnestly seek him.

Scripture Prayer: Blessed Assurance

Holy God
Visible in Miracles Angels and circumstances. True and faithful deliverer of answers and requests to know you more. Beautiful revealer of all that is and all that is good. Beautiful Creator of knowledge, of WORD flowing alive.

Holy Ghost
I see and seek you more. In your kairos moments you reveal the truth and love. Holy are your revealings. Unfolding are the dealings. Forever present is Your signature of significance to the world.

Holy Jesus
To see your face, to know your place to follow you in possibility. Faith eyes receive faith hearts believe I come to you inclining. You are the gift the price in lift, to You my life resigning.
TBTJC Savior Smiling

APRIL 5

PrayStill

John 14:2
My Father's house has many rooms; if that were not so, would I have told you that I am going there to prepare a place for you?

Scripture Prayer: Castle Streams

Faithful God
Heaven and earth adorn your glory. Stars and castles and countless rooms of adventure spread into eternity. Undoubtedly, the signature of Heaven waits for the longing and abiding souls.

Convincing Spirit
Just a glimpse of the palaces and castles assures. More and more rooms to explore. Follow the sound and see the light in this room. This one reveals and this one conceals, in each view a comfort the heartwarming feels.

Jesus The Way
A tap on a shoulder a whisper in ear a hand full of grace to know you are near. I turn and I follow to you as the lead. Your yoke is easy your path true in deed. You take me in dreams to Heaven to go, assuring your presence is priceless to know
TBTG Jesus God 3in1

APRIL 6

PrayStill

Matthew 6:6.
But when you pray, go into your room, close the door and pray to your Father who is unseen. Then your Father who sees what is done in secret, will reward you.

Scripture Prayer: This Place

Heavenly God
Creator of places to pray. Maker of channels and pathways leading to prayerful meditative pastures. Holy and powerful signatures in time and space throughout eternity abound.

Prayerful Spirit
You teach me to commune in your presence. To stay a while and surrender all. To unlock the earth in me and fill with the holiness from you. Warm my soul you your providential plan surrounding in light streams.

Jesus Teacher
Your invitation is pleasing inclination to my soul. Wherever I am, You are. You train me to crave the peace beyond. You melt my physical you calm my emotional you focus my concentration. Feed this human vessel spiritually.
TBTJC Author of Prayer

APRIL 7

PrayStill

Mark 4:31
It is like a mustard seed, which, when sown upon the ground, is the smallest of all the seeds on the earth.

Scripture Prayer: perseverance

Gardner God
The substance that grows one hundredfold. The energy and genes of expansion. The DNA of cells replication. The scientific order of things explained and unexplained. The master of the universes.

Spirit Growing
Lord sustain me. Give me courage and strength. Comfort and assure and assuage my ways in you. Let me give more of me away to get more of you. Only in Your strength can I sustain. You remain my strength to behold my fortress my Rock. I am weak and needy and only you know my comfort. You persist and insist I follow you. You are my life abundant. With through and in You, Lord Jesus, I can do all things.

Lord Jesus
You remain in me past exhaustion and defeat. You waken me to fullness in bold transformation. You crucify my pride and see inside my intent and motive. You fuel my incentives and purify my ways. Waves of your inspiration enthuse my spirit to Yours. You have me all and reveal my unknown as your beautiful spirit reveals.
You grow on me you glow in me you take and make me yours. You know me and show me and bring me to these tears. You flow in me and go through me a channel for my ears.
Forever with me. endeavor in me to praise and worship near. Draw me in.
TBTJC

APRIL 8

PrayStill

Acts 4:31
When they had prayed, the place in which they were gathered together was shaken; and they were all filled with the Holy Spirit and spoke the word of God with boldness.

Scripture Prayer: Thunder Voices

Lord Jesus Father
You shook me into this awesome communion with You! So very grateful... +++
You opened and awakened my soul to Yours. I am shaken by no other thing now. All hope all faith all joy is in You. You build me up from Your solid foundation. You make this vessel unshakable.
To the left or the right I will not go. This faith You make will not be shaken. I boldly declare You my savior. You are my never changing foundation. My rock, my redeemer and fortress of Holy Angels.

TBTJC

APRIL 9

PrayStill

1 John 2:15

Scripture Prayer: Vessel Dust

Heavenly Father
God Almighty, Maker of Heaven and earth. Master craftsman molding and making each vessel custom for adorning goodness. Beautiful Creator, Architect, Designer-in-Chief.

Heavenly Spirit
Vision of beauty, vision of life, master o'er pride master o'er strife. Let me see light, blind me from sin, open my heart, let love begin. Empty me clean and fill me pure love, overflow my heart with love from above.

Heavenly Jesus
Fully God and man. Take away the flesh and pride desires of self and self-focus. Steer me with thy comfort. Thy rod and staff are easy yoke. Let me not look back to selfish pride. Mold, make and fill this place overflowing.
TBTJC Author of Salvation

APRIL 10

PrayStill

Acts 5:7
After an interval of about three hours his wife came in, not knowing what had happened.

Scripture Prayer: Direction

Lord Jesus
When I hoard and don't share, I die. When I lust and envy I die a little more. When I lie, I die.

Lord God
Your gratitude in me gives.
Your grace in me makes me content.
Your truth in me is always revealed.

Lord Spirit
Make me a cheerful giver in gratitude and truth. Let me place others before myself in good thought and deed indeed. Your steward is listening.
TBTG

APRIL 11

PrayStill

Acts 5:14-15
Yet more than ever believers were added to the Lord great numbers of both men and women, so that they even carried out the sick into the streets, and laid them on cots and mats, in order that Peter's shadow might fall on some of them as he came by.

Scripture Prayer: Reflection

Whose shadow am I under?
Whose shadow do I long to be under?
Whose am I?
Lord Jesus, I am yours. You own me and I love it. What joy in your comforting custody. You have no shadow. You are light perfect in every shade of brightness and every direction. Your nearness is the healing.
Shine away the darkness. Illumine the areas in my life that need to be examined and given up to You, Lord Jesus.
I can see from the darkness of my shadow into light. You reveal the light is present and I can see into it.
I cannot see into darkness. I need your directed light. Shine in through and with me to reveal the things I do not see that need revealing. In Your great name, Jesus, for your glory and clarity.
Amen
TBTHS

APRIL 12

PrayStill

Acts 5:38-39
So in the present case, I tell you, keep away from these men and let them alone; because if this plan or this undertaking is of human origin, it will fail; but if it is of God you will not be able to overthrow them—in that case you may even be found fighting against God!

Scripture Prayer: Direction

Lord Jesus Christ
Author of succulence in enjoyment.
Let my yes be yes.
Let my no be no.
Let me spit out tepid lukewarm.
Light my path and discern my ways. Guide and protect my path. To the left or the right I will not go. Look me straight to You without sinking. Always in focus. Discern and direct my ways to yield to Your ways.
Lord Jesus, slow me down to speed up You in me. Let my rest reward rule away the rushing and redoing. Keep my motives simple and pure.
Through and in Your great loving mercies, Jesus God.
TBTHS
Amen

APRIL 13

PrayStill

Proverbs 17:9
Whoever would foster love covers over an offense, but whoever repeats the matter separates close friends.

Scripture Prayer: Forgiving

Good God
Giver of goodness mercy and forgiveness. Inclining to meet at the place. Ready to welcome and include. Insistent to do likewise in return.

Good Spirit
Take away my pride worry fear and anger. What if my what if worry became what if glory. What if it's all ok. You are already there. You take away the worry of the world.

Good Jesus
Great teacher and lover of souls. Forever friend, You lay down your life to forever show the power of forgiveness. We know not, we need a lot, You are the saving grace of ages. Reign over in righteousness forever.
TBTJC Savior divine

APRIL 14

PrayStill

Psalm 145:18
The Lord is near to all who call on him, to all who call on him in truth.

Scripture Prayer: Worthy

Approachable God
Calm peaceful and patient in the realm. Always inviting always exciting always waiting for return. Welcoming saunters and sojourners forever at the gates.

Convincing Spirit
You hear the pleas of the contrite. You welcome the calls of the right. Always receiving never deceiving, the humbling of those through the night.

All knowing Jesus
How near to my soul is Your heart. You know me before I start. All through this life you carry the strife and lift and draw near in the calling.
TBTJC Friend Forever

APRIL 15

PrayStill

Acts 7:51
You stiff-necked people, uncircumcised in heart and ears, you are forever opposing the Holy Spirit just as your ancestors used to do.

Scripture Prayer: EGO

The covenant of faith. The portable tabernacle with no inheritable land. I have placed my God in Vagabond transience in the creation homeland. The son of man has no place to lay his head. Persecuted in wandering.
Lord in this vessel you gave to me as an inheritance, my natural inclination is to allow EGO to creep in.
E ase
G od
O ut
Lord make and let me be a strong advocate of Your Holy Spirit manifest in me.
Let me listen and hear through my ignorance and denials and ego pride. Commune with me always making my King Your Will and Ways known to me throughout each day+++
Open my eyes of faith to see you.
Open my ears of trusting hope to hear you.
Renew my mind and heart to know and love you more.
TBTHT
Thanks Be To Holy Trinity

APRIL 16

PrayStill

Acts 8:1
And Saul approved of their killing [Stephen].

Scripture Prayer: ACTS

When will the killing stop?
Pray they receive the Holy Spirit.
Pray we receive the Holy Spirit.
Pray I receive the Holy Spirit.
Once the beautiful, mighty ever-present Counselor is in the human the conviction of changing movements to God occur.
Lord Spirit you patiently persistently insistently wait for the slivering crack of human ignorance to open. You are relentless in washing and igniting the love and pursuit of God within us.
Have your way. We wrestle like Jacob and you win. Always for Your sovereign victories.
Your gift of free will is our gift back to You when we submit and surrender to Jesus.
Amen
Acrostic ACTS
A dornation
C onfession
T hanksgiving
S upplication
Lord Jesus, beautiful, loving, embracing Savior
I am weak and You are strong.
Thank you for your enduring unconditional love.
I pray we stay.

APRIL 17

PrayStill

Acts 8:13
Even Simon himself believed. After being baptized, he stayed constantly with Philip and was amazed when he saw the signs and great miracles that took place.

Scripture Prayer: Pining

Open the eyes of my heart Lord. I want to see you. I want to see you. Expel any fearful unbelief before it arrives. Baptize me in faith overflowing in abundance.
My willingness, Lord Jesus, is your opportunity.
My stubbornness is Your opportunity, Lord Jesus.
Holy Spirit, Mighty Comforter, Counselor and Teacher. Stay constantly in me with me and around me as Your wonderful mighty miracles unfold. Wash and rinse me into your quiet still and clean place of renewal. Fill me with confidence and expectation of your beautiful embrace.
Be my guide, mark my steps, guard my mouth and thoughts to be Your ambassador today.
Let me be as warm and welcoming to others as your presence is in surround of me.
This I pray through Jesus Christ my Savior and Redeemer. The Deliverer of souls.
Amen

APRIL 18

PrayStill

Acts 8:29-30

Then the Spirit said to Philip, "Go over to this chariot and join it." So Philip ran up to it and heard [the eunuch] reading the prophet Isaiah. [Philip] asked, "Do you understand what you are reading?"

Scripture Prayer: Amazing Invitation

Love Isaiah's prophesy
Holy Spirit come.
Rest in this place a while. Make your presence known. Surround and fill this vessel with Your Mysterious Ways. Work in my willingness Your wild Wonders. I surrender. Have it all. I comply with Your inclining and deciding. Take me where you will have me. We transcend space and time in prayer and meditation and presence.
Selah
Lord Spirit be my light shadow through the shadow of the valley. Guide, direct, protect and illumine Thy Word. Your servant is abiding. Lay Your grace hands on. I am willing to receive Your free Freedom. Fill me make me mold me. How I believe with all my heart.
TBTHS

APRIL 19

PrayStill

Acts 9:18-19
And immediately something like scales fell from [Saul's] eyes, and his sight was restored. Then he got up and was baptized, and after taking some food, he regained his strength.

Scripture Prayer: rebuking

Lord Spirit Mother
You lovingly break me from my prideful fear and ego driving my motive to judge and persecute. I want my way, I want to be king. I want to usurp your loving authority.
Why do I persecute you, them, others? What harm have they done? My unyielding confrontational stubborn hurt must be broken. Immediately if not sooner.
You present before me the naked truth of my motive driven in fear. Holy Spirit, my Maternal God, reflect in me the transforming and transcending that must occur. Melt me to ground zero. Descale my vision to clarity. Baptize me in Your Holy cleansing shower of renewal. Wipe me away clean and fill Your Spirit in me. Rename my soul to be Yours alone.
Selah
Lord humble this restless heart and reign over my intentions. Break away the persecuting spirit within that serves self and false pride. Replace my human instinct with Your holy magnetism. Empower your will in me and make me your own. Fill me with the manna from Heaven that serves Your holy and gracious purpose. Transform me into my new and peacefully loving and inviting agency. Mold me into messenger for your abounding and overwhelming love and mercy.
This I pray in confidence and assurance that you will always watch over my intentions and inclinations in motive. Make and implore me to channel love always in all ways.
TBTHS

APRIL 20

PrayStill

Acts 9:39
So Peter got up and went with them; and when he arrived, they took him to the room upstairs. All the widows stood beside him, weeping and showing tunics and other clothing that Dorcas had made while she was with them.

Scripture Prayer: Arise

Loving Spirit, care and call for urgency. Impress upon this heart the power of resurrection. The urgency and immediacy of knowing those I grieve raise up with You. Life is never denied. Tabitha Dorcus lives as do all other believers. Shower life in Your Mighty WORD of Salvation.
Be the WORD of power alive and walking healing and reviving. Just say the WORD.
Be the WORD. Live the WORD. Convey and deliver the Spirit of life truth communicated.
Holy Spirit Mother, Your living WORD weaves resurrection life. Arise and live. Make me a powerful channel of your living Word. Breath this pure Word to earth like fire and flood to give us life in Your embrace. Mama God you deliver life through resurrection. Breadth and breath of powerfully spoken life in word to lift and raise souls.
Revive me in You.
Jesus, You draw and deliver the pathway through the cross of earth to eternity. You live You reign. You make it plain and simple. I make it complicated in doubt and hardness. Simplify my unbelief. Fill me in faith occupied to brim to spilling over in contagion. Spread Your surprising and welcome miracles here on earth. Continue to reveal your mighty power of miraculous life eternal.
TBTHS TBTG TBTJC
Amen

APRIL 21

PrayStill

Acts 10:15
The voice said to [Peter] again, a second time, "What God has made clean, you must not call profane."

Scripture Prayer:

Invoke Meditation Lentamente
Lord God, King of Kings, Queen of Queens, hear my silence.
Arm me to alarm me
Defend me to intend me
Protect me to inject me
Holden me to bolden me
Surround me to impound me
Shield me to yield me
Guide me to be inside me
Surrender me to tender me
Clean me to glean me
Renew me to eschew me
Imbibe me to abide in me
Purify me to justify me
Surround me to impound me
Make me holy to make me wholly. Yours, Lord, I surrender.
Lord, hear feel and know my pining for you, my longing for Your residence in my soul.
Prepare me more for You. Surround Your green fertile flowing fields, You pasture me to lay
in absorption of your presence.

Warming, numbing, relaxing waves spread in circulation as You meditate me to your awareness in silent still calmness.

Selah x breathe.Take me with You where you have me go. Cleanse the thoughts of my mind and the inspiration of my heart. Renew me. Fill my desire. Assure my longing. With You, I am one. Whole again. Present with You.

Selah. Lord Your vision cleanses me. You implore me to peace. You rest me assured.

All ways always through your Loving Holy Spirit desiring my all I am yours.

You are my need.

Remain in me.

Selah

Amen

APRIL 22

PrayStill

Acts 10:28
And [Peter] said to them, "You yourselves know that it is unlawful for a Jew to associate with or to visit a Gentile; but God has shown me that I should not call anyone profane or unclean."

Scripture Prayer: Invitation

Lord, hear my prayer You knew before I spoke.

Arise and shine, raise and roll the rock of salvation. You. Lord, speak in signs and messages of conviction. Your Spirit descends and thrives and fills the earth. Your messengers tune my senses to your angels imploring. I say ok to obey. I put everything my pride knows aside. The weight of the wait is in Your obedience.

The rules are returned to their human creators empty from exclusion. Pride in rules most certainly sets aside in divide.

Open minded and exploring for you Lord always returns your presence. I receive this inviting message. I seek and am welcomed.

Lord Jesus, You reign.

Include every soul from every sin and every religion.

Lord Jesus, you want us all. The invitation is always open. You attract to You, the Way. You are the Way. You illuminate the Way. You give the Way freely.

Let me be in your way, in the Way, in a good way. Yes way! Your Way is the only way and everyone is welcome to come. Invited to attend, attracted to stay.

Lord Your Way reigns the only way with no other way. SO AWESOME. Assurance and conviction wipe jealously away. There is no other God. Abba, Mama, Lord Jesus, Trinity divine, have Your Way.

Amen

APRIL 23

PrayStill

Acts 10:46b-47
Then Peter said, "Can anyone withhold the water for baptizing these people who have received the Holy Spirit just as we have?"

Scripture Prayer: Presence

Lord
You find me wherever I am. You seek me out in all places. I think I hide in the secret from you however you know me before I was born. You know my days ahead.

There is comfort in knowing your baptism is perpetual. You tend to me in renewal. Every day you bring scriptural nourishment gifts and renew my soul. Wash me cleanse me make me new in You. The truth in the life in the light of Your surround is inescapable. I am guarded in your loving embrace.

God, You please in goodness, love, mercy and grace. Descend your embracing spirit fresh on me. Shower enjoyment contentment and peace. Meet and take me to our warm place of peace. Exhaust myself of me into you. Kindle flames of dance. From the inside pour over me. From touch you walk in. You abound in everywhere. You meet me here. You are my now. I know now this present in presence is Yours, Lord. I remain.

TBTHS

APRIL 24

PrayStill

Acts 11:16-17
And I remembered the word of the Lord how he had said, "John baptized with water, but you will be baptized with the Holy Spirit." If then God gave them the same gift that he gave us when we believed in the Lord Jesus Christ, who was I that I could hinder God?

Scripture Prayer: Cleansing

Lord Holy Spirit, come. Descend afresh anew. Renew me to You. Receive and glorify Your great name, awesomeness on breath tongue and lip. Flowing Spirit reign.
Spirit Mama God
You always have your way with me. I surrender expectedly. Yoke me in your easy and light. Draw me through the flame warmed and purified for You. Dedicate and pass me through the waters breathing in Your life. Descend in my unknown and captivate me to you. I withhold nothing. I hold only You.
Born in need for Your cure of sin, You take me from within. You turn it inside out. You place me with Your glory within. Surround my in and out.
Purifying Font, burn away the chaffing sin. You shear my sin away and clothe me close in colors, inside out outside in.
When I go heavy and laden make me easy and light. I delight my ways in your ways, Jesus. You fulfill Heaven's desires in my heart.
TBTHS
Amen

APRIL 25

PrayStill

Acts 11:29-30
The disciples determined that according to their ability, each would send relief to the believers living in Judea; this they did, sending it to the elders by Barnabas and Saul.

Scripture Prayer: Giving

Lord Jesus Spirit. +++
There is trust in giving. Teach me to trust completely in giving and give anonymously. This removes my fear and pride. Make me confident in humility offerings.
Jesus, you gave all of You to death to give abundant life to us. Your payment is sin. I pay You my sin debt and You give me life abundantly abounding.
You love me first so I can love You always by loving first others. At the end of me I find you. You begin and end me and everything between.
Today Lord, I pay this free gift in eternal perpetuity back in cheerfulness smiles and contagion to attract Your harvest to You. Make me Your instrument. Let me cast freely the love You first bestowed upon me to those You have me meet.
Let me give freely my time and ability and resource. It's all Yours from the beginning. Implore me to give of me to others to create room for You to enter and renew me. I let go to let You in. I surrender a colorful Heaven's coat gift to those in need.
May the words and actions in my travels and encounters today be Yours. Giving is a gift both ways, reflexive of Your great weaving first love.
TBTJC through the Holy Spiritess.
Amen

APRIL 26

PrayStill

Acts 12:7

Suddenly an angel of the Lord appeared, and a light shone in the cell. He tapped Peter on the side and woke him, saying, "Get up quickly." And the chains fell off his wrists.

Scripture Prayer: Freedom

Lord you guide in the suddenly. My instinct is Your way. You are lightning to my path alert. Your urgency beckons my reply. My startle is for You, my yes is yes. My awakening is in tune for your direct. I see hear feel and know you are authentic. You are true and right. Your messenger angel deliverer assures in confidence.

Infiltrate my chains. Escalate my desire in your expanse. Elevate my pitch to your freeing frequency. Your messenger angel, Lord, sets me right straight. Unbind me from what I have no awareness. Whisper me away from sins' shackle. The hidden shackle holds back no more.

Quickly suddenly prepare me to Your freeing graces expanse. Uncontainable lightning cracks the stone of restraint to currents and waves of sands. Ride me from my limited reside.

Crystal Clarity,

Crackling pitch,

Light to Your expansive universes of Your Kingdom's realms.

Free from me to free with You

TBTHS TBTJC TBTG

Amen

APRIL 27

PrayStill

Acts 12:22-23

The people kept shouting, "The voice of a god, and not of a mortal!" And immediately, because he had not given the glory to God an angel of the Lord struck him down, and he was eaten by worms and died.

Scripture Prayer: Reverence

Lord God Jesus

I am dust. My prideful usurping way thieves your Glory. I am dusted back to dust when I claim Your glory. May my pride boast in you alone. Reverence revering Your sanctified holy name.

Let me be the first to praise you in the joys and successes of the day. Make the pride in me just enough to deflect the praise You create in me back to You. Protect me from my desire to claim the praise that is Yours. Meet me where I am.

Make me want to give it all back to You. My worth resides to you. I give you the pain. I give you the praise. You are the author of my foundation creation.

When praising and lifting others, let the accolades reign upward as a flowing effervescent stream to your ears. Beat rhythm and cadence of our inspirings scented back to you. I exalt You.

Your redirected pride in me is my shield and strength. My pride in me is my fear and weakness. Pride me to the level of estimable only. Nothing more. Nothing more is needed than to wear loosely this life given back to you.

May the words of my mouth the actions of my mind and the intentions of my heart be always and only two and four You, Lord Jesus, Spirit of my soul. Be my fervent continual prayer. Be the salve of my salvation. Make my wild recklessness elevate in You.

Amen 3:16

APRIL 28

PrayStill

Acts 13:7-8
[A false prophet] was with the proconsul, Sergius Paulus, an intelligent man, who summoned Barnabas and Saul and wanted to hear the word of God. But the magician Elymas (for that is the translation of his name) opposed them and tried to turn the proconsul away from the faith.

Scripture Prayer: genuine

Lord Jesus, Holy Spirit, Mama Abba. Hear my prayer.
Conviction in truth discerns genuine versus counterfeit. Make no mistake about it, do NOT be deceived. truth is always revealed. Sense the abiding Lord Jesus. Know the victory is won. Test the integrity knowing God's truth spoken.
Jesus, You are mighty strong and humble champion of my soul. I adore Your holy avenging desire for me. Relentless assurance in pursuit of my every need.
I confess my weakness in the lustering world.
Praise in the prize of Your surprise.
Bask me in your great and merciful grace.
Your graceful mercy insists my renewal.
How grateful am I Your redemption rules.
Supply my sustain. Cleans my stains of falsity and counterfeit. Provide discernment. Make my sensitivity understand to You. Remove the facade of the imposter. light shine, light Divine.
My trust and faith in You, Lord Jesus, shall always be first. You are my genuine guiding guardian. My inheritance always and forever, eternally unending.

Thanks
Be
To
Father
Son
Holy
Spirit
TBTFSHS

APRIL 29

PrayStill

Acts 13:40-41

Beware, therefore, that what the prophets said does not happen to you: "Look, you scoffers! Be amazed and perish, for in your days I am doing a work, a work that you will never believe, even if someone tells you."

Scripture Prayer: Enlighten

Jesus Spirit God

Free my perishable perception of You. Amaze me in You.

Willing me my reception of your ways. Broaden the scope of understanding love and relationship with You. Miracle my every belief exponentially. Guide my trust and love in you beyond wonder ability and expectation. Abide my comprehension with Your fathom. Transform me away from me.

The excitement is in the not knowing. The trust is in faith and the joy is in acknowledgement and reception of Your sensation.

Your magnificence overwhelms and breaks my containing beliefs. You guide my expansion. Explode me to Your ways. Focus my God-gles to submission beyond your pervasive light. Enthuse my desire to infinite communion. Meet me here and now to take me outside here and now.

Selah

Pleasure Your alluring consuming vehemence in eminence. I am made new. Made never the same. You are perpetually changing eternally expanded, forever loosed in wild uncontainable, spread surpassing sensation.

I am released from me. Take me, make me, break me, unmold me with You.

Selah

Amen

APRIL 30

PrayStill

Acts 14:11-12
When the crowds saw what Paul had done, they shouted in the Lycaonian language, "The gods have come down to us in human form!" Barnabas they called Zeus, and Paul they called Hermes, because he was the chief speaker.

Scripture Prayer: Adorning

Look and see my desiring intention from desperation. I beckon Your awesome healing. Chain me to your freedom. You make me walk from my lameness, healed in hailing the new. Lift me in the wholeness, raise me from the gravity of the situation Inspired.
Selah
Celebration
Holy Spirit, pervasive attraction, universal ambassador liaison, grab me where I am and take me to Trinity infinity. Welcome, invite and occupy my every essence. You, Lord, abound in flavorful colors. Your lighted spice permeates and softens me. I receive.
Stimulate my adherence in your obedient presence. You come to me through every channel. You submit my idle gods to Your will. All my receptors are aligned and reset. Capture me in rapture of your ravishing activation.
You reveal in me the insistent truth of Your ability to own me. Instigate in me continual completion in, with, and for Your proclaiming purposes.
This I pray in full assurance and confidence. Through Christ Jesus our Saving Lord.
Amen

MAY 1

PrayStill

Acts 14:27
When they arrived, they called the church together and related all that God had done with them, and how he had opened a door of faith for the Gentiles.

Scripture Prayer: Endurance

Lord Jesus, God
Delight me in your ways. Enlighten my desire to share Your Good News. Wash off the dust of the day to refine the message of Your loveliness. You Lord are the greatest Greatness News that takes away the sin of the world.
Selah
Embolden my share and conviction. Make me magnetize to you in attraction. Enthuse and inspire to alter at Your altar. Renew my soul to make me whole. Holy is Your presence. Awesome is the attraction. Beautiful is the embrace of comfort. Live my life in me to show Your life in me to others. Channel through me Your desire.
TBTHS

MAY 2

PrayStill

Acts 15:8-9
And God who knows the human heart, testified to them by giving them the Holy Spirit just as he did to us; and in cleansing their hearts by faith he has made no distinction between them and us

Scripture Prayer: Whelming

Holy Spirit, You are....
Jesus... Is....
Mama Abba God ... forever was and will be.
You are mighty strong and relentless. I am weak and needy. Be my need fulfilling.
In Your presence is light and peace and strength and hope and contentment. grace and mercy, you own me. You are my surrogate advocates. You reign in me. I am adopted back to original. You are my well beyond and above expectations comprehension. Live me in your will.
Holy Trinity, let me love all unconditionally. Help me to meet and accept my encounters today exactly where they are without expectation or judgement. Reveal the spiritual keys that tie and blend us. Our blood, breath and water are all the same. Meet me where we are. Allow me to humbly submit to others to wash their steps in your glories.
My conviction is You. You are my power my presence my relation.
Thanks be to Holy Trinity, Three in One, mightily awesome Author of salvation.
Amen

MAY 3

PrayStill

Acts 15:28
For it has seemed good to the Holy Spirit and to us to impose on you no further burden than these essentials.

Scripture Prayer: Boundary

Lord Jesus Spirit
You speak to my soul in conviction. You discern and reveal my right and wrong. You keep me in the realm of your green pasture. Your shepherded fence surrounds my intention. You subtly convince me to process sin thoughts healthfully.
You deflect my anger and turn it into focused kindness.
My greed energy is suddenly replaced by generosity.
You take my gluttony and over indulgence and show me less is more.
My envy, ... You turn into contentment and gratitude.
My lust is purified.
My hesitation becomes diligence.
Take my pride in self and fear and insecurity and humble me to expressive love in Your will be done.
Lord the rules are legal religion. My abidance is written by Your Spirit on my heart. Ignite my willingness to surrender all to you. Powerfully before knowing, my sin is removed by you before asking.
Lord Jesus, God, when I am weak, Channel and redirect my sin natures to you. You are mighty and strong and overwhelmingly receive from my willingness to let go. Intrude in me when stray. Set me straight to in with You.
Free me, free love, free gifts to give and receive freely.

Your awesomeness in surround smiles my presence.

TBTHS, thank you Jesus God!

Amen

MAY 4

PrayStill

Acts 15:38
But Paul decided not to take with them one who had deserted them in Pamphylia and had not accompanied them in the work.

Scripture Prayer: Beginnings

Lord Jesus Christ, Son of God Alpha Omega, Mighty Creator, Never-Ender.
Grateful am I in the glory of Your kairos moments.
Break up my linear thinking trapped in timeline and hope me in your circle of life. Your refresh surprises.
When I think it is over You show me otherwise. My conclusion in expectation is uprooted in Your miracles.
Your will of surprise and enlightenment convicts my soul of Your Great presence. I expect the mundane while You reveal Your surprising delight in different endings.
Lord Jesus Spirit
You have rooted my ending in Your great beginnings. Turn me upside down. Let me go into letting go. No matter in Your circle, all endings are beginnings to Your means. This ending in my boundary is breathed as beginning every day.
Lord, You are...
You are the continual beginnings of hope and renewal journeying in the wild relentless authorship of precious moments. Seared into the print of the picture you paint on my soul.
Prune me, Lord.
Grow You in me.
Chaff away the dust of the day. Grow me to You. As I insist my will, You persist Your will around me.

Permeate my ways.

You, Lord, have written on my soul "there is no end.". What I thought was ended is begun again. The love never ends. The love begins again. No matter encircled, I am loved loved LOVED... I love You. 143,459,831

143 = 1 Letter-I, 4 Letters-LOVE, 3 Letters-YOU

459 = Phone Digits I, L, Y

831 = 8 Letters, 3 Words, 1 Meaning

Amen

MAY 5

PrayStill

Acts 16:15
When [Lydia] and her household were baptized, she urged us, saying, "If you have judged me to be faithful to the Lord come and stay at my home." And she prevailed upon us.

Scripture Prayer: Invitation

Guardian, Parent, Jesus, God
Your light word path attracts. Drop the confines of space. Uncover and draw my surround. Peel away the substance to draw my understanding. Reveal in me the placelessness of your nature. Everywhere is already there. The there is here. Omnipresence reigns unbound.
Lord Jesus, Spirit
With you there is no traveling required. No rushing or waiting. In being, I dwell with You here. Lord my comfort is... you pervade always every here.
Attraction and adhesion like droplets of water drawn to connect draw engulfing. Permeate Your presence invitation.
From within, you ignite. light with light, water with water, flesh with Spirit.
Be with me in steps. Stay in me in travels. Be my every destination. Constrain prevail and convince me beyond your presence. Transcend My place to know with you is spacelessness abounding.
Amen
TBHS
Amen

MAY 6

PrayStill

Acts 16:16-17

One day, as we were going to the place of Prayer: we met a slave girl who had a spirit of divination and brought her owners a great deal of money by fortune-telling. While she followed Paul and us, she would cry out, "These men are slaves of the Most High God who proclaim to you a way of salvation."

Scripture Prayer: Good News

Light of the world, flesh of the son of man, truth of the grace of redemption, You shine through the darkness. The whole world sings out and declares Your great glories uncontainable. The cry of the world is heard. The darkness declares the light. The hidden obvious is declared and revealed.

Lord Jesus, Author of redemption. Your unfailing love shines through mountains declaring God alive. You persist salvation in eternity alive. Even the darkness worships the light.

Let everything that has breath praise the Lord. Let the trees in the field lift their arms to You. Let the hume over the earth grow Your sanctified glory.

Lord Jesus, God

Declare in me discernment to know the intentions of the declarations. Allow me to know the root of the intentions. Grant me Your truth in motivations. Genuinely reveal authentic motives.

Light bright the fleeing darkness. Your Awesome light truth purifies the messengers' intentions. Even the wolf the scorpion the snake are tamed and dismissed. The dove, the silk weaver, and Thy staff elect and Shepherd righty Your Way Lord Jesus.

Forever rule in love this reflection of darkness to darkness. Convert it to colors of hue adorning arraignments. Shine Heavens victory Godspeed surpassing lights' discovery.

Holy Holy Holy is the brilliance of Your Glory.

Holy Holy Holy is the Lamb.
Holy light, Holy Bright, Holy Three in One.
Amen

MAY 7

PrayStill

Acts 17:6-7
When they could not find them, they dragged Jason and some believers before the city authorities, shouting, "These people who have been turning the world upside down have come here also, and Jason has entertained them as guests. They are all acting contrary to the decrees of the emperor, saying that there is another king named Jesus."

Scripture Prayer: Turn It Over

Jesus you reign by ruling release. I grasp the comfort of knowing. Habit sloths me stagnant. Uncomfort me in unknown assurance.

The change, for, in, with You is the excitement. The change changes every day. Never the same and always new in You. Grow me in Your pastures' field of food.

Lord, you give me just enough free will for me to be upside down in sin self-will. My free will is truly only free in You. My self-will usurps pridefully deceived. Always resorting back to you. You boundary me awesomely. By default design, You masterfully let all free will dissolve to Your Freeing Will.

Make no mistake about it, You will not allow deceit. My perception deception steers to you for alignment.

The wind sounds like rain

The rain looks like colors

The rise and the set sun the same

My yes brings more no

My no knows more yes

Surrender in you is to win

Slowing down I speed up

In silence I'm heard

A setback is now a set up

Lord you turn the upside-down world right side up. When You're at the table the enemy flees and all truth flows from Your cup.

Lord Jesus. Perceive my deception into truth. Weave my steps in your safe field. Direct my thoughts and actions.

My Guide, My comfort, My Deliverer. Your reign in me washes my breath of your horizon. TBTG TBTHS grateful in You Lord Jesus the only True King of kings. Reign on!

Amen

MAY 8

PrayStill

Acts 17:19-21

So they took [Paul] and brought him to the Areopagus and asked him, "May we know what this new teaching is that you are presenting? It sounds rather strange to us, so we would like to know what it means." Now all the Athenians and the foreigners living there would spend their time in nothing but telling or hearing something new.

Scripture Prayer: love New

Lord Redeemer,

You reside and revive. You naturally draw and attract. The beauty of your essence cannot be contained. love is always in all ways.

Jesus let me love Your love. Simply receive, simply know, simply feel. Easy to know and share. The greatest love is You. There is no greater.

Lord Savior, there is no other.

Your fragrance lingers insisting. Erase my complication. Simply know You love all of me as I am. YOU KNOW. You made me. You placed me where I am. You love and are love.

Love surrounds every word, You are there. I welcome, you are here. I believe Your love continually visits. love is always new.

Lord Jesus, you love me first I love you back. Clear love, Free love, Wild love. Overwhelming uncontainable always remain-able love.

Only Your love saves eternal, Jesus.

Amen

MAY 9

PrayStill

Acts 18:26 [Apollos] began to speak boldly in the synagogue; but when Priscilla and Aquila heard him, they took him aside and explained the Way of God to him more accurately.

Scripture Prayer: Bold Tuning

Jehovah Psalm,
Song of my heart, You pulse my heart. The lifeblood beat of the rhythm of my soul. Boldly proclaim in me the wild compellation masterpiece You sing in creation. Delight me to your tune. Bend my pitch boldly to proclaim Your glory. May it be a sweet, sweet sustaining effervescence. Linger in my calm. Take me to Your stillness in the noise.
Selah
All for You I give to You to be Your song. Make me Your instrument. Channel flow and deliver your honeypot attraction. Inhabit my ability.
Thine, not mine, be the Glory.
Let the fragrance flow in, to, and for You, Lord of creation, vibration of life, warmth of the world.
Selah
Living word alive in praise. Raise and weave Your harmony and melody beating to the rhythm adorning You. Raise the elevation to point to You. Plug in Your lightning. Illuminate and bolt to You the street signs of desire. To You, the page comes alive. Thy Word alive sings out.
Jesus, Messiah, Jehovah Jireh
Jehovah Psalm, Make me an instrument of Your song. Live in me my days in you, to the melody of Your tune.
Selah
Amen

MAY 10

PrayStill

Acts 19:24-25
A man named Demetrius, a silversmith who made silver shrines of Artemis, brought no little business to the artisans. These he gathered together, with the workers of the same trade, and said, "Men, you know that we get our wealth from this business."

Scripture Prayer: Purity

Lord Jesus
You are authentic genuine and true. Everything else is chaff. Worship me not in idols. Earn my keep in genuine living rooted in wholesome initiatives. Let the wheat and the tares grow where they may. Let my steps flourish the wheat and crush the tares. May the seeds I foster profit Your great kingdom, Lord Jesus.
I am weak and needy. You are the cure. You are the solution to anything ailing. Hail Your mighty fortress of love prevailing. Jesus, Master, Author of Salvation. Direct Your Heavenly Kingdom through the shadows of tares and darkness. Flourish Your abundant golden wheats of lights flourishing all to You.
Amen

MAY 11

PrayStill

Acts 20:29-30
I know that after I have gone, savage wolves will come in among you, not sparing the flock. Some even from your own group will come distorting the truth in order to entice the disciples to follow them.

Scripture Prayer: Beware

Lord
Spirit
God
Watch over Israel. Never slumber never sleep. Learn me into learning to discern. At any given moment the thief can enter in. Rebuke with your powerful word the enemy attempt. Convict us in wholeness to fend off and flee off and crush the enemy's false fleecing.
Selah
Lord you grant the ear to hearing. Suddenly realize us in the revealing that takes away the sins of the world mercifully. Do not let the imposter be. Scattered the enemy away.
Check my motive ... am I fear or am I love? Refine the truth root to the master weaving vine. Nourish the truth to shine in the sparkling rains that washes sin away. It takes Your grace to know a thief so take the thieves away
Not an inch can be given for compromise. No surprise for the diligence intelligence. Wisdom reigns over power and power cannot ascertain. Yes is yes and no is no. Flee the foe from here to get behind.
Incur understanding and insight, Lord Jesus. Give Hear ring in my ear, to learn and discern Your true lightning words. We are safe in You, Protector, Lord, Father, Son, Majestic Spirit.
Amen

MAY 12

PrayStill

Acts 21:12-13
When we heard this, we and the people there urged him not to go up to Jerusalem. Then Paul answered, "What are you doing, weeping and breaking my heart? For I am ready not only to be bound but even to die in Jerusalem for the name of the Lord Jesus."

Scripture Prayer: Em-bold-ening

I give it all to You, Jesus.
I live my life like a prayer for You. I tithe x 11 my life for You. Everything I have, do and know, is for You.
Rest Selah
My mission submission is Your incision decision to make me whole in you. Reside abide and stay with me, in me, through me. I am Yours again and again spinning in braced comfort of Your love. Start and end, birth and death, Alpha and Omega, You so reign. Everything in the middle is Yours.
I think I'm mine, so You let me be free will, to decide a way. All that I do is really stepping for You. Whether I know it or not, good or bad is all raised up to you. Be in my instinct. Be in my intuition. Inspire my desire for You.
I surrender, I submit, I cast in loosely away. All that I have, all that I am, and all that you'll have me to be. How awesome is that You love and guide and comfort and provide and deliver me from my distress. Your love magnified, purified inside melts with warmth this vessel supplied.
Grant me your love grant me your wisdom grant this in tuition paid forward. Beyond my comprehension thought or retention, just a portion of You overwhelms!

Thanks be to the Father, the Son, the Holy Spirit that lives and reigns in gentle convincing persuasion.

Yes way, Yahweh, always in all ways.

Amen

MAY 13

PrayStill

Acts 22:6-7
While I was on my way and approaching Damascus, about noon a great light from Heaven suddenly shown about me. I fell to the ground and heard a voice saying to me, "Saul, Saul, why are you persecuting me?"

Scripture Prayer: Powerful Magnificence

Holy Spirit, embrace me. Blind me erase me and redirect my ways. In the warmth of Your holy engulf, the assurance of faith change numbs my stance. Instantly melting my resolve I am.

Selah-bration Selah

Present Your pre-sent messengers of glorious transform. Melt and mold new, redirected to You. Surrounded in peace light I relent. Blinded of my ways I repent. Drawn out, dried, and enlighten. Shiny new reflection of Your mighty forgiving assurance of extravagant love. Free from me at last with no conditions. Shone in colors and hue to reflect Your magnificent hues of life. Huge in all in all surrounded. Take my all surrender. Own my soul.

Jesus, Lord of all, you see hear and feel me beyond my understanding. The true right mothering soul within planted in eternity. Direct, redirect and infect my will alignment. Beautiful is Your way. Sealed protected obeyed. Never again to stray from staying powers You rule. My desire and Your fire desire refining glow my warmth rekindled. Ember this sender to touch my lips and cleanse and send me new. My feet and eyes are covered in your pure truth. My sight steps I relinquish. Your wings lift my soul aright. Your scented sense essence is clear

Send me, send me, I am, here I am, You in me.

Amen

Thanks be to God's glorious holy messenger angel, Spirit of light and truth. ^^+++^^

MAY 14

PrayStill

Acts 23:6
When Paul noticed that some were Sadducees and others were Pharisees, he called out in the council, "Brothers, I am a Pharisee, a son of Pharisees. I am on trial concerning the hope of the resurrection of the dead."

Scripture Prayer: Attraction

Lord Jesus
You draw and persuade me. You attract and convey to me. You convict and assuage me. Forever inescapable. There is so much comfort in knowing I am heir to you. I inherit your love and forgiveness. grace and mercy abounding in abundances. Meet me beyond where and when I am.
Selah
You marker my life with moments of loving grace that steer point and direct to You. Your mercy reigns in my direction. I am set to You.
My faith steps leap, landing on Your promises. Secured assured and cured of what ails. Fear no more, Faith's at the door. Pride aside and place humble beside. You Lord yoke and strengthen in your easy light way. Moments of forever pass through that beyond understanding peace.
To dye red my sin to you is to gain. To live in you is gain. Again, and again you reign.
TBTG mighty savior and Author of Salvation, Master of Creation.
Amen

MAY 15

PrayStill

Acts 23:12
In the morning the Jews joined in a conspiracy and bound themselves by an oath neither to eat nor drink until they had killed Paul.

Scripture Prayer: love Wins

Abba Father, ruler of all. You take away the sin of the world. Receive our prayer. You alone are the most high Jesus Christ in the Holy Spirit. Have mercy upon us.

I am who I am with. Alone I need help direction and correction. Let me not be on conspiracy and motives of pride fear. Accompany me Lord throughout my days watching through alliances and associations and friendships and loved ones and spiritual prayer partners. Guide direct and infect your holiness in me. Let me not be deceived. May your word sword though the tares.

Let the truth be not deceived by the crowd. Let Your truth always light illustrious paths to You.

My strength in Your revealed truth multiplies exponentially Your Great Deity. Let ignorance blow chaff away to the dunes. Purify Thy way immeasurably. Magnify truths transforming love of souls from the pit of disparagement to the glory of Your great communion in community of love.

Lord Jesus, the willful enemy is unjustified in result. Your mighty fortress shall never be denied nor trampled. Your holy pasture, Heaven, converts wicked to willful in Your grace redirecting transformed and supplanted.

You are so, so awesome, Lord. I melt in awe at the sound and imbibing of Your great name Jesus. Take me with to You.

Amen

MAY 16

PrayStill

Acts 24:5
We have, in fact, found this man a pestilent fellow, an agitator among all the Jews throughout the world, and a ringleader of the sect of the Nazarenes.

Scripture Prayer: Genuine

Lord Almighty, Jesus Christ, in the Holy Spirit!
May the...words...meditations...thoughts...prayers...and actions of my heart be always pleasing and true to You LORD.
The calm peaceful truth delivers in love and agitates the soul to conviction. Rightfully so the truth be told. Lord does it need to be spoken now. Does it need to be said at all. Does it need to be channeled through me. Harness and bridal my lips.
Patience in my delivery. Listen more and more. Let me hear and know this moment. Let me hear the words falling down before they are spoken. Root my motive and message in peace to the effervescent sweet sound of your voice rising in-sense. Fold away the noise of the world in the stillness of the calm deep surround.
Selah
Can I speak your truth in love, with love, surrounded and wrapped in care? Can I deliver with planted peaceful agitation motivation stirring currents to You. Sword: Your Word in Your truth healing.
Let the Word taste easy on the ears and sweet on the soul and convicting on motives. Let the spoken truth reign down o'er me. I love you, Lord. You make my hearing sensitive and true. Quick to listen, slow to speak, fast to showering love.
TBTG
Amen

MAY 17

PrayStill

Acts 25:12
Then Festus, after he had conferred with his council, replied [to Paul], "You have appealed to the emperor; to the emperor you will go."

Scripture Prayer: Adamant

Lord Savior Jesus
Your unending pursuit of my soul comforts in obedience. Your incessant desire for me, unceasingly
surrounds my life. You are King of me and my ways. I love submitting in conviction to your Word alive.
Say la
Lord flow deep. Lord surround complete, Lord be in my head Lord be in my heart. Lord be in my left hand; Lord be in my right hand. Lord be in my whole body. Thanks be to God
Jesus, armor is my sanctuary refuge rock. The Lord protects and defends. I refuse to let the lies of the world enter my being. I no longer can retain or absorb the lie. The truth is spoken. The lie set behind and the battle over and won. There is no compromise.
Jesus, You Indicate indictment of truth love unending. No law can stop or contain Your Holy Word. It convinces in conviction. Like the melting crackles of shattering glass statues of statutes, love replaces, back to dust, the molten lava of refining fire to seal Your complete holy wholeness.
Jesus, God, You are... Spirit of Life, Ruach Elohim, Jehovah Jireh, King, Lord God above all names, You are.
:-) X Infinity ^^+++^^
Amen
TBTHS

MAY 18

PrayStill

Acts 26:24
While he was making this defense, Festus exclaimed, "You are out of your mind, Paul! Too much learning is driving you insane!"

Scripture Prayer: Inverted

Lord All Mighty Son of Man and Son of God you awesomely rule this world in the silent threads of belief. Lord Jesus wash away my unbelief to in-belief. You are everything always everywhere.

You in-escape me. I am comfortably bound to your loveliness truth and honor. Be my every. Lord

Turn it upside down inside out make it true and true. Turn the worldly ways of life around and back to You. What's true is false what's false is true it perishes away. Today's the day I have to say... Lord Jesus make Your way.

My faith in you is planted every day. I look for your precious signs. I see you here, I see you there; your works are the Divine. You shower, reign and deign the way and open eyes to see. You make the way that other say insanely has to be.

Whose perspective is it anyway when truth is false and false made true the sheep just fade away. Find 'em bring 'em back to You unveil the truth as true.

My sane for you Lord is insanity for truth. What others say is not my way I'm insanely in love with You. All day long I pray and talk and listen for Your signs. All day long and nighttime too you comfort in reply. Your always there in more and more unending love of new. I give it all I live it all I give it back to You.

Trinity, God in One, lover of my soul. I come to you all ready there, You make me whole in whole. I'm overtaken in love surrounded in peace, renewed in mind and soul. I'm crazy for you Jesus crazy for your love. All ways with your hand on me always from above.

Lord Jesus, God

Today I am

Today I am sane

Today I am sanely in love with. You

Today I'm in sane for you!

Amen X Foreva. :-) X ^^+++^^

TBTG

MAY 19

PrayStill

Acts 27:9-10
Since much time had been lost and sailing was now dangerous, because even the Fast had already gone by, Paul advised them, saying, "Sirs, I can see that the voyage will be with danger and much heavy loss, not only of the cargo and the ship, but also of our lives."

Scripture Prayer: Embolden Change

Blessed Spirit
Take me from this comfortable place of stagnancy. The habit of the day is so easy to fall in two steps. The waters are calm in the Port of familiarity. It's so easy to recoil from life in the mundane bay. The door to daily sameness cries.

Lord Jesus, make radical in me the change in my inspiring. Stir boldness and faith in my unknown steps to You. Maintain strength in being outside the boundary. Fear get behind me. I step right over the frigid freeze of dormancy.

Ignite in me holy good, stillness, peace sharpened into action change. New! New! New! I crave the new knew pristine. Every day presents a known unknown. Let me look for the true uncomfortable to You.

Let me try the new food. Meet the new person. Take the new way. Make me desire Your daily freshness of opportunity.

Risking in you is rewarding my faith. Step me into your change of heart and direction. Renew my mind to Your pleasing and perfect will. Enlighten and inspire my conviction to the uncomfortable enough to make it delightful joy.

Embrace this vessel to journey beyond this port to destinations where your open arms already reside. Hold me in Your boldness. Tiller the rudder to righteous regatta. Replace this lingering fear with excitement for your blessings succeeding.

Through your great masterful navigating design, Lord Jesus. Amen

MAY 20

PrayStill

Acts 28:24
Some were convinced by what (Paul) had said, while others refused to believe.

Scripture Prayer: Attraction Spirit

Little by little certainly by surely Lord you peel away my doubt confusion and stubbornness. You melt me in refinement. You sift me like wheat. You knead me to need you. You peel me to praise You. You hold me, You heal me, You love me, so I loosen my grip on me. I am drawn and bloom to your light.
Rest
Lord Jesus, Spirit
Fall fresh deliciousness, Feast and overwhelm my soul. Rage the inferno to quelling kindled flames of warmth. Calm the raging roaring waters to calm placid paths of cool refreshing sips on my lips. Filling fresh overflowing.
Selah
Stand me on your feet, Jesus. Dance me through this valley. Carry my surrendered weakness transformed. Float my inspiring to call and be saved upon Your name. Make me worthy to be saved. Rest peacefully my soul. Calm inviting lightens my way. Melt and mold my soul refined. Presence in your Spirit remain.
Thanks be to the awesomely, mighty Holy Spirit, Counselor, Friend, Protector. Everywhere waiting to present Holiness.
TBTHS X infinity
AMEN

MAY 21

PrayStill

Matthew 12:22-24

Then they brought to him a demoniac who was blind and mute; and he cured him, so that the one who had been mute could speak and see. All the crowds were amazed and said, "Can this be the Son of David?" But when the Pharisees heard it, they said, "It is only by Beelzebul, the ruler of the demons, that this fellow casts out the demons."

Scripture Prayer: Discernment

Lord Jesus Christ,
Peel away the scales of injustice on my eyes that block the truth. Enlight my conviction to know your voice and hear your calling. You are mighty and powerful, and I am weak and needy. I fear the unknown so only my faith in You, Jesus assures my strong peace and comfort in Your steps.
Your powerful Word in the world allows me to face the unknown. I prayerfully test the unknown spirit. Test in this. Test in that. Reveal the genuine motives, uncover the lie. Reveal the honesty to free enslavement from the darkness. Confine the prowler in locking chains. Unchain the truth to bold expressions of conquering wisdom. Reign on, Lord Jesus. Praise God.
Lord Jesus, your light is uncontainable. The evil is weak and overcome at the speaking of your name. The Word of love overcomes all fear doubt and confusion.
With you Abba Jehovah, there is assurance, peace and victory.
Faith, love and hope drag the deceiver to light every time. At the Cross the darkness dies to light. The tares and goats and seeds of lies are scattered. Yes, yes, yes, powerful Lord Jesus.
Lord Jesus, God, Mighty Defender, Awesomely Empowering, Author of Salvation...guide protect and reveal the tested truth to reign eternal.
TBTG TBTHS TBTJC, Amen

MAY 22

PrayStill

Matthew 12:33-34
Either make the tree good, and its fruit good; or make the tree bad, and its fruit bad; for the tree is known by its fruit. You brood of vipers! How can you speak good things, when you are evil? For out of the abundance of the heart the mouth speaks.

Scripture Prayer: Flourish

Jesus
Author of salvation, lover of my soul, Devine fruit of my heart. Open grow and tend to my ways. Watch over words and steps and intentions. Motivate my motive to You
Lord in Your inescapable overwhelming grace. Make mercy and hope cheer the days.
Lord in the morning I direct my prayer. Let my words lift up your presence and be a pleasing and effervescent cool refreshing sound.
Seek and delight always in the word of the LORD. Grow and abide in the root of Jesse. Sustain me in the vine of Your Word. Branch and prune me daily to your will. Bloom me where I am so I may prosper all to You.
Lord attach stem and multiply your way in the veins of renewal and flowing graces.
Your mighty attraction binds flourishment in nourishment sustained.
Through with and in Jesus abiding.
Amen

MAY 23

PrayStill

Matthew 12:47-48
Someone told him, "Look, your mother and your brothers are standing outside, wanting to speak to you." But to the one who had told him this, Jesus replied, "Who is my mother and who are my brothers?"

Scripture Prayer: Agape

Holy Spirit come!
Lord Jesus save!
Abba parent redeem!
There is agape love everywhere. I see it in you, you, and you. I find it here and there and everywhere. TBTG
Lord you have your way with the world. The silence love quiets and quells the barking unrest. The town criers bark out the fearful news exhaustingly yet all I hear and see is...
the free reigning,
never ending,
all encompassing,
forever welcoming,
Love of Jesus overwhelming the world.
Everyone is the 99. Everyone is the one. The flock is family unending. Silence listens still on and on. WORD sings signs of melody and harmony loves. Hear, feel and know to provide in the Abide. Stay remaining unending.
Pastures of deep abiding love beating from the heard and understood heart. The compassion of you before me... The uplifting of one another.

Lord, make a gaping hole into agape love. Fill my desire and reception of you to the flame that flows. Unknowing where it comes or goes, Lord weave it in your breath of life.

Fill Words of embracing transforming formation into informing the light in the world.

Jesus, you call me friend. Jesus, you call me family, Jesus, you call me saved. Jesus, I call you Savior.

Redeemer of my soul.

TBTJC TBTHS TBTG Agape Style

M A Y 2 4

PrayStill

Matthew 13:29-30
But [the master] replied, "No; for in gathering the weeds you would uproot the wheat along with them. Let both of them grow together until the harvest; and at harvest time I will tell the reapers, Collect the weeds first and bind them in bundles to be burned, but gather the wheat into my barn."

Scripture Prayer: Golden

Master Spirit
You dance the golden wheat in rhythms and waves of showering air. I know not where you come from or where you go. I see Your effect in the current and feel your sensation around me.
The field is rich and softly plentiful.
Guide and direct a path to uplift the wheat and tear down the tares as the moment becomes. Grow me taller beside the tare to strengthen and provide perspective. Make this wild infringing weed turn to benefit for the golden wheat prosperous. Make flavorful this substitution benefit. The barn field store is beautiful.
Let this foe be a weapon against itself dividing. Let the weight of the shadowing tare struggle for light bellow me. Use its energy to take resolve into protection from the other elements and adversaries. Make the surrounding moat of darn Darnels inadvertently cause protection.
All things work together for Your good harvest. Master, realize this focus to your angling light rays, pattering rains, and refreshing blowing winds. Plentiful abounding sustenance embraces the surround.
Grow me up where I am planted to vest me in Your surround. Harvest and glorify Your goodness and prosperity in fruitfulness. Germinate the garden genesis for Your purpose.

Master Owner,
Master Planter,
Master Grower.
Master Harvester
Master of my soul Jesus you reign o'r me
Amen

MAY 25

PrayStill

Galatians 5:9
A little yeast works through the whole batch of dough.

Scripture Prayer: Holy Magnitude 3 in 1

Jesus
Delicately place your WORD alive on my comprehension so it kindles back to God's purpose. Grant me the understanding to capture receive and multiply Your magnetic attractive creation. Make this leavening leave the state of stagnancy to grow Your kingdom. Delight your ways of truth and light to the expansive sustaining leavens.
Lord you are the reagent agent that transforms the ignorance into graceful Favor. You are unending food and nourishment swelling beyond consumption. Never ending, lavishly spending, forever sending souls back to You.
Selah
The love in the oven seeps Heaven's scented aroma.
The staring starving world feasts on Your never ending, all sustaining, comfort, placed to grow to within. The Holy Feast table sponges absorbing words to the world in peace.
The acquired taste of your WORD craves my heart to imbibe more and more. In your leavened feast is yeast that sets in motion the transformation of souls. Your escapable flavor dips like a seeping dye, tainting away the indifference of the world.
Your awesome kingdom is the banquet of Lordship sparking the dynamite of peaceful truth light food.
Reign on perpetually. Expand swell and grow me back to You.
Amen X Mamma Abba, Son, and Spirit ^^+++^^

MAY 26

PrayStill

Matthew 13:37-39

[Jesus] answered, "The one who sows the good seed is the Son of Man; the field is the world, and the good seed are the children of the kingdom; the weeds are the children of the evil one, and the enemy who sowed them is the devil; the harvest is the end of the age, and the reapers are angels."

Scripture Prayer: Parallel

Teach me your parable ways, oh Lord. You know how I learn, Teacher. Explain in my heart what to see. How is it related to me. Teach me how it will be. Talk to me in colorful pictures.
Jesus Army Angels,
Messengers of God's will. Plant in me reception. Reveal the moments in just your perfect instant instance.
I think I know until you show me your way. In your time in your space in your moment of grace more is revealed.
Angels and archangels and a company of Heaven's principalities forever do Your will. Let the angelic part in me stay remaining in your will Lord Jesus. Let it rule over my will. Emotions and animal instincts. Humble my humanness from hume to purpose and guide in comfort my ways. You are powerful I am weak. You are loving I am abiding.
Lord Jesus
The picture you draw I see a a thousand times over in your courts. Always new always with different perspectives. Turn my light on Lord lead me home with you to know you. Your pictures take me to Heaven in the world.
Set aside my understanding and erase my tabla rasa. Draw a fresh on me the picture delivering a thousand words. Hear my inclinations to set me fresh anew. Better is this moment with you now than everything elsewhere.

Selah x 7

TBTJC

Amen

MAY 27

PrayStill

John 3:8
The wind blows where it chooses, and you hear the sound of it, but you do not know where it comes from or where it goes. So it is with everyone who is born of the Spirit.

Scripture Prayer: Trinity Sunday

MammaAbba, Jesus Spirit
Maker of Heaven and earth. In the beginning the end and everything in between. All powerful present and knowing
Omni-potent, present, niscient. How You custom fit Your essence to my being.
GOD
Mighty magnificent creator. Powerful mountain moving universe creating, star naming, law commands creating Yahweh. I am tiny and insignificant to this magnitude. Your expanse overwhelms me I know you are for me.
JESUS
Author of salvation, son of God and man. Loving brother, image of God on earth, I relate to You calling me friend. My teacher and guide my example supplied. The cleanser of every sin in the world from beginning to end. My closer walk with thee to free me.
HOLY SPIRIT DIVINE
You are in me around with through and for me. Fire igniting, Wind reuniting, Water washing whitening. Counselor force providing angelic host inviting. Falling the world into place.
Three in one all easy to see revealed in my journey nearer to God. You give me my breath, You save me from death. You named me and knit me within. You love me and lead me my advocate plead free my Comforter, Jesus, God ... love.

Selah X 3
TBTG TBTJC TBTHS
Amen ^^+++^^

MAY 28

PrayStill

Matthew 13:51-52

"Have you understood all this?" They answered, "Yes." And [Jesus] said to them, "Therefore every scribe who has been trained for the kingdom of Heaven is like the master of a household who brings out of his treasure what is new and what is old."

Scripture Prayer: All In

Jesus is. JESUS is in, All in, paid it forward, backward, all in. For everyone everywhere all in. Amen

Jesus you are. You are my jealousy demanding. I find you and I want all in. You signed it on my arm and wove it in my heart. I am inescapably written. This is good. This is very good.

I found me in my youth. You love me into growth in You continually. I pine and long and adore the more of You. In losing the precious small things the greatest value is declared. The joy of finding Your signature preciousness daily are rewards sustained.

The stain is removed and granted grace I'm improved. mercy's seat a throne of esteemment. These beautiful gifts designed to uplift and save me from me cuz I love You. You love me more before I knew. I languish in in your surround Spirit God. I believe and transform to You. I surrender. I render it all For you.

Selah

Love is all. You, Lord Jesus, have it all. You give it all, You exchange it all. My complete book you find and refine into Your kingdoms worth. Beyond gold diamonds, beyond fragrant rising frankincense and smooth silky myrrh, Your treasure, Lord, is found anew. I want You, I believe You, I receive You.

TBTG

MAY 29

PrayStill

Matthew 13:55-56

Is not this the carpenter's son? Is not his mother called Mary? And are not his brothers James and Joseph and Simon and Judas? And are not his sisters with us? Where then did this man get all this?

Scripture Prayer: Faith Imbibing.

Lord Jesus

I have faith in you, learn me where it lacks.

I see you... lighten me where I do not.

I hear you... Teach me where I am deaf.

I follow YOU... Lead me from this stray.

I feel you... Touch me where I am numb.

I taste YOUR fragrance Lord! spice me where it is worn.

You are present here Lord. Let me not be alone.

Peace

In this vessel, You astound me. Submit and insist in me more of your goodness.

Lord, you are my expansion. My next escalation. My assurance of salvation. You reign and rule and deign the revealings. Fill my emptiness brimming with Your love. I believe my unbelief is filled helpings from above. You Lord are the assurance of hope and things not seen. You, Lord Jesus, fulfill and redeem me.

Amen

This is the day the Lord has made. Let's be rejoicingly glad in it, cheerfully living abundantly giving.

TBTG

MAY 30

PrayStill

Matthew 14:8
Prompted by her mother, she said, "Give me the head of John the Baptist here on a platter."

Scripture Prayer: love Inextinguishable

Lord
You help me through the double negatives. Evil kills off evil. Negative negates negative to make positive conquer.
Just prior, Jesus said to them, "A prophet is not without honor except in his hometown and in his own household."
Just next is the 5000 feast with Jesus and growing with plenty left over. The love of more love and more power in love is unleashing to the world always. TBTJC
Evil writhes and gashes at the success of love. love wins every time. Herod evil in lustful courts is deceived in lustful flesh deals in a desire to justify worldly sinful existence. Darkness never overcomes light. How temporally mistaken is the darkness.
Love wins every time. love heals and realigns. Realize that this effort to stop a tidal wave of love is fruitless.
John the Baptist, this wild-haired temple exploding, locust eating, to the ends of the earth propagating, harbinger of truth, is already winner of the war of love's contagion.
Amen
Jesus
The Lord's Prayer You speak invites me to be with You, the Holy Spirit at God's table banquet feasting with blessings and honor and glory and truth and righteousness and peace. How precious to be with You all ways.
You, Lord, have overcome the world. Awesomeness X Infinity X love
TBTG

MAY 31

PrayStill

Matthew 14:16-17
Jesus said to them "They need not go away; you give them something to eat." They replied, "We have nothing here but five loaves and two fish."

Scripture Prayer: Gratitudes' Abundance

God is Gracious, God is Good,
Let us thank Him for our food.
Amen!
Giving thanks in grace and gratitude always fills the heart soul and mind. I want what I have and I want to share it. Lord you sustain and provide continuously. Take from me my fear of being without and multiply it into assurance of abundances overflowing.
What I think in fear, is not enough, turns into much more than enough. Praise in the plentiful and in the paucity. With less is more. How can this be. God you provide more and more. There is more now than ever before. Feed me.
Let me worship You the provider in thankfulness rather than the gift of the provision. Keep my eyes on You above the waves of doubt. Abundance resides with gratitude's contentment. More is satisfied only in You, Lord. More of the world's material never does.
Lord Jesus Christ,
Please feed me. Your word sustains me. Your endlessness fulfills endlessly.
Amen
TBTJC

JUNE 1

PrayStill

Matthew 13:33
[Jesus] told them another parable: "The kingdom of Heaven is like yeast that a woman took and mixed in with three measures of flour until all of it was leavened."

Scripture Prayer: Marker Moments

Lord of power and might, Jesus, you reign almighty. You have me before I am me. You light the fuse of your Deuteronomy recipe in my heart and life. Explosive unchained power deliver in your kairos Infinites of love x grace x mercy.
That moment I surrendered to You, Lord, You lit the yeast fuse of life in my flour.
I set my life in the powerful Words of a small prayer Your Spirit Fire signed on my heart from your Angelisa,
consecrated, devoted, given to God.......
Jesus I take you! You are my Lord and Savior. I take me off the throne and place me at your feet. Amen
A lifesaving marker moment. Everything changes to saved in that second.
I detected no presence. No immediate sign no receipt or confirmation.
That surrender though, The yeast of your leavening life Word baked into my soul. Your transformative force emblazoned my ignorance of Your presence into the desperation of my need for You all in.
You pick me up and set me straight back to You. You grow in me your leaven of Heaven.
Lord make me in Your oven of love-raising, Scripture-grazing, transformational-praising a messenger of Your tasty life.
TBTJC Amen

JUNE 2

PrayStill

Matthew 13:36
Then [Jesus] left the crowds and went into the house. And his disciples approached him, saying, "Explain to us the parable of the weeds of the field."

Scripture Prayer: Why? Test me in this.

Lord, you search me out. My heart is yours. When I stray, the mighty Counselor convicts my quenching spirit. Thy rod and staff of truth and forgiveness wakens my wonder back to safety. Beside these still water streams flourishes your grazing wheat fields of safety.
My belief in you Lord requires receptive faith eyes knowing assurance. The truth unravels and falls right into place revealing Your true and holy will, plain to absorb. You give me free will to explore and align back to you and choose Your will.
Asking why the faith mystery is required or, why it is, requires faith itself. Acceptance of Your will removes my attempt to fill in my faith for yours and proudly play God usurping the Deity throne. Faith fills the gap between my will and Yours. Acceptance is patience in the unanswerable. Whys will reveal in Your perfect time. My faith is Yours.
TBTG

JUNE 3

PrayStill

1 Samuel 3:1b
The word of the Lord was rare in those days; visions were not widespread.

Scripture Prayer: Patience Circle

Lord
Are you present. Of course You are present. You always are. I wander in wonder. I'm so busy doing, I need to spend time being with You. My pride in busyness eases out the stillness to drought. Slow me in the world to still me in Your communion
My stillness gently floods with your soft warmth. I meditate and receive your numb flowing relax waves continuing. Fill this renewal. Ease and relax me. Open and secure my soul. Breath me deep to exhale my heart to you. Pant rhythm to receive lights pure love.
Selah
Waiting in patience to receive You, Lord, anticipates comfort. Here I am Lord listening in silent stillness. Complete submission in wonderful attention. truth light and love surround embrace and relax my spirit into yours. Magnify and multiply me in me in You.
Selah x 11
TBTHS

JUNE 4

PrayStill

Psalm 44:6 For I do not rely on my bow, and my sword does not give me the victory.

Scripture Prayer: Surrender

Lord Jesus

Help me. My sword and bow are useless. My battle is lost yet let Yours be won. You are Guardian Supreme. You protect and guide and lead me from my foes distress. The enemy appears large in my eyes. To you Lord this enemy is small. My cheek is turned and tuned to You.

Let me rest in Your peace and be the first to forgive and break bread rather than bone. Make my sword be Your Word of truth. Let my sword hand be made plowshare. Make my flaming bow hand be down and tune to peaceful lyre. Unconscious me from this writhing fight drowning in futility.

Mighty strong unchanging and just, Lord you make the foes friends when the pride slides aside. Calm the heart of the restless. Mend the anger to love and forgiveness. Peace be in the gaze of the lost and broken. Fall us into place. Towering cedars calm the raging winds and rains to your Heavenly pastures laying down.

TBTG Amen

JUNE 5

PrayStill

Matthew 13:55
Is not this the carpenter's son? Is not his mother called Mary? And are not his brothers James and Joseph and Simon and Judas?

Scripture Prayer: Focus

Jesus
Let me be attentive and learning. Teach me to hear and understand. Close my eyes and preconceptions and wanderings. Open my vision to you. Open my precepts to your way. Walk my faith life in line to you.
Let me set aside everything and listen and be led. Allow me to be drawn to your calling purpose. Make me new.
With you Lord all things are. Possible. With you Lord all things are known. Cleanse and inspire me to the flowing of your rich valuable Words of life directing this journey of faith in You.
In with and through the Holy Spirit drawing near in presence and conviction may the fathers will be fulfilled.
TBTG Amen

JUNE 6

PrayStill

Ecclesiastes 3:1
For everything there is a season, and a time for every matter under Heaven.

Scripture Prayer: Vanity

Jesus
Walk me with You when I need not be carried in Your arms. The sands of time are fading to the shift of your beautiful rhythm of seasons. My feet dance like a child on Yours. You embrace me when I'm faint. Your rod and staff guide my footprints.

Selah

Take me from the frozen tundra to the melting cool waters on a hot hot day. Wash my feet in the
beautiful crystal white sands of the azure blue seas. Prepare me and The Way for the changing seasons of purpose and reason. Erode away my fear to reveal steps of boldness courage and conviction. When all is yours you are all I need. Delight the sparkle of sands and tingle of sounds to to Your greatness and expanse. Your power transcends and occupies my soul vessel.
TBTJC Amen

JUNE 7

PrayStill

Matthew 14:20
And all ate and were filled; and they took up what was left over of the broken pieces, twelve baskets full.

Scripture Prayer: Hunger and Thirst

Jesus

You are my portion. You refresh my soul. Thirst first in You refreshes my wholeness. Let me commune and abide with your satiation soul food unending. I come back for thirds and fourths and it spices differently with the flavor of Your teachings. More is enough. Designed in Your master creation for each moment, The lingering scent to taste and see. All the days long the aroma of Your feast fills the air. You prepare the table and welcome the banquet. Preparing prayers propose Your Way as the favorite flavors imbibing. Cleanse from within with the washing of my steps to the anointing of my thoughts! You are in me. My sustenance and essence are permeated with Your presence.

Still

Stay and nourish my soul. Feed my all in all with tender Mercies, forgiving and bountiful graces savoring. New life is You refreshing. Less of me is more of you. More of you is the Feast of life. Your life in me makes for life anew sufficing in multiples to share and give freely.

TBTG TBTHS TBTJC Amen

JUNE 8

PrayStill

Matthew 14:27
But immediately Jesus spoke to them and said, "Take heart, it is I; do not be afraid."

Scripture Prayer: Judge

Jesus, you own my heart. I spend a lifetime knowing you intimately and sensing Your Holy Presence. When you suddenly appear and present my instinct to you is true. Not a word need be spoken. The overwhelming awesomeness of your suddenly immediately is known. Together and trusted the yes is yes. The bless is the rest.
Let my yes be yes and my no be no. Let me know it Is you. The grey area is out. Make no mistake about it. Only the true You is genuine. Self-preserving instinct judges friend or foe. You call me friend I call you life. Your pure veritable essence showers in assurance and conviction. You reign in me, alive me and instill me.
Let me see know and trust in Your presence Jesus. Assure and rest my soul. You intercede the foe with protective immediacy.
You, Lord, are my guard, my rock, my salvation. The ever-living director of truth designed woven in the hearts of believers. I believe you are suddenly always present. Your servants attentively listen in silent instinct receiving.
Selah
TBTHS TBTG TBTJC Amen

JUNE 9

PrayStill

Galatians 3:28
There is no longer Jew or Greek, there is no longer slave or free, there is no longer male and female; for all of you are one in Christ Jesus.

Scripture Prayer: Unique

Jesus
Walk with me on your common ground. Invite and welcome me to Your table of worship. Let the eternity keys you place on our hearts tune back to you in design. Bring out our pieces to the faith table to fit in the mosaic of Your placid path to faith.
Building trust links is easy in twos and threes with you Lord as my focus. Let me seek and see You in them. Let me be attraction, to You, for them. Lord liaison me to every soul I meet. Help me discover the cover that veils Your intimacy.

Selah

Lord
Trust me to Your leveling pasture fields. Introduce me to the doors opening to your reside in want and fellowship. Plant in the Fallow soil of grace your fellowship following redemption. Bring me through, with, in, Your holiest of guided moments.
In Christ who reigns ultimate eternal.
TBTG, JC, HS, three in one. Amen

JUNE 10

PrayStill

Genesis 3:9
But the Lord God called to the man, and said to him, "Where are you?"

Scripture Prayer: Secret

Lord you know my fear of being found out. You gently knock at my gate with loving persistence. You are patient and insistent. My hiding place speaks echoes of your searching my soul for the light of day to break through. I am surrounded and surrendered.

Lord Jesus, you always know what I am up to and what my motives and inclinations are. You know my soul before it happens and offer the cure to what ails me. Intercede my desires for Your inspiring.

Lord Jesus Christ my Savior,

My soul reviver, my what I strive for, my truth in knowing what is pure. My delight in the right You overcome the night with the joy inherited daily. Fill me and cleanse me and make me to receive you, revealing in me strong conviction. Abide me and ride me and cleanse from inside me every fear doubt and lie. The truth when spoken illuminates what's broken and places Your love truth inside me. My heart is Yours. You have it all.

TBTG

Holy Spirit consume me. Jesus you find me, enter rejoice and come in. Amen

JUNE 11

PrayStill

Acts 11:23
When [Barnabas] came and saw the grace of God he rejoiced, and he exhorted them all to remain faithful to the Lord with steadfast devotion.

Scripture Prayer: Well Pleased

Truly devoted, unwavering Holy Spirit
To see the manifestation of Your revealings in people joys the heart. The Lord delivers, powerful true and just. The goodness people reflect, the goodness of the Lord the faithfulness of healing, and the joy of surrender and conversion are You alive in us.

Free will reaches diminishing returns, and the only recourse is to fall into the arms of the steadfast lover of our souls Jesus. Your will, Lord, fills the desires and pinings. Your grâce, Lord, cleanses and renews anew for me and you to flourish

Jesus your way is revealing our hearts are unsealing to graces appealing the goodness of your love. Unending and sending your love is my mending I cannot deny Your relentless. You transform my heart right from the start to make me aware of your presence. Abiding between us Your love so instills us with certainty, certainly steadied in fastness

Come Holy Spirit come. Dwell in this place in this stillness Amen

JUNE 12

PrayStill

Matthew 15:34
Jesus asked them, "How many loaves have you?" They said, "Seven, and a few small fish."

Scripture Prayer: Fast Fill

Lord Savior savoring,
Focus my vessel on you. The sustenance of your Word imbibes in me my heart's content. At the hearth of the table flames fulfilling contentment. Peaceably, less is more. Replace my physical with spiritual.
Replace this guttural disconnect for eating to satisfy feeling with prayer and meditation. Slow down my physical to increase your spiritual meal. Time speeds to faster. Feasting with you is warm space less timelessness.
Feast me on the smallest taste of Your Purity. Seal my lips with purifying embers of transformation.
Deny me my mouth to stomach pleasing with soul to heart increasing. In Your presence we are one.
Fill me with Your Word bread with water as well and air for yeasting into communion at the focus of your calm still.
Speed me up in You and slow this world around me. Seal my heart to purify and proclaim the goodness of the flavorful feast of Heaven leaven.
With you Lord there is plenty. I am full up and ready. Digest in me this restful peace meal. Make me crave Your truth aware.
TBTHS surrounding Amen

JUNE 13

PrayStill

Galatians 5:14
For the whole law is summed up in a single commandment, "You shall love your neighbor."

Scripture Prayer: First

Lord, you love me first. Before and after time begins and ends. You make me and sign me into Your Realm. My soul spirit and mind are very very good. Fearfully for you and wonderfully made. A craftsmanship in an image of your awesomeness Incarnate.

Make me a sweet and pleasuring sound flowing back to you. You planted in me, Lord Jesus, the love seeds sprouting back to reflect this love love LOVE.

Love smiling, greatly forgives.

This power to live to forgive overcomes the pride You set aside. Ease in on me Lord and let this first love prosper and reflect all back to you.

Make me to...Give first too... love first too...Forgive first too... Just like You

Cherish first too...Honor first too...Lift first too...Smile first too... Just like You

Motivate and activate my love.

Selah

Lord

Just like you love me, Jesus, let me love myself unconditionally. Let me turn and love my neighbor with that powerful mighty overwhelming unrelenting always transforming love.

Let that power from you turn to melt the enemy neighbors into rivers of kindness.

Perfect love from you passes through and casts out all fear. Without fear there is love, love, LOVE.

Lift this love abounding and make it love surrounding and show the You in me to all.

TBTJC who created and loves first. LOVE is already there. Reveal and revel it. Amen

JUNE 14

PrayStill

Psalm 74:16

Yours is the day, yours also the night; you established the moon and the sun.

Scripture Prayer: Potent Omniscience.

Bless the land and all the people in it. Your beautiful pasture is defiled by the darkness enemies. The ruins erase the ravages in hatred replacing the empty loneliness of prides hollow victory perceived. Do not be deceived by this moment.
Lord
Your nighttime cannot hide the joy of the morning. Your spurning buds germinating cannot be contained. There is life always living in the roots of your fallow ground. Generation Genesis proclaims the glory of Creation uncontainable.
The light of day reflects the night sparklings that cover and shields the land. The darkness of night is deceive to believe that the darkness will overcome light. The light of the night is right in the sight of the strong and persistent creation.
Lord Jesus Spirit
You spoke this dry parched land into flourishing. The Eden day is nourishing the night sparkles alluring and the pure dark sees in the twinkle. This lonely despair of isolation can never ever remain. It washes away like the tide to dawn sunrising. The whole creation shouts victory unending revealed in the sending of loves craving adorning and praising. The light of the world is yours Lord the darkness is no more.
TBTHS Jesus Lord Amen

JUNE 15

PrayStill

Galatians 6:2
Bear one another's burdens, and in this way you will fulfill the law of Christ.

Scripture Prayer: Move

Move me with compassion Lord. Move me to your plateau. Meet me with souls at your leveling table, the banquet feast where all God's creation points to celestial Heaven's praising.

Lord Jesus, you meet me where I am and transport me to your feast. My hunger for You moves motivates and molds me into you.

Every moment of Your perfect pureness pulls me back from my inclination to match your inspirations. Magnet attractive and very reactive to your glory.

Sensitize me, Lord, to the longings of my loves and families and friends and strangers to move to them like you come to move me. Channel your compassion through me and meet me in communion union back to You.

Lord, Your love compassion magnifies the comfort Scripture words, lifted and uplifted. Your love attention lifts up the shared burden into blessings of redemption rising.

Jesus walk compassion with me to look listen learn lead and love over and over and over again all for Your glory in passionate desires. Make progress point towards Your perfection. TBTJC my Passion Savior Amen

JUNE 16

PrayStill

Matthew 17:4
Then Peter said to Jesus, "Lord it is good for us to be here; if you wish, I will make three dwellings here, one for you, one for Moses, and one for Elijah."

Scripture Prayer: Purified

Lord of dazzling lights, Jesus, You reign. In me is fear uncertainty and doubt. You wipe away the sins of the world and cleanse my palate. You white wash clean the scars of earth in the shadow of decay. The saving beam of love transforms and instills this dwelling place. Your temple in me illumines to your presence. Stay me in this numb warmth. Respire to inspire my desire for you.
Much Selah
Honor and blessings and truth and love and forgiveness and consolation swell my heart. It is well with my soul with You.
Colorful hues of sparkling dew glisten listening to the ringing silence. Waves of warmth roll me to surrender. Ride me with you to the smooth rock foundation in Your castle room turning.
You Lord Jesus are awesomeness imbibing the sweetness of creation planted. Be staying within my soul. Magnify and give me to live me. I worship you always praising Your name above all names always, Abba Father, Spirit, Yahweh Jesus.
Amen

JUNE 17

PrayStill

2 Corinthians 5:7
For we walk by faith, not by sight.

Scripture Prayer: Focus

Lord Jesus
I close my eyes to see you and You are present. I close my eyes to focus center you.
Take away the sight of the world for Your faith vision reflection. Silence my imbibing to your surround. You love me and feed me. I receive.
Jesus wash my trodden steps back to your feast. Fill me up with regular 3 in 1 Holiness. Wipe away all my fears uncertainties and doubts. Replace them with Faith Assurance and Certainty.
Faith Eyes searching Convincing Hearts sharing
Certainty Foundations building.
You lord Jesus transform me to right where I am within you. Surrounded in love and comfort you strengthen me. Your power to love overflows my soul and makes me whole in the Holiness. Wholesome mindful presence of your spirit warms numbs and reigns my soul. I am yours Lord and there is nothing else. Succulent sweetness fills my heartbeat flowing Your love magnified
Selah
Set me free walking to do Your Will and to be Your will doing.
Amen

JUNE 18

PrayStill

Matthew 17:20b
For truly I tell you, if you have faith the size of a mustard seed, you will say to this mountain, "Move from here to there," and it will move; and nothing will be impossible for you.

Scripture Prayer: Key Building

Jesus
Lord of my life,
Rock solid assurance,
my water air and nourishing sustenance. You overcome my fears. You quell my unease. Your bring me to Your peace. I can do all things through You.

This natural belief You key in my heart is growing to You and for You. Overwhelming assurance fills the future of Your presence. Now in peace, project this peace forward to the futures' rest. Make my unknown fears Your opportunities excitement. Only love and hope are present. Encompass my direction.

I can move this mountain. I climb avert and break through the rubble of fears Lord. Break this rock of resistance to grow my roots around this obstacle. Make it be my rooted stronghold.

Atop the precipice is the light of Your salvation placing life perspective. Unlock my unbelief. Lock me in your belief.

The altitude is Yours. The air is thin and my faith eyes feel Your direction. I will go, I will follow, I will stay with you.

FAITH freeing
Father
Always
In
Thy
Hands

TBTJC Amen

JUNE 19

PrayStill

Numbers 11:9
When the dew fell on the camp in the night, the manna would fall with it.

Scripture Prayer: Savory

Lord
Save me with You, savory host. The anticipation of your host makes my mouth water. Before you come to me I can taste the texture. Precious sustenance of Lord melting in my mouth and melting my wash away. Moist dew cleanse me from the inside. Take away my longings for the world and fill me with your graces and mercies abundance. Dance me in the light of your holiness. Let me have a glimpse of knowing Your purity.
Selah
Jesus
I want and love what I have. I am provided for and watched over in your great nurturing embrace. You hold my contentment communion. I appreciate just where I am. Every day your new mercies change and mold me closer to You. Peaceful waves of Your glory fulfill my desire and plant my motive motif to you. Own me and guide me in my blindness. Call me to the still silent whisper luring union.

PrayStill Stay Still TBTHS AMEN

JUNE 20

PrayStill

Matthew 18:7
Woe to the world because of stumbling blocks! Occasions for stumbling are bound to come, but woe to the one by whom the stumbling block comes!

Scripture Prayer: Inheritance

Lord
You are mighty and strong and I am week and needy. Heed and herd me with your rod. Protect me and block me from the wrong direction with your strong strategic staff. Save me from the pit cliff. Redirect and retrieve my wandering to Your protection with the crook. Anoint my head with Your protective oils to stop the sinful contagion from entering my mind heart and soul. Clarify my purpose. Set me right and true straight to You.
Selah
Make my thoughts words and actions strong defender and promoter of Your WORD alive, truth.
Reflect your wholesome goodness to reveal the true lie of sins. Shine light bright upon the cowering trembling liar that thieves and leaves abandon. Idols get behind. Flee this Holy Presence.
Jesus
Retrieve and receive and bring to believe the good-hearted souls into the loving kindness of showering glory praise and worship. Embracing arms surround. Perfect are Your mysterious ways of enlightening truths
Reign on and on. It is the Lord God Jesus I serve.
TBTG Amen

JUNE 21

PrayStill

Matthew 18:20
For where two or three are gathered in my name, I am there among them.

Scripture Prayer: Surround

Lord Jesus
Your prayer surrounds me all ways. Especially whenever I'm in prayer position with knees to elbows face in hands, You surround me. Jesus in Heaven with me, filling in the Holy Spirit mighty counsel in surround. We are 3 in 1 before Lord Abba God absent space and time and substance.
Empty me from within. Fill me with You from without, this is strong calming bonded union. Breath.
Bring me to another to make me two with both of you before God. Share, commune, and relate, the great manifestation of Your glory. Magnify and praise your name in thought word and deed. Grow and go the Spirit of the Lord always. Dance me in your waves of ways. Be my automatic nature. Make my default state be You Lord. Make in me, worthy esteem to humbly present your kind loving glories to others.
Initiate and spark forgiving love uniting. Bond in us Spirit attraction to open Your pathways of fellowship. Be with us in Your great relate state.
Amen TBTJC Amen x 7

JUNE 22

PrayStill

Matthew 18:21
Then Peter came and said to [Jesus] "Lord if another member of the church sins against me, how often should I forgive? As many as seven times?"

Scripture Prayer: Live to Forgive.

Lord Jesus saving salvation,
Am I to proud to forgive since pride screams for justice.
Am I to afraid to forgive since fear screams for authority.
Holy Spirit mighty counselor,
Your forgiveness of me melts away my self-anger.
My forgiveness of You Lord heals rightly my humbled accepting heart.
My forgiveness of me wipes away my self-anger.
My forgiveness of the trespassers balms with the salve of salvation
Lord forgive me... I forgive You...
Lord forgive them...I forgive them...
Let us forgive them before they even trespass!!!
Forgiveness reigns in loves' peace tranquil. Lord take away any and all hints of subtle resentments harming my soul. Heal my judgement heart and break my prideful unforgiveness.
7x77 I pray to forgive yet only in Your great wisdom and mercies in Kairos moments do I awaken to the joy of Your washed and cleansed freedom in forgiveness, You Lord are mighty and strong, and I am humble from my stubborn resistance to relinquish. Take away the comfort of clinging to the pain. Make me free again. Your lesson is learned.
Selah x 77

Lord you illumine the path with power to forgive. Let me be in You to overcome the tall order of the little and big places to forgive. The Beauty and Wonder washes the SON filled side of the street to shadow over the choke hold of unforgiveness.

The victory is yours Lord Jesus. Only in Your great Mercies am I a receiving reflection of Your awesome and merciful heart of forgiveness to others.

4givN=LOVE
TBTG TBTHS TBTJC

JUNE 23

PrayStill

Psalm 90:17
May the graciousness of the Lord our God be upon us; prosper the work of our hands; prosper our handiwork.

Scripture Prayer: Sprinkle Colors

Master Spirit Provider,
Lightly shower this adventurous desire upon my soul. From stillness to glories, Nourish and fulfill free comfort in your beckoned extoling. Inspire my desire to receive and magnify all of your glories in me that they may be wholesome, grown and developed, and presented as Your great glory.
Receive x Selah
I am all yours. You come to my soul and magnify the gifts of your presence offered up to You Lord magnifying as my greatest uncontainable gifts back to Your altar. My life is not my own. All is Yours shown in always exceeding beyond expectation into rewarded glory. The prospering handiwork develops from the seeds of creativity rising upward.
Know me, show me, persistently grow me, flow in me, this know in me and never let go of me.
So gracious precious and beautiful are the gusts of gifts bestowed upon us by Your creation in us. Make us exceedingly confident to break boundary and examine and conquer the beyond our growing expectations. Adventure invention beyond comprehension to this place of limitless boundlessness.
Praise God from whom all blessings flow forward exponentially. Lord Savior and motivation multiplier come.
PBTG PBTHS PBTJC

JUNE 24

PrayStill

Mark 4:38
But [Jesus] was in the stern, asleep on the cushion; and they woke him up and said to him, "Teacher, do you not care that we are perishing?"

Scripture Prayer: Hush

Lord Jesus Christ my Strength and Redeemer. Whom shall I fear?
The storms of suddenly are at the gate. The weight of the wait for your intercession is imminent. I am at the end of myself. Overcome in a sea fear uncertainty and doubt. I cry out. Help me I'm drowning in exhaustion and breathlessness.
I do not want to wake you in the waves of my insecurities. My failing esteem says I am not worth the possibility of a no answer or an answer of no.
My stinking thinking is sinking my soul. My only grace is the saving rescue line to you. I grab on and cry out.
Breathe
The trauma and the shock have set me on autopilot. My God positioning source sets be back tou you. I'm writhing in the raging sea. I render senseless in agony. I grab Your hand to rescue me.
This mountain under me is Your growing faith from you to me. My breath of life is given to me to walk and see your love for me.
Even when I wander from You, sinking in disbelief....... You rescue, save, heal from the grave and instill life living.
Breath and carry me to the light of Your life. Warm calm fill me with your life of life.
Hug hold embrace and tell me I am loved loved LOVED. Wake me to suddenly life anew with YOU LORD JESUS.
Lord Jesus, mighty to save, rescue and renew in the suddenly of a cry out.
TBTLJC Amen

JUNE 25

PrayStill

Luke 1:66
All who heard them pondered them and said, "What then will this child become?" For, indeed, the hand of the Lord was with him.

Scripture Prayer: Magnify the Lord.

Lord of the dance, Author of joy, Song of my songs,
magnify the Lord in my soul. Break me out as a beacon to the world I meet today. Take all there is on the worldly earth and bring the temple to it. Let the whole earth rejoice and be the temple of the LORD.
Jesus
Turn me out. This is the day the Lord has made rejoicingly to enter. Let me break down the obstacles of communion of saints to bring the washed word of God to the world. Make me part of the disciple of nations delivering the mikveh cleansing to all I encounter. Let me use your words if I must. Redirect and magnify all to You.
My soul sings dances and rejoices at the joy of joining your presence. Replace my iniquities with your precepts.
Guard my words and steps.
Make me a protector defender and example of Your Word. Discern my thoughts and actions. Smile my life to others to magnify multiply magnetize Your kingdom.
Amen

JUNE 26

PrayStill

Matthew 19:26
But Jesus looked at them and said, "For mortals it is impossible, but for God all things are possible."

Scripture Prayer: Divine Savior

Holy Spirit
Fill my vessel desire, open my willingness doorways to You. You are all of me. I am empty without you. Connect and inject saving graces and mercies. Make me whole again. I surrender.
Selah
Jesus
My free will has strayed to believing I can heal myself and be living. I swim in unknowing circles in deceive I'm progressing better.
The only full circle is You to me. Be my beginning and end and everything in between. Excite my soul to reverence the Saving Savior authorship of souls in creation. Indeed, my purpose back to You.
God in Heaven, the fear of losing me to surrender to you levels my pride's esteem. The gravity of the grave overwhelms. Fall me into Your loving mercy arm to the embrace by Your loving grace arm. Carry me tight to right. Your eternity key unlocks me. Yes, yes, yes; the freewill given up for Your purpose sustains me and returns to You, Lord Redeeming Savior.
Thanks be to Trinity's foundation salvation creation, in the falling into the grace of mercy's embrace. Mighty to save. Free from the grave. Holy be thy name above all names.
Amen

JUNE 27

PrayStill

Matthew 20:10
Now when the first came, they thought they would receive more; but each of them also received the usual daily wage.

Scripture Prayer: Gratitude

Heavenly Father Savior Son,
Guiding Spirit, fill my soul with Your bountiful graces and mercies in dancing abundances. Flooded with gratitude there is no envy coveted jealousy. love gratitude reigns.
Your economy is currency in love. Realize my coffers to pay extravagantly from Your redeeming bank that saves souls. Let me take wages from my souls reserves to pay forward the last worker into the Heaven field of life.
I will pay gladly anything to see the last one on to be the first one saved and lifted to Your glory. This is most precious and important commerce. Save to save the unsaved You bring to the harvest field workers.
Selah
Help my focus purpose and direction to point to you Lord. Make me cheerful for others joys and successes. Make my heart kind and generous always giving first. Giving without reward for giving. Living for giving in gratitude of grace rather than obligation of wages.
Learn that my yearnings are really my earnings paid forward for Your purpose in Heaven. My days wages are focused on my field for relating and not comparing. Help pay forward Your grace wage. My mercy bank is full with the greatness of Your inheritance of riches adorning reflecting your sprinkle sparkling all to You.
TBTG TBTJC TBTHS
Amen

JUNE 28

PrayStill

Matthew 20:26
It will not be so among you; but whoever wishes to be great among you must be your servant.

Scripture Prayer: Whose I Am

Lord

Mighty and powerful to the weak and needy. Open my perceptive senses. Bring me to realize the real you. Let me deserve to serve you.

Let me choose this day whom I shall serve. I will choose something. Let it be you Lord.

Throughout this day let me lay down my idols and fears and follow the pining and Longing for You.

Let me cast out the dust of the day that that the world magnifies. The threatening weather man the fear instilling news man. The murmur of bad news acclaim. Let that lower power slip away. Un-paralyze the spectators to turn and serve your Words.

I reserve the Good News of Your higher glory elevated to the raising praise and worship. Let me know the cost and the reward is Yours, God. Hang on the cross the sin of the day to cleanse and wash away.

What can separate and come between. Whatever I put between us is lost. No power formed against can surpass this bond of life. This healthy cure of healing what ails, is the serving deserving conserving reserve of Your mighty power indeed.

TBTHT HOLY TRINITY 3IN1 Amen

JUNE 29

PrayStill

Ezekiel 34:11
For thus says the Lord God: I myself will search for my sheep, and will seek them out.

Scripture Prayer: Return

Abba Father, Savior Son, Mama Spirit, Trinity adored,
You give me just enough free will to be lost and drowning in the sea of self-centered desperation. Before you form me, You know the destination of my steps and wanderings in the seas of deceptive pleasures toils and snares. I search for me as my own saving source and the king of my destiny. I am lost in king baby me.
This is the self-will I surrender to Your will aligned. Let Your will be my will. Let my will be realigned. True my soul to you. Plumb my worship and praise for Your beautiful purposes. Energize my lightings brightly to your washing altar table. Reclaim my soul.
You, Lord Jesus, redirect revive and restore me. My soul rests in the cool warming breezes of Your sanctuary implanted in my heart.
Revitalize and revamp my resign to relinquish responding to Your call. Render me in renew. Reserve and revitalize relation resolves. Right and rule the reigning in my heart.
All these requests reassure through the Redeeming blood of righteous ruling Christ.
Rejoice relentlessly to remain and restore the reward of receiving Your revelation reflection recreations.
TBTHS Amen

JUNE 30

PrayStill

Psalm 33:10
The Lord brings the will of the nations to naught; he thwarts the designs of the peoples.

Scripture Prayer: Powerful

Mighty, powerful and filled with grace are you, Abba Yahweh. Be my strength and comfort, my shield my protector. Reign over me. Set nations right.

My Little kingdom I sometimes mostly have control. The kingdoms of other I can sometimes influence. The kingdom of nations you rule. Your Kingdom, Lord is unchanging in the unchaining of hearts back to You.

My self-will was out of control. Now I'm out of control back in Your control.

Resign my design of life to the singing signs of praises raising and glory.

You Lord God have me in new song each day. Overwhelm me in blessing and favor of the assuring inheritance of your precious kind loving steadfast rescue.

TBTHS

JULY 1

PrayStill

Mark 5:36
But overhearing what they said, Jesus said to the leader of the synagogue, "Do not fear, only believe."

Scripture Prayer: God Tuning

Lord, hear my Prayer: I believe x Trinity x Harmony. Exhaust my fear. Fill me with Your Rock of fortitudes' beat. Dismiss my doubt. Break forth Your powerful assurances' symphony. Unchain my uncertainty. Let my yes to you be YES to You indeed in tempo kairos.
My strength, my salvation, my Redeeming advocate advisor, You fill overwhelm and brilliantly place me in Your womb of faith. I am surrounded in surrender salvation. Rhythm my heart to your song.
Selah
Spirit mother consuming, Abba father shielding, saving Son embracing, guard and protect the cracks in me that are sealed to sanctuary strengthening. Flood me in faith flowing streams of melodies overflowing.
Just the thought of a drop of your pure FAITH moves mountains of fear. You are my strength enabler.
Only pure love Faith is allowed. Faith so present it is automatic. Faith so powerful it overwhelms and consumes. Faith so invisible I only know I have it in recollection chorus. Pure love my assurance in clear fresh pristine. Wholly Holy shield in armors of truth and righteousness. Protect from the dust uncertain. Guard me in invisibly from the enemy. Seal in Faith this assuring conviction.
TBTHT

Acrostic:

FAITH: Finding Assurance In truths Healing

FAITH: Fear Aside In Trinity's Healing

FAITH: Father Always In Thy Hands

AMEN X ^^+++^^

JULY 2

PrayStill

Matthew 21:12-13
Then Jesus entered the temple and drove out all who were selling and buying in the temple, and he overturned the tables of the money changers and the seats of those who sold doves. He said to them, "It is written, 'My house shall be called a house of prayer'; but you are making it a den of robbers."

Scripture Prayer: Mammon

Lord Jesus
Let the anger and greed of love of thieving money idols be set right. You Lord are cleanser of souls. Your conviction speaks in suddenly. Your revealings lighten up abruptly. Your replacement economy of love patience and kindness expels the greed of the worlds' greed in life.
Rest the settled dust of mammon to the alter of dirt. Whip to the ground and snap into right reverence the desiring motives to Your magnanimous Kingdom's purpose.

Lord
All the mammon of the earth is yours. Turn and alter the altar in the world's ship upside down to turn the keel into the ridge beam of Your house in us. Turn it over, let it go, what falls out... ¿¿¿
Let the drizzle of lust for the luster of the world fall from the rooftops to the earth. Transform its woeful purpose to watering your beautiful purpose of adornment in Heaven. The mammon is ALL yours.
The value of Your economy Lord supersedes all others. In peace and patience, the storms of anger and lust greed fall to the ground in shame.

Let the payments of love Peace Patience Kindness Humility and Generosity motivate and register my soul's payment systems to Your Great Glories.

The value of your presence in the barter of life is Truly amplified in magnified and well supplied for your awesome ride inside the glory of Your great bank of overflowing abundant life given freely.

TBTJC

Author of salvation

JULY 3

PrayStill

Matthew 21:32
[Jesus said to them,] "For John came to you in the way of righteousness and you did not believe him, but the tax-collectors and the prostitutes believed him; and even after you saw it, you did not change your minds and believe him."

Scripture Prayer: Fresh

Lord
Set my words and deeds fresh daily. Guide direct and imbue my heart to You, in Your ways. Let me be Your Living WORD to those I meet without saying a word. Mirror my reflection to Your truth. Be my mediator advocate and truth interloper. Protect and guard my thoughts and words and deeds to truth in love showering.

Selah

I believe You are here present. Spirit of God manifest in Jesus living powerfully in God Almighty. To know the warming wing of Your embrace comforts and sustains me. Hold me tightly. Guide me rightly. Insight me brightly to to your leading. Be my destination. You reign, sustain and remain in me.
TBTHT
Amen

JULY 4

PrayStill

Matthew 5:46a
For if you love those who love you, what reward do you have?

Scripture Prayer: inflame

Lord Jesus
Mighty Lord Author and Savior.

Spark and Kindle this campfire for Your Awesomeness. Wake me up to my dreamed first thought of Your filling Grâces. Make Your reality my presence. Your loving invitation caresses away my unsettled fleeting fears. All that remains is warmth in relaxed numbing. Remain here present in and around me. Infiltrate and permeate my affirm for Your Heavenly firm firmament.

Rest
Selah-brate

Let me love Your first love of me back first to you Lord. Let my purpose and desires be Yours. Surrender me to greater love than comfortable love in stagnancy.

Thank You Lord Jesus
You make broader my borders to meet my detractors and enemies and love-forgive them where we are.
Resign me to inherit your great mercies. Be the author of the lovely resolving outcomes. Conquer and dispel the unease of disease relationship.

Help me to forgive like you forgive. Make strong the bonded ropes entangled in your peaceful plains of resolve. Anoint my silence stilled in authenticity of your attractive aura. Holy Spirit reside with, in and through me. Convict my heart and soul to your beckoning love's healing.

Amen

JULY 5

PrayStill

Matthew 22:14
For many are called, but few are chosen.

Scripture Prayer: Crux

Jesus, Welcoming Inviter,
The truth of the matter of my soul is, You want my whole soul. Half measures expedite expulsion from Heavens Eternal Banquet Feast. At the cross, the crux of the matter is.
I surrender all to you. Take away my worn idol clothes in the changing room of your transforming powerful WORD alive.
Adorn me in your Grâce coats to prepare the Way. Your Way, the only Way.
Eternal finality is chosen in the call to surrender everything I have, own, think, do, and am to You.
Pleasing pleadings refine me to Your feast of life abundant at this banquet preparing.
No laws or weapons can form against, feasting on living fruited spiritual blessings. Place in me, the consuming desiring and quenching thirst for Your
Love,
Joy,
Peace,
Forbearance,
Kindness,
Goodness,
Faithfulness,
Gentleness,
Self-control

Focus the gnashing of my teeth to bite away the sins of fleshed desires and crucify worldly pride. Cleans and restore my soul to satisfy the call choices in this earthly valley. Elevate and sustain truth and Clarity within and without to the importance of wearing the Grâce coat gracefully.

Let me hear listen and understand the calling of Your voice to answer to You always.

Yes Lord

Yes Lord

Yes Lord

Yes

TBTJC

JULY 6

PrayStill

Matthew 22:21b-22
Then [Jesus] said to them, "Give therefore to the emperor the things that are the emperor's, and to God the things that are God's." When they heard this, they were amazed; and they left him and went away.

Scripture Prayer: Enrichment

Lord
How amazing and awesome some awe in you. Especially when the worth of your free reaching riches are discovering spiritual payments and blessings beyond any comprehension.
Living vessels fill up with the jewels of mercy, forgiveness, trust, honor, and glory. In Your Kingdom we advance payments and offer freely to give back to You each moment for Your Glory.
The beauty of Your profits of renewal and peace continually direct deposit. They accrue and invest. They multiply in dividend and insure and secure peace. They are in stamp of spiritually and they account for and deliver this most precious gift,
Jesus

Jesus
Your eternal love payment has great universal magnitude across cultures and generations past present and future. Your mercy payment suffices the world.
I am paid handsomely in the riches of your merciful grace filling wealth flooding my reserves abounding.

I take this Trinity coin key to reconcile my debt and pay forward Your glory filled life
giving purposeful payment in perpetuity
The pin to my soul is three in one in me.

TBTHS in Trinity
Amen x Selah

JULY 7

PrayStill

Matthew 22:37-40
[Jesus] said to him, "You shall love the Lord your God with all your heart, and with all your soul, and with all your mind.' This is the greatest and first commandment. And a second is like it: 'You shall love your neighbor as yourself. On these two commandments hang all the law and the prophets.'"

Scripture Prayer: None Shall I Fear

Lord
You love me before time was created. You love me in any matter in any place. You created love and you created me in love. Let me love you back knowing your intimate desire for me. Your love is greater than any other. love more powerful, more rewarding, than any other.
I am overwhelmed in love from You Lord God love from Jesus love from the love Counselor Spirit. Reign all over me, unending gainfully again.
Whole complete unconditional found love.
I give you all of me. My heart beats in your rhythm. My mind obsesses in You occupying my thoughts. All my energies build in this faith relationship. My soul is locked onto You, the Way, Jesus.
This persistent perpetual love reigns my days. You Lord are first, and nothing can be between us. The joy is mine in turn to you. I am full and complete. Use this love you teach in me to show and give to others.
Be my strength and courage to risk and be vulnerable and love others first like You love. Your love is in me first and always,

Love expelling all fear, love continuously seeking, love perpetually healing, love powerfully advocating, love strongly steering, love that can only be partially described in a lifetime of Your revealing. You Lord move in waves currents and floods of love moving me beyond the small love I know right now. Expand my expanses of love to Your great Kingdom love. Through with in and around the Mighty strength of your Holy Spirit dwelling boldly in my soul for You +++ Lord my guiding inheritance directive.

TBTHS TBTJC TBTG

Amen

JULY 8

PrayStill

Mark 6:4-6a
Then Jesus said to them, "Prophets are not without honor, except in their hometown, and among their own kin, and in their own house." And he could do no deed of power there, except that he laid his hands on a few sick people and cured them. And he was amazed at their unbelief

Scripture Prayer: Open Minded

Lord Jesus
Take away any doubt or contempt for Your new Kingdoms. Make me learn to embrace investigate and invigorate with Your new possibilities. Continue to instill me to be still me and receive your presence. Let me be bold to embolden others for Your glory.

Rest Selah

Meditate me beyond my understanding to know confidently Your Will manifest. I am transported from familiar to new pasture horizons braced in comfort embraces for Your Glory.
Out with the old me in with the new fresh WORD. Continual refreshing feeds my need for You Lord. Bind my imbibing with Your Word alive.
Set aside everything I think I know and crush my stubborn. Bear me freshly into open mindedness receiving. Nourish Your transforming WORD in me.
The unknown is familiar with You already there. Carry me and bring me to every new. Awake and retake my every day to your beautiful glory manifest in your living WORD beaming.
Through the precious loving Jesus,

Amen

REIGN God you REIGN
Rejuvenating
Enlightenment
Inspiring
Graces
Nearing

JULY 9

PrayStill

Matthew 23:11-12
The greatest among you will be your servant. All who exalt themselves will be humbled, and all who humble themselves will be exalted.

Scripture Prayer: Truth +++

Lord Almighty, Jesus Christ,
Maker of Heaven and earth. Let my glory be your glory. Let every good glorify Your Great Name. I deserve only to serve in Your Name.
Graceful humbling guide learnings of Your Ways. You guide direct and implore your true spiritual axiom law. Keep my deserve to serve in cheerfulness. Let each moment be a sweet and fragrant offering up to You at Your table.
Release from me any prideful motives usurping and stealing praise. Let Thine not mine be the glory.
Release from me my Insecure desires to reign and make any pride in me be pride for You. Only in through and with you is anything possible.
Purify my motives intent to glorify Your WORD name. Align my will to exalt your holy and great name. Let me praise and raise all to you.
In my humbling stumbling moments let the exalting exultation revere your praise and glory. Forgiveness slays worldly pride and moves on. You are the Author Divine, instilling desire in me to Your approval.
Let's worldly approval slip away. Direct any earthly praise to your love in creation.
You Lord guard and protect. You seal my heart lips from anger and envy and greed and lust and pride and glutinous sloth.

You let the floodgates of kindness contentment gratitude humility chastity diligence love peace and sufficiency in You, channel through my words thoughts actions and intentions. All is Yours, Jesus. I am gratefully surrounded in surrender. Keep me kind gentle meek and reverent, exalted only by Your design, Jesus, and not by the world.
TBTG Nobis Pacem Amen

JULY 10

PrayStill

Matthew 23:23-24
Woe to you, scribes and Pharisees, hypocrites! For you tithe mint, dill, and cumin, and have neglected the weightier matters of the law: justice and mercy and faith. It is these you ought to have practiced without neglecting the others. You blind guides! You strain out a gnat but swallow a camel!

Scripture Prayer: Loosening

Great God in Heaven, Jesus
You know my pique. You sense my irritation. You feel my unease. Make them all fall to ground dust for cleansing and release. Take away the broken shoelace frustration and the little tiny seeds of resentments that cause me to hold back your great encouraging love. Let me smile and move on over the little insignificants that stumbles my way to Your Magnificence.
Jesus
Crack open the nutshell of my desire for this perfection stronghold in me and me making my own kingdom come.
Let it slip away as cast to the stillness of love.
Open my senses to the loving kindness that looks beyond the little jabs, the little self-perceived imperfections, the little distractions drawing me away from Great graces in Your Glory.
Fill me with Your powerful WORD when monitoring the comments, the traffic, the distracting little nuances of things not the way I would have them.
Let me see all the beauty in the mosaic. Let me focus on the wider grâce view in mercy and Forgiveness to see all the beautiful greaters than the small imperfections,

Lord

Boldly emblazon my heart to conquer the unforgiveness of myself for where you have revealed the consequences of my decisions, that draw away from Your great Kingdom. Let me see Your design in my hindsight justice and truth You reveal gracefully to my soul. Through with and in the strength of Your mighty living WORD, manifest surround and guard my thoughts lips, and motives.

Amen

JULY 11

PrayStill

Matthew 23:27-28
Woe to you, scribes and Pharisees, hypocrites! For you are like whitewashed tombs, which on the outside look beautiful, but inside they are full of the bones of the dead and of all kinds of filth. So you also on the outside look righteous to others, but inside you are full of hypocrisy and lawlessness.

Scripture Prayer: Inside Out

Jesus
Render me senseless to my own sin. Reveal the unhidden secrets. Wash and cleanse this vessel from within.
Let my insides match my outsides. Deliver me from my own devices to the place where you grant me peace surpassing all understanding.

Lord Jesus
You designed me. You know my inner machinations. You take and make me true to you. You have this insistent persistence that craves for me to grow faithfully towards your transformation.
Let the resistance in my contempt become the consistent close distance in Your loving embrace. Heal my human nature to match Your Spirit nature.

LORD SPIRIT,
You make the truth shine. You illuminate the joy in being cleansed from within. You are my Redeeming escort to Your firm foundation.
You break open the tomb I build around my selfishness in desire and make it into a selfless desire. You teach me in service to You that I deserve Your free gifts fill up.

My reservoir of reserves is your abounding gifts given freely passed out gratefully in faith knowing assuredly all surrender is to you. Yours is the key to release all my selfish worldly desires. You make me wholesome and the world leaves me emptied from holes of selfish centered desires.

Teach me Lord to have faith growing to know in trust showing that the love glowing in Your heart for me can match the love I have for others first.

TBTG

JULY 12

PrayStill

Psalm 18:17
He reached down from on high and grasped me; he drew me out of great waters.

Scripture Prayer: Delight

Abba Mamma Spirit Jesus
I am weak and needy, You are mighty and strong. You are my life rescuer; my bold shield beat of life. My instilling, refilling, rebearing womb.
My drowning unconscious faints into space less divide. I am numbed to movement. Your lifeline warms my comfort. I am not alone. You render me sensitive.
Breathe
Selah
Delight me in Your life. Your first delight in me reflects delight in You Lord. With you there is powerful peace in content melting away my Fear. I pant at peace arriving. The desires of my heart are full of overflowing. You baptize away my iniquities. You restore my soul.
Lord of saving graces,
Life line me to you. Reel in my reality to your expansive plains of sands washing in scouring cleansing. Pull me through the font of wisdom cleansed eternally to your light Way in WORD.
Suddenly my adroitness to your frequencies of love manifest showering over hatred. Pure love reigns dancing in delightful.
You revive me, You alive me. My pride in sin drowning turned to pride of love abounding.
My new shield surrounding protecting guiding in cleansing to breathless.
Thanks be to the living Lord and Savior, Jesus Christ, Almighty.

JULY 13

PrayStill

Psalm 16:7
I will bless the Lord who gives me counsel; my heart teaches me, night after night.

Scripture Prayer: Touch

Lord Jesus, Parent Spirit, Mighty Heavenly God
Touch my soul indescribable. Crazy love me every way I can receive. Double and triple your magnitude in every moment. Beyond any worldly sense is the conviction you plant in my soul. Open every gateway to know and be with you. Ask seek and knock my soul beyond escalation to your elation.
Rejoicingly glad in You am I. My contented peace in presence fills, remains, and explains, assurance, in blessings of You Lord Jesus. in your uniquely loving way of whispering I am taken care of.
Selah-brate
You, Lord, are watching over me in slumber and sleep in coming and going in moments revealing.
Even in my focus independent, you guard protect and assure convincingly. You are mighty strong and faithful comfort in each thoughtful step and each deliberate intention. In my thoughtless reactive unplanned movements, you surprise in suddenly the gifts of your presence and approval.
Lord
You approve me as I as I am. You create and deign my days. In Your glory, praise raises the day and speaks clearly hearing ringing for Your acceptance.

You Agape love me. You physically mentally emotionally and spiritually mark my soul as your servant. I ask, seek and knock boldly for Your boldly, and everything else falls into place.

Be my days, be my ways, be my everything I say. Fill my nights make my sight only in you delight.

Through with in and especially because of Your first love of me You place before me.

Revere my countenance always to you.

TBTJC Loving Savior

JULY 14

PrayStill

Matthew 24:36
But about that day and hour no one knows, neither the angels of Heaven, nor the Son, but only the Father.

Scripture Prayer: Mighty Lord Almighty

Heavenly Jesus, Son of God, Author of man: You number my days. You author my beginning. You sign my end. The mystery of life, the mystery of faith, the mystery of death concealed in unknown.
Convict my truth to knowing all is well and as should be. Hear my pleading pleas Lord.
Please fill my unknown discomfort with your assured comfort.
Receive my Selah
Within You is being... glimpse of my eternal. No more want no more mercy require. Full throttle faith floods and transfixes the broken fallenness. Your way gateways turnstiles of beautiful rolling verdant pastures unfolding in undulating elation.
Selah x rest
Let the fear and uncertainty swap out from my heart to the reality of Your infinite momentless. Before and after, time is no more. Evaporate to condensation presence in feeling and knowing unseen.
Guide my days in and on Your Word. Breath on and in. Inject life to the sponge of my word leaning learn in Your Bible ... to Heavenly courts of sustaining light perpetual.
B asic
I nstructions
B efore
L eaving
E arth

Beautiful Invitation Before Leaving Earth

Reveal in your intimacy the Longing of my heart's desire to know and be knowing. To hear and be hearing, to sense and be sensing. Saturate my porous absorbing soul in Your living merciful grace, glowing warmth embrace.

Selah x amen x 77

TBTJC

JULY 15

PrayStill

Mark 6:26
The king was deeply grieved; yet out of regard for his oaths and for the guests, he did not want to refuse her.

Scripture Prayer: Appeasement

Lord
I am weak and needy, reactive and submissive, compromising and relinquishing.
I surrender to the wrong peace sometimes rather than stand boldly for Your truth.
In silence, unspoken to the compromise, I slip into people-pleasing rather than God-pleasing.
Help my firmness in resolve. Empower me in the standing and saying the right thing when it is even more difficult than the condoning.
Wrap in kindness the knowing when to say no. Provide your awesome patience in the how to deliver the please hold.
So much better is one moment in your presence green pasture courts. Let the elsewheres slip away.
Cast aside my pride obstacles and let me forgive first, guide me to love more, and meet more deeply, the true Jesus that is in every encounter.
LORD
Let my countenance be true.
Be my fluent influencer.
TBTHS x 3 Amen

JULY 16

PrayStill

Matthew 25:3-4
When the foolish took their lamps, they took no oil with them; but the wise took flasks of oil with their lamps.

Scripture Prayer: Vessel

Lord All Mighty,
You are healer, healthful thought revealer. You mend and bind my cracked cistern. My treasure chest God box can restore.
You renew and repair where the gravity thief draws from the crack, contents substance of Your filling. Empty me of me!... to seal my brokenness leaking. Make me worthy to hold and overflow. My life for yours!
Selah
Sealed stronger in the mended dry bone fracture, You Lord create a worthy retainer.
You protect the value of my contents to pour out from the top the impurities refined and separated. I am more worthy in your repair than my despair.
Lord keep me mindful of all the beautifully oiled fuels you sustain. Prepare and guard in my drowsiness. Slumber nor sleep can keep me from Your loving insistent pursuit of my essences. Purify my refine.
Trim and ignite the light of desire for passion for provoke. Take the mend in cistern for Your exchange to bright cheerful deliberateness.
Smile to peaceful enjoyment the attractive way You author salvation lighting.
TBTJC Healer Amen

JULY 17

PrayStill

Matthew 25:25
So I was afraid, and I went and hid your talent in the ground. Here you have what is yours.

Scripture Prayer: Multiply Talents

Heavenly Spirit
Inspire every gift of smiling bestowing upon to share in multiples. Remove from me every fear of failure and judgement. Replace bold urgency in giving back Your Kingdom. Refrain not my success desire in You. Restrain my inhibition. Reveal and free all the beautiful abilities You give to reflect Your kingdom.
Let not the dust cover up the light shining brightly through.
Embolden in confidence!
Emblazon Your will to flourish and shine delightfully to your adornment. Let it all be given freely in deliberation expanding beyond expectations.

Selah-bration
You lord Jesus are the author of so many beautiful gifts of love and service and uplifting.
Write through hearts the uncontainable desire to reflect these gifts as Your blessings.
Lord make cheerful giving in cheerfulness.
TBTHS flowing through Your Glory. Amen.

JULY 18

PrayStill

Matthew 25:45

Then [Jesus] will answer them, "Truly I tell you, just as you did not do it to one of the least of these, you did not do it to me."

Scripture Prayer: Omnipresent

Jesus

You are awesomeness everywhere. You reign supreme. Every eye I see opening into a world of Your beautiful design.

I confess I am blind to things on any given day. I am weak and needy and selfish sometimes. You strengthen my resolve stronger.

Thankfully, You occupy me with Your Spirit ways and persuasions. Gratefully, You enlighten to Your presence in each soul longing for Heaven's love. Be the Master mediator liaison in every encounter.

Lord Jesus,

Realize my knowing you reside in each broken soul. Let me see beyond the black in the eyes to see and lift. Let me lift the weak and strong, comfort to poor and wealthy. Compassion with the sick and healthy. Find the lost and the directed. Soothe the angry and kind. Fill the hungry and full. Enjoy the fearful and trusted.

Everywhere Your Healing Leveling Loving Spirit flows today, may I be your ambassador of open armed embracing love without judgement.

Let me be You for them and let me see You in them to make us Us as three in one gathered.

Glory be to Mamma Abba Spirit Jesus The Supreme elicitor, solicitor provoker and passionate advocate of the Way, the truth and the Life. Amen

JULY 19

PrayStill

Matthew 26:6-7
Now while Jesus was at Bethany in the house of Simon the leper, a woman came to him with an alabaster jar of very costly ointment, and she poured it on his head as he sat at the table.

Scripture Prayer: Sacred Adornment

Precious Savior Jesus
Mighty and powerful loving deliverer of souls. Most worthy of praise and honor and respect and adornment. Highest in Heavens authority most reverent.
Lord
You show now how to praise and glorify. In giving we receive in anointing we are anointed.
Let the floodgates of adornment oil cleanse and protect the valley paths in safety. Open up meandering moments of graceful mercy and merciful grace flowing all back to You. Let the tears of gratitude joy and grief fall fresh and flowing.
Rest, Selah, Peace, rejoice,
Half-heartedness steals away the whole gift. Teach me to praise all, full, complete, to hold no thing back. Surrender all to you. Surrender all to peace. Surrender all to win. In spiritual discernment let the already, already won, battle be Yours.
At Your table altering, the enemy eats truth. truth reveals peace. Peace love points to Heaven's gate calming. Silence listens, in anointing praising, with raising adornments in each, loving.
Lord

You make me worthy to receive love redirected back to you. Help me to deflect and redirect enemies back to dust. Give all my love in service all back to You. Receive all my love from everything of You. Pour my life as a prayer to you.
TBT Precious Lord Jesus Amen

JULY 20

PrayStill

Romans 12:12-13
Rejoice in hope, be patient in suffering, persevere in prayer. Contribute to the needs of the saints; extend hospitality to strangers.

Scripture Prayer: Goodness Aglow

Precious redeeming Lord
Installer author of instilling grace. Mediator of every fragrant circumstance, beautiful is your name Jesus
I am senseless to the unknown. My actions motivate in fear sometimes. I do not know the outcomes. My hesitance holds me down. Here I am, Lord.
Thankfully the assurance in Your WORD steps comforts to knowing it is well. Rejoicingly gladden the excitement of Your unknown revealing light. Help me wait peacefully in humbly as opportunities are for rest rather than anxiety. Pray/connect with me in moments unpassing. Surpass my understanding in/with/for the unknown saints and strangers. Entertain the unknown angels through me.
Seeking treasures in the eyes of the unknowns. Looking for Your reference, Lord, in the hearts of the newly greeted. Finding favor in listening hearing and understanding how you present each situation revealing your unique and changing signature.
Let me boldly meet the stranger and the saint at Your table equalizing the flesh facades to health Heavenly encounters.
With your beautiful loving Spirit all things are possible, through Jesus Christ our persistent mediator.
TBTG Abba Mamma navigator. Amen.

JULY 21

PrayStill

Psalm 30:2-3
O Lord my God I cried out to you, and you restored me to health. You brought me up, O Lord from the dead; you restored my life as I was going down to the grave.

Scripture Prayer: Breath Life

Holy Jesus blessing healing redeemer. You breathe life into bodies ailing. Your life air of WORD uplifts and dances at the joyful in communion with God. Your ear inclines to the soft whimper of my cry. Your WORD in me is life expanding. I exalt you in exultation increasing.
Breath life
My body is dying yet my seeded faith spirit grows stronger. You embrace my wholeness with your holiness renewing Envelope for this worldly transport slipping into dark.
You shout light surround breaking my walls down. Your authority eternal reigns true to my soul seed of faith. You pour out life blood and flesh for rescue. Your eyes on me twinkle reignbows of life treasure in You. You capture my essence. You pulse my heart back to YOUR life. I'm alive anew in You.
Praise eternal, God Spirit Son singing dancing praises.
TBTHT Amen

JULY 22

PrayStill

Mark 6:31a
[Jesus] said to them, "Come away to a deserted place all by yourselves and rest a while."

Scripture Prayer: Still

Selah x 7
Holy Spirit, come and be with. Take me from myself to You.
Physically my heart slows. Insides become numb and warm as in sleeping trance. Your calming presence aware to receive.
My mind's eye tabula rasa in clearness paints Your picture inviting.
Jesus
Pure implicit forgiveness wipes away the inside pride clamoring to be heard. Peaceful emotion waves wash away tides of fear to deep pools running faith's strong current.
All is well
In the presence of my allies' implicit love revives receiving.
Absolute union is knowing without approval. Words need not be spoken. Feel the Agape.
Perfect assurance in souls uniting. Blessing calm remaining.
Stay
Take me to one glimpse of Your palace place. Nothing can compare. Ivory and pomegranate mixed rose seals mark the sounds of sparkling eyes hearing. Sweet smooth signals humble grace attending. Fill You in this empty place.
You and I are one.
Be this place always ready. Bring me throughout the day. Signal this place here in in your moments pouring down beauty. I sense aware Your here.
TBTHS

JULY 23

PrayStill

John 20:16-17
Jesus said to her, "Mary!" She turned and said to him in Hebrew, "Rabbouni!" (which means Teacher). Jesus said to her, "Do not hold on to me, because I have not yet ascended to the Father. But go to my brothers and say to them, 'I am ascending to my Father and your Father to my God and your God.'"

Scripture Prayer: Revealing

Lord. Teacher. Friend. Jesus.
You are mighty strong loving and everywhere. You lift and humble those in need. You rule to love and patience unending. You raise conscious contact revealing.
You present your presence in signature moments. I love when you show up and give your present of life abounding. You teach in beautiful creation moments. You bless wisdom knowledge recognition and understanding in grace flows.
Teach me to search for your WORD and sacraments. Abide me in your ways to paths of pastures grazing. Fill my soul with your yearning for more soul food feasting.
Keep returning in those special moments assuring my soul. You surround me. You watch and comfort. You protect and save. You never let go.
Teach me to receive these graceful encounters of Your living WORD in gifted presents. You teach my heart true.
What is mine is yours. What is yours is mine. You exchange my earthen sin dust for True life. You exchange beauty in love. Teach me in the leaning in Lord.
TBTJC the Living Lord Amen

JULY 24

PrayStill

Romans 14:7
We do not live to ourselves, and we do not die to ourselves.

Scripture Prayer: Authorship

Saving, soul-sanctifying Jesus, You never ever let go. Beyond forever sealed in love. Overwhelming in your passages of beginnings and ends are your signals. Satisfying soul providing sweet is your name alive, Jesus.
Receive Selah
In grief, love comforts. love exchanges pain of loss and love reveals truth. You, Lord, comfort my unknown. You assure my not alone. When all is gone, just you and me, I see. You take me where I need to be.
Breath Selah
Life alive, in thrive in You. Death alive resides no more. You conquer darkness. You shine light alive to every doubt fear and discomfort.
Great is your faithfulness in growing faith assurance. Comfort is Your inescapable relentless presences freeing. You relieve my soul. How simple and easy You make my surrender. In Your grace, mercy, and love is life eternal.
TBTG Awesome Designing Mighty Creator. You own me. I am Yours.
Amen

JULY 25

PrayStill

Matthew 20:26b-28
Whoever wishes to be great among you must be your servant, and whoever wishes to be first among you must be your slave; just as the Son of Man came not to be served but to serve, and to give his life a ransom for many.

Scripture Prayer: Hostage

Lord Deliverer, you take away the sins of the world. Hearer listening to prayer: You make my matter. The substance and the issues are Yours.
Teach me, Teacher Rabonni, to serve as You came to serve the world. All purpose and matter are for and because of You. You reign in soul redemption. I am, no longer a hostage to sin. You free my soul. You pay my ransom. You captivate my renew to You.
Selah
Lord everyone is my boss. Let me cheerfully serve. Obey me to your serving style in esteem with boundaries. Make me emulate and imitate your essence. Relieve me from the shackles of selfishness and self-centeredness.
Lord Jesus
Help the sin of pride out of the pulpit to the rail at the altar for transformation. Speak life of redemption and conviction and confession of self will to wash away the self-sin in the world.
Peace,
Selfish sin fighting in the pulpit divides. Sin confessed at the rail changes slave to free.
Let me serve others as You serve me Lord Jesus in gently powerfully convicting insistences of truth, mercy, Forgiveness, grace, and love.
Guard my lips and intentions.
TBTJC

JULY 26

PrayStill

Romans 15:1-2
We who are strong ought to put up with the failings of the weak, and not to please ourselves. Each of us must please our neighbor for the good purpose of building up the neighbor.

Scripture Prayer: Inspire

Lord Jesus Christ,
Author of love and of life. Creator of communion within.
True and simple are Your teachings. Beautiful are your ways. Precious are the moments You teach in love and encouragement to lift.
You take away the wrong and make it right. You take the right and make it great. Great are Your ways and precepts. Help me to dispel the negative and flood with positive.
Let the garment of giving good be what I want most to give. What I give comes back. Let listening and kindness be circling back.
Guard my motive in giving for Your gift not mine. Let me seek always the least of these and lift to more. Stamp away pride in accomplishment and direct it back to you for Your glory especially others good.
Let inward selfish aloneness prune away into blossoming and flourishing closeness. Weed away prideful seclusion leaving to humble intrusions.
Insist your ways in me.
Let the giving and receiving of Your grace gifts be to Thy glory.
TBTJC TBTHS TBTG 3n1

JULY 27

PrayStill

Psalm 40:1-2
I waited patiently upon the LORD; he stooped to me and heard my cry. He lifted me out of the desolate pit, out of the mire and clay; he set my feet upon a high cliff and made my footing sure.

Scripture Prayer: Uplifting Inclining

Holy Spirit, come.
Revive my soul to joyfulness. Instill in me peace knowing where I am is where You want me. Where I'm going is where more of You is. What You want for me is Your glory saturating my essence.

Selah x breath x repeat

Lord Jesus
I know You get up and continue always. You help me to get up and continue. You rev my inspire to motivate. You shower peace calm flowing. Deep is Your still silence raging victory over dust. I am lifted and sifted for goodness. Inspect my strands for purpose. See me through the obstacles.
Mama Abba parent God
Your new song sings to my soul. Intimacy abiding through Christ with You sets my feet upon your cornerstone rock. Elevate my strength. In You Lord be strength for goodness and graciousness. For Your sake my esteem is lifted to humble enough to wait in confidence knowing all is well all ways always with You.
Strong in pursuit. Strong in patience. Powerful is your force surrounding, abounding as pounding comfort, sounding sweet vibrato to my soul's ear.
Thanks be to Trinity everlasting TBTTE

JULY 28

PrayStill

Psalm 139:6-7
Where can I go then from your Spirit? Where can I flee from your presence? If I climb up to Heaven, you are there; if I make the grave my bed, you are there also.

Scripture Prayer: Aware

Lord of surrounding completeness, you surround and engulf me, Lord Jesus. Inescapable is your presence. Comforting is Your touch. Beautiful is Your inquiry. You lead and plead my ways. You guard my very being. With You, there is no without you.

Selah

Every day I am born again to you. You fire my soul to You. You turn my pit pot upside down and pour me into Your Heavens place. It Is all yours.
Erase away the days into Your Will. Capture my wholeness to make it more holy. Resign my resistance to belief
You draw near, and I am here. Trusting in knowing You are there also. Escape me not from your embrace. Hold me tight to right me. Never let me go. In my dry absence from you who moved? Wander me back to you.
Always in Your loving pursuit I all ways am reclaimed. mercy and grace are welcoming back to You.
TBTHT 3in1

JULY 29

PrayStill

John 6:8-9
One of his disciples, Andrew, Simon Peter's brother, said to him, "There is a boy here who has five barley loaves and two fish. But what are they among so many people?"

Scripture Prayer: Hunger

Lord Jesus
Beautiful power within. The joy is in You. You feed the spirit of the soul healthfully. You sustain me and retain my allegiance feeding. I am welcome at the table.
Taste and see the beauty of Your food. Sweet is the sound of your voice calling for meal. Plenty full are filling moments with you. You require my desire to be in You. Honey to my lips is Your WORD of life. Nourish and satisfy.
Ember sealing tiny taste of purity. All is given for leaven. Heaven's host of the most provides for my inside thirst and hunger. The belly of pleasure resides. The loaves of warm and tasty remain
Lord Jesus
You are fuel for full. With you there is no want. You sustain me to thirst and hunger no more. Overflowing is your peace meal.
Prayers and blessings, Joys and lessons, filling hearts with contentment. Willing to take, willing to eat. Willing to give it all.
TBTJC

JULY 30

PrayStill

Matthew 27:24
So when Pilate saw that he could do nothing, but rather that a riot was beginning, he took some water and washed his hands before the crowd, saying, "I am innocent of this man's blood; see to it yourselves."

Scripture Prayer: Idle

Lord
You illuminate the truth. You reveal the motive, You unfold the fear. You wash away the sins of the world. You are merciful.
Lead me to action, not idleness. Let the truth be spoken. Let all my thoughts words and deeds be motivation for truth living out. Take away my idling in idols.
Make strong conviction be a place of residence. Take away the sin in silence and resignation. Desire me to do your will and not mine. Grant me strength and courage to see feel and speak truthfully
With You, faithful Lord it continues. It is never over. You reign supreme. You make things right. You take away the fear replacing the enthusiasm for truth. You are awesome indeed.
You make me smile in your revealings. Your dealing is truth love mercy forgiveness and uplifting powerfully.
You still my fear to calm. You place my anxious in excitement for truth revealed. You turn my worry into worship. Your will reigns supreme.
TBTJC Amen

JULY 31

PrayStill

Romans 16:17-18

I urge you, brothers and sisters, to keep an eye on those who cause dissensions and offences, in opposition to the teaching that you have learned; avoid them. For such people do not serve our Lord Christ, but their own appetites, and by smooth talk and flattery they deceive the hearts of the simple-minded.

Scripture Prayer: Genuine

Lord Jesus
You make motive clear. You clear away the false pretense of getting what I want. You motivate truth and inspiration for Your glory only. Guard my lips and vision steps.
Jesus provider
You love in the lifting. Inspire the desire for truth in me. Make the motive pure. Let the gentle kind flow out. Keep the worship in the holiness rather than the pride. Direct the praise to for and with You.
You, Lord, urge distance from the loud drama and the people worship.
May the words of my mouth and the meditative inclinations of my heart be acceptable for You, Lord Jesus, my rock and my redeemer.
TBTJC

AUGUST 1

PrayStill

Judges 3:12
The Israelites again did what was evil in the sight of the Lord; and the Lord strengthened King Eglon of Moab against Israel, because they had done what was evil in the sight of the Lord.

Scripture Prayer: Persecution

ABBA Father
Three in one ruler of nations. Maker of Heaven and earth. How mighty is the kingdom of Heaven. How precious is the Son and Holy Spirit. How beautiful are your ways.

Lord
You present the question that levels away pride on the road to Damascus.
Why do you persecute me?
That stops me in my tracks every time.
I am flawed, and I sin. I realize this when I know You and Your way, through the Helper Holy Spirit conviction.
You open my eyes to the painfully obvious. You let me see on me my wrong steps. You mercifully set me straight. You heal my imperfections. Only with you am I complete
Son of God, You hold me. Son of man, You show me. You meet me where I am. Holy Spirit, fold me make me and mold me make me one complete.
Abba Mamma Father Jesus, how powerful your ways. Step me through the valley worshiping your way. Lead and direct me guide me and protect me. Show me where I'm wrong. Set me and let me follow you along. Your path of righteousness let it be the song
Amen
Thanks be to Trinity, Spirit Son and God

AUGUST 2

PrayStill

Matthew 27:55
Many women were also there, looking on from a distance; they had followed Jesus from Galilee and had provided for him.

Scripture Prayer: Nurture

Great Spirit love,
Great are You Lord. Sustaining life force weaving through the tending to each other's needs. You teach how to lift one another. Mamma Abba nurturing God, you are preciousness in outreach.

Lord of empathy and concern. You draw the loving tender touch of healing. You lift and hold the longing soul. You make the pain waste away. The languid is no more. Your humble servants raise and sustain. You take away the sin flaws of the world to lift the needy. You are fierce to protect. You do not relent.

Nurturing God of solace. You elicit and solicit healing. Your merciful tending is sending love beyond compare. You restore and revive, You make love alive. I am in comfort from nurturing nursing. You sooth and remove, anoint and improve, protect as You and I are one.

Numb warm flowing relaxation, Lord Jesus, Spirit, You slip away the pain. love conquers hates hurt dirt in the balming salve ointment anointment. The sand grain is removed in the gentle blink of an eye. The smile of peace resides.
TBTHS

AUGUST 3

PrayStill

Psalm 69:22
Reproach has broken my heart, and it cannot be healed; I looked for sympathy, but there was none, for comforters, but I could find no one.

Scripture Prayer: Speak Life

Lord Jesus, Author of WORD. Creator of WORD life. Motivator of showering graces speaking to existence. lover of souls and giver of praises lifting high the power to lift. Your kind uplifting words turn away anger to dirt. Falling praises fall fresh on lips uplifted.

Lord, let me arrest all incoming anger. I speak out my soul. My words fall before me. Make me hear them in completeness before I speak.

Sometimes I hear what I say, and I know it comes out wrong. Sometimes my words are wrong and hurtful. The shame of my words spoken hastily in anger sinks in.

The mighty Spirit of life in convicting reproach wants hurtful words unspoken. The hurt of the harm is only healed in the kind, loving, graceful Spirit conversion.

Lord, Your kind words spoken kill cruelty. Your fiercely kind love dispels fearful anger to its knees. Turning cheeks and shields of love deflect the words unspeakable. The contagion of anger dies.

Let the hurt of my soul be transformed to showering graces, Jesus.

Lord

Your calm, kind, king words, spoken gently, open channels of peaceful flooded mercies.

Make song and music multiply tones to kind sweetness sweating words pouring out.

TBTHS

AUGUST 4

PrayStill

Matthew 28:15
So they took the money and did as they were directed. And this story is still told among the Jews to this day.

Scripture Prayer: Mammon

Lord Jesus
You are provider. You are the wealth of nations. Your currency is electric and valuable. You register with the abundant and the paupers the same. In Your economy God the wages of life are leveled to love. The dividends of Heaven's Glory conquer and divides the love of idols mammon's monies lusts.
Lord
Money motive makes mindful my desires that serve and worship me or serve and worship Your kingdom. Check my payment statements. Does it go for me or does it go for You. Does go for fearful greed, does it go for Your good.
Jesus
Make me a cheerful giver that does not fear with pinch and hoarding. Turn the greed into gifting and lifting the need. Pay it forward without need to receive. Blessings in angel EFT break the banks of fears' full need. Envy pride and greed make the color of dirt's' dust payment to self-red.
When the cup is running over, I want a bigger cup. Let me pour out blessings instead. When my cup is half full I want it fuller not realizing it's full of both Your lifegiving water and air.

You sustain me. You retain me with your prepaid salvation credits. You charge me ransomely. You pay me handsomely. You save me in gracious and mercifully. I am rich x 77 in Your wealth and blessings abundant.

TBTJC

Lord and Savior saving.

Amen

AUGUST 5

PrayStill

Psalm 51:3
For I know my transgressions, and my sin is ever before me.

Scripture Prayer: Conviction

Holy Spirit
Teaching advocate lover of my soul. Masterful creator of redemption and renewal. Gentle lover of truth and revealing. Perfect substitution for the flaws. Hear my prayer
Lord Jesus
You bless with the gift of, as much free will as I want. I take it and learn and come crawling back to You. You convict my soul home to you.
Against You, Lord
Against me, Lord
Against others, Lord, have I signed sin or let sin slip in or fall unknown to sins win.
My indiscretions, harms, and flaws are grievous on my heart. I can sense when I judge I can sense when self-pride wins. Take this prideful heart for trade in.
Change out the sin unease with your spiritual free and easy. Chains of sin are set free to the dropping shackles ring
Help me so,
I forgive others
I forgive myself
I forgive even You Lord for letting it be this way
Jesus Spirit living,
I go, I go and sin no more. I go and sin no more with You. At my side You keep me safe.

Turn my sins into singing. Let my heart rejoice. Bring me to the rail to drop and let it go. Turn my eyes scales to scales of justice. Wash away and bring contrite. In Your loves moments, You make it right. Repent repeat repents.

Fill me with Your spirit. Surround my hearts intent. Lift and cleanse and set me strait. Direct me all to You. Your love heals and binds, forgives and washes new.

Bring me to that field steam of right newness righteousness. We start again anew.

TBTJC

TBTHS

TBTG

AUGUST 6

PrayStill

2 Peter 1:13-14
I think it right, as long as I am in this body, to refresh your memory, since I know that my death will come soon, as indeed our Lord Jesus Christ has made clear to me.

Scripture Prayer: Named

Lord Jesus
You are beautifully humble truth alive. Words adorn grace's spoken and the whole world rejoices in you. You are mighty and strong and powerful God force Spirit. You reign and deign the days.
Lord God
I am weak and needy. You sign me into Your presence with a whisper. You gently assuage my soul to know You more. You know my every fiber intimately.
Lord Spirit Holy
You set my days before me. You know my waking and sleeping. You know my wrong turns and right turns. You meet me in the portal of here and now.
Just in the moment the here and now is gone. Alive with you in perpetual. You author my first and last breath. You cleanse my trip through the valley and streams and deserts. You guard protect and inject life in my life. I am yours before during and after life. You are beyond my Alpha and Omega, eternal Spirit, three in one.
Beautifully designed. Heavenly aligned. Spirit of life contain me. Maker of redemption, in line my souls' intentions to love and serve you in the eternal newness. My fleshly vessel journey is yours. You assure me that to die is gain.
Amen

AUGUST 7

PrayStill

Acts 3:6
But Peter said, "I have no silver or gold, but what I have I give you; in the name of Jesus Christ of Nazareth, stand up and walk."

Scripture Prayer: Healing

Jehovah Jireh
Healing provider, beautiful author of abundant life. Strong persuading balm of the ailing world. Brilliantly gorgeous present reviver. Giver of gifts of life. Powerfully eminent is your name Jesus.

Lord
You heal me. My firm firmament is cast away. Breaking the boundary of complacency in sameness. You Lord restore my soul in many multiple news, one new at a moment. Open my heart in change to You.
You take away the dim sin of the world. My sin pain is gone. You heal redeeming. My physical pain resides. My mental anguish agonizes no more. My love hurt subsides. You reside in my reviving. My spiritual pain transforms to spiritual gain.
I inherit this mind body spirit soul emotion that is made to heal by Your awesome design. Let me bring all to Your renewal. You revive alive.
My self-pride trouble is reduced by double in graceful pride in You Lord. You heal me. Your grace in mercy balm brings the calm. Within and through You Lord is the cure. Your pure truth love reigns.
Amen

AUGUST 8

PrayStill

Acts 3:25
You are the descendants of the prophets and of the covenant that God gave to your ancestors, saying to Abraham, "And in your descendants all the families of the earth shall be blessed."

Scripture Prayer: Inheritance

Lord Jesus
Root of Jesse. Son of God and man. Beautiful Savior and Creator. Beginning, end and in between. Maker and judge of all things. Deliverer of salvation. Cleansing agent of the world.

Lord God
Redeem my ailing. You are
Merciful adorning keeper of my days. Bless guide and surround my soul. Reveal the truths of love inherited. Take away the binding of detouring mistake. Set right the missteps of wandering from Your will covenant.

Holy Spirit presence,
The truth is always revealed, never concealed always at my heart. In waking and sleeping in praying and stillness its relentless at my side. The whole world knows but the one to whom it goes, bout the love deep inside you have planted.
You have it all. My heart is Yours.
Forever Amen
TBTHT

AUGUST 9

PrayStill

John 1:46
Nathanael said to him, "Can anything good come out of Nazareth?" Philip said to him, "Come and see."

Scripture Prayer: Enlighten

Jesus Lord God
King and author indescribably brilliant in set aside holiness. Creator of miraculous motives of loves pure design. Your supreme sovereign reality brings contrite to our knees. Precious is the sound of your name, Jesus.

Son of God and man, You save. Mighty hands wring clean the soil of dirt's dismissive dust. Dripping taint falls to streams of washings renewal. Deceit is no more.
Now is knowing, time standing still and stopped. Communion into your Holy essence fills this vessel fleshly refresh unending. Angels are ascending and descending Holy Spirit showers unending, Jesus.
Being in with around and through You Lord completes keys to the heart of my soul. Have reign over me.

Lord
You are suspended animation of my current. I am forever surprised of my misjudgement of You. You continually exceed my expectations. You bring more and more and more of love WORD.

You are the fulfilling desire. You require my intention. You demand my attention. You maintain my retention of Your LOVE. This time with you alone. Removes all of the unknown. I set aside every thought I know.

Have me, I submit.

Amen in You, Lord Christ,

Jesus

Amen

See also July 8th

Jesus rocks and reigns

AUGUST 10

PrayStill

Acts 4:13
Now when they saw the boldness of Peter and John and realized that they were uneducated and ordinary men, they were amazed and recognized them as companions of Jesus.

Scripture Prayer: Astonishment

Lord Jesus
You are power to the weak and needy. Relief to the strong hard hearts hearing. You reign on the parade of life. You are sustenance to the masses and miracle to the believers. The wonder of it awes.
Author of suddenly. Revealer of truth. Redirector of wills. You take the common theme of life in want and set it free. The loudness cries of mammon pride injustices is silenced and the unspoken speaks without a word. love is revealing all ways.
Lord Spirit God
You sign names and call gentle invitations. You are solution resolution to any who ask. Seeking your presence knocks out pride inside my soul. You, Lord Jesus, have the key to my heart indeed. Unlock me.
Amen
TBTHT

AUGUST 11

PrayStill

Psalm 87:6
The singers and the dancers will say, "All my fresh springs are in you."

Scripture Prayer: Delicious

Lord of all needs come bursting forth. Freshness falls from on high. Fountains of busting blessings cool lips in praising. Cool crystals clear my panting soul, painting to raising praises.

Forever always present is your surround of ocean streams thirsting. Only in Your rivers fonts of upward currents is my soul refreshed. Fresh gentle sounds of bubbling streams dancing, cry cleansing sips inside.

Arcing colors of reignbows reflect diamond crystal clear. Only is this life by renewal. All the days long I come to you. Dancing to the rivers of rhythms. Falling in surround of pure refresh new. Is You, quelling for the unquenchable fire of delight roaring in You.

TBTHS

AUGUST 12

PrayStill

2 Samuel 18:33

The king was deeply moved, and went up to the chamber over the gate, and wept; and as he went, he said, "O my son Absalom, my son, my son Absalom! Would I had died instead of you, O Absalom, my son, my son!"

Scripture Prayer: Tears

Lord God

Comforter of shocking and sadness. Pain grief sorrow regret are yours upon this shadow valley without light. Blinded in the darkness of loss there is nothing to hold back tears. Every bit of conflict turns to remorse. The waves of sadness cannot be denied. There is no peace in the maelstrom of torrential grief stricken.

Lord Jesus

The loss of love in my family friends and foes is only repayable with Your love. You Lord wring out the injustices of mournful pain. All the fear is real. All the pain is great. I want it all back. Every bad thought or word. Make it all only be love. Heal the pain in the sting of unresolved discords and negative emotions come to truth light.

Jesus, Son of man,

Only you know death like no other. Only you can make the pain go away. You are risen conquering son. You are substitution for the death of the world dying. Even to the least of these and the greatest of Thine enemies. truth in love demanding passes through the grave.

You wipe away the death of the world in triumphant resurrection. Mighty is your power to overcome. The victory is Yours. The sting sings no more. Rejoice in your victory again and again rejoicing. True light in life reigns eternal.

TBTJC Lord and Mighty Savior

AUGUST 13

PrayStill

Psalm 89:1
Your love, O Lord ever will I sing; from age to age my mouth will proclaim your faithfulness.

Scripture Prayer: Steadfast

Lord,
Your Agape unending love proclaims my lips. Unending praises engulf my days. Overwhelming and ever present are the signs of pure love flowing surround. Your love is steadfast for my heart. Mine waits in expectation always languid by Your side.

Steady and pure are the ways of Your love presenting. Fasting away my self wants my longing is filled with You. The music in my heart sings praise all the day long. Thank You Lord thank You Lord grateful is my heart.

Always are you near me. Inclining in my ear. These godly loves appear. Whispering stillness beyond the 7th Heavens of love. Philia Agape and Pragma, Eros Storge and Ludus, all in Philautia esteem. Your love is powerful beyond any person place or thing.

You came to love me first in an awesome special way. Forever faithful and true to the truth. Singing signs of praises, praying glory rising sounds of jubilant joys. Joy pours out from my lips in praises unending. You slow my fast in me to speed my feast in You. Steadfast are you for me, forever, I'm for You.
TBTJC TBTHS TBTG

AUGUST 14

PrayStill

Judges 13:3
And the angel of the Lord appeared to the woman and said to her, "Although you are barren, having borne no children, you shall conceive and bear a son."

Scripture Prayer: Fruitful

Holy Spirit

Mighty powerful presence of God, come, fill this place with great messages of healing. Brush gentle adorning words of comfort across the horizon. Expand the awareness of your prophesy.

Angel messengers carry God's will forces undeniable. Tune to the rhythm of holiness. Overwhelm in assurances, in enduring presence proclaiming. Prayers unending transcend time and space.

Jesus
Lord of all master of Heavenly wisdoms, guard and protect these hearts. Watch and guide Your trails to Your place of peace surpassing. Enlighten lift and straighten narrow pathways. Reveal all the goodness.
Messengers Angels of God heal and reveal. Deliver and liven eyes to see the glory. Make my story your glory alive. Resound in me the words and deed to be Your will. Blaze flames of refining fires to the cleansing ash of beauties polished songs of praises born anew.
Amen
TBTHT

AUGUST 15

PrayStill

Galatians 4:4-5
But when the fullness of time had come, God sent his Son, born of a woman, born under the law, in order to redeem those who were under the law, so that we might receive adoption as children.

Scripture Prayer: Child

Abba Mamma God
The love beyond belief. The power that sets free. The eternal family of embracing welcoming. Always inviting in.

You Lord are the inheritance of ages. Forever persistent in owning and welcoming me home. The true family of angels always present and endearing. My champion of life in vibrancy. The place I call home that is, in all ways with me. I reside my songs' dance in you.

Mighty comforter, Peace giver, my true family of origin. My home welcoming wandering soul rejoices at the embrace of returns. Ever present, always loving, forever at my side. Reside through, within, beside me, and make me whole.

Lord, You turn my prodigal around. You take me from the ground and lift me to your table. My every need desire and want are filled with your passion of ownership. I am yours before birth and after death and always in between.

You know me, You own me You love me all the way. You desire me to free me and bring me to Your way. Around me, surround me and bring me to my knees. I fall down and worship the crown of deity you attract to me.

Agape God love is powerfully forever.

TBTHS 3in1 Divine Trinity of Angel and Saints in Holy Family.

Amen

AUGUST 16

PrayStill

Psalm 105:1
Give thanks to the Lord and call upon his Name; make known his deeds among the peoples.

Scripture Prayer: Claim

Lord Jesus
King of justice, ruler of nations, creator of Heaven and earth. Mighty redeeming savior. Beautiful power within, refreshing and true.
Cleanse the thoughts and words and meditations of my heart. Wash away and cleanse my anger. You are mighty strong and able to absorb all my woe. Take and replace my flaws and sins and replace them with your holy place within.
Turn my heart. Help to let the goodness flow in like rivers of goodness meandering through my veins. Fill my heart with your greatness if only for a moment. The taste of your desire in me makes me long for more of thy grace and mercy that washes away iniquity and shame.
Praise and proclaim till just the Lord will remain. The glory and justice Yours forever. Make our masks holy with love from the start to the end from inside to outside You cleanse me. The justice is Yours the peace returned is ours. I proclaim You claim me as yours. Forever inescapable in loving arms embraceable. I surrender all to you.
TBTJC lover of justice. Author of creation.
Amen

AUGUST 17

PrayStill

Acts 7:23
When he was forty years old, it came into his heart to visit his relatives, the Israelites.

Scripture Prayer: Discerning Hearts

Mamma Abba Lord
Manna of all the earth. Sustenance of all creation. Nutrition of nurturing love. Fill in the heart's desires with Your completeness.

Lord Jesus
How precious and true is the discovery of discernment. Right or wrong good or bad known and unknown You weave the right truth to those who seek You. Let my seeking be finding. Open the right doors and close the wrong doors. Let my yes be yes and my no be no. Direct this ocean pathway proper.

My vision and perspective is in need of elevation. You see beyond the realms of earth and guide protecting steps and words. Waiting patiently on You, The Lord of Lords And King of Kings peacefully directs Your will. Give me strength and courage and wisdom and assurance to know Your will more than my own. Jesus, take the wheel.
Amen

AUGUST 18

PrayStill

John 5:5
One man was there who had been ill for thirty-eight years.

Scripture Prayer: Surrender

Good Lord
Master of all things, creator of time. Author of free will. Convictor of the truth. All ways present and revealing
You are King of Kings.

Lord Jesus
Help me to surrender my infirmity. I'm stuck and freezing in inaction. Your grace frees me from my lock chain. Change me to Your follow. Let me be away from me to grasp onto you.

Mighty Healer
Let me proclaim Your healing in your medicine. Let me boldly proclaim and not be ashamed to speak truth of Your salvation. My lips confess how you heal this mess and my intention is the peace that You author
TBTJC
Amen

AUGUST 19

PrayStill

1 Kings 3:9
Give your servant therefore an understanding mind to govern your people, able to discern between good and evil; for who can govern this your great people?

Scripture Prayer: Counselor

Lord Spirit

Mighty counselor and doctor of truth. You are powerfully persuading in bringing light to darkness. You make wise in the eyes of your loving perspective. You make certain the wavering. You weave in, welcoming the truth revealing.

Holy Spirit come fill this place. Be the next wise choice. Navigate in newness with much assurance c,onsidering all perspective. Wiggle not into appeasing appeals for less than. Justify not into the grandiose. Keep the true straight and narrow

Lord of true, reveal the new and shine light on the motive.
Unfold in certainty and remove uncertainty and certainly bring truth to fruition. Let it go and make it so and lead without directing. Quiet love convincing or loud fear barking let the love of truth settle wisely in suddenly.
TBTHS
Amen

AUGUST 20

PrayStill

Acts 7:59
While they were stoning Stephen, he prayed, "Lord Jesus receive my spirit."

Scripture Prayer: Life

Open arms Jesus
Creator of eternity, lover of souls, author of free will. Beautiful is your assurance of life removing fear of death to give life so abundantly in You.

Lord God
Sweep away the valley. Swoop in with the familiar knowing of your presence. Heaven here on earth knows the hint of Heaven in Heaven.

Holy Spirit
Rushing waters roaring flames, winds that sound like rain. Dusk and dawn begin and end with love all in between. Surround within and take without and lift it all on high. Surpassing everything revealed so far the best is yet to come.

TBTJC TBTHS TBTG WORD BIBLE
B.old
I. nfuence
B.efore
L.eaving
E.arth

AUGUST 21

PrayStill

Psalm 124:7
We have escaped like a bird from the snare of the fowler; the snare is broken, and we have escaped.

Scripture Prayer: Gratitude

Lord Jesus
Son of manly toils, overcoming pain and fear. Son of godly freedom releasing to the free. Beautiful strong and powerfully healing, freeing is the way. Your truth and light are. They bring life to the light of the world.

Father God
You break open pathways of delight. I am poor and floundering. I do not know my flaws. I am trapped in this cyclical vortex circling the pit. This is my only knowing. I have no worth and my strength is weak and closing in.
Breathe

Holy Spirit
Lover of souls, maker of God's ways, developer of situations, the Architect of souls convertible.
Just a sliver of silver shining reflection of God turns these groans to gold. Fly me free. Permeate the shell of the valley and nurture me back to health. Doctor Divine, my pose is supine for Your salve of salvation that heals me. Revive in alive You make my stride strive for the free key you place right inside me.
TBTHT
Amen

AUGUST 22

PrayStill

John 6:13
So they gathered them up, and from the fragments of the five barley loaves, left by those who had eaten, they filled twelve baskets.

Scripture Prayer: Suffice

Lord of abundance, Jesus. Master of contentment, Designer of enough and plenty. Creator of satisfaction in fasting. Deliverer of peace and truth and joy and love. Abounding dances all around in Your welcoming in.

God of all. Supplier of more, answer to my need. Take the fragrant fragments and place them into place. The pieces of peace surround and envelop sustaining every need.

Delight me in Your ways. Settle me where I am with what I have. My full cup runs over and I want a bigger cup. My more hoard creeps in collecting and storing away.

Combining and giving I live. More of you and less of me. Empty me my need. Delight me in the truth and love and all I want is You. Nothing can surpass the place you have in me. The only thing that fills me up are the things You give for free.

Contentment reigns in satisfy and satiate, You trigger my enough. You make the need no more, the want to give, the key to my content. The Left overs of not enough more than well suffice. You, Lord, make easy and facilitate the fire consuming quenching, in Holy Spirit food.
TBTG

AUGUST 23

PrayStill

Job 1:21

[Job] said, "Naked I came from my mother's womb, and naked shall I return there; the Lord gave, and the Lord has taken away; blessed be the name of the Lord."

Scripture Prayer: Blessing

Lord God

Bless and praise the name of the Lord. The one who is worthy and adored. Beautiful the sound of your name, Jesus. Precious in the ways of the world. Heavenly is Your presence here on earth.

Bless and raise the name of the Lord. A love all else, is mostly all restore. The only thing remains is You. Your great loving mercy, grace, kindness, and forgiveness.

Given away, taken away, fasted into empty. Still I say your love remains and blesses more and more. It is well, it is good, it is glory in Your name. Empty me, and fill with You, I never am the same.

Lord Jesus in the deserts of life you convert and change me. I need You. I am weak and needy. You are powerfully strong and providing.

You take and make my.......

Trash into treasure

Waste into witness

Ashes to Rose's

Test into testament

Pain into power

Shame into sureness

Guilt into gratitude

Failure into fortune

Weakness into wealth

Hiding into hailing

Defect into reflect

Lies into learning

Lonely into love

My selfish into selfless

With you, without me, I am everything I am to be.

TBTJC Lord of mercy.

AUGUST 24

PrayStill

Psalm 91:11
For he shall give his angels charge over you, to keep you in all your ways.

Scripture Prayer: Jehovah Jireh

Lord provider,
Maker and judge of all things. The sweet sound of Your name, Jesus rings true melodies in harmonies ways. Draw dear to the glorious sound of your waves pouring over. Your legions are faithful true and renewing

Angelic hosts proclaim your name continuously insisting. This is God's will, this is God's will, this is Thy will be done. His grace, His grace, is always in place, communion continues on. All needs provide in riches and glory, sufficiency in grace all around. Riches and glory in charge over me, I hover inside His reside. Spiritual , discover from inside.

You know my name, you hear my voice, my tears are only joy. Guardian messengers, celestial passages, staging for Your force. Powerful glory, powerful might, powerful never ending. Angels armies, angel legions protecting in all ways.
TBTHS Advocate Master
Amen

AUGUST 25

PrayStill

Job 3:20
Why is light given to one in misery, and life to the bitter in soul?

Scripture Prayer: Hope

Lord God of light,
Glimmering hope of all ages. Strength of the surrender. Comfort and love of the soul. Key to communion contentment in the breath of the WORD of life.

Lord hear my cry,
There is no hope from within me to live. My light is extinguished, and embers remain. My omega day is calling. My pity reigns as I defend my misfortunes. My desire is vanishing in vanquish.

Lord of life and light
Resuscitate my soul. Revive me to life in hope in you. Give me breath and breadth of hope and life. Erase away my pitiful pain grasping at my sorrow. Pour through me Your Holy Spirit hovering over my essence. Breathe life into this shatter clay pieces of a vessel. Float me to Your shores of rest and peace and comfort and warmth. Shine dry your light on me. Fill this strong cup up overflowing. Fill Your will in me to reflect Your mighty awesome signature on my heart.
Make me channel your light loving healing touch in all my days to come.
In through and with your Holy Spirit comforting advocate,
Jesus Lord.
TBTHT 3IN1

AUGUST 26

PrayStill

John 6:64

"But among you there are some who do not believe." For Jesus knew from the first who were the ones that did not believe, and who was the one that would betray him.

Scripture Prayer: Obvious

Lord of all knowing, Jesus. Master of the heart's heat. Discerner of truth and intentions. Maker of all motives surrendered up to You. You let the truth freely flow in yes and no. No desires or secrets are hidden.

Spirit of situations, all things come full circle back to you. Your reflection is shining inescapable. The truth is undeniably surrounding. Free will steps from wandering out of green pastures safe boundaries come homing back to You.

Teach me Your ways convicting my heart. Lead me in my free will intention back to you. Witness my life as your testimony. You, Lord, reign me into open arms welcoming.

My prodigal pride is set aside. Outlandish living leaves falling to dusted grounds. The riotous living rebellion of determined self-will retreats.

Your channel remains pathway to renewal.

Lord of merciful forgiveness and oceans of love, take and make me new. Fill surround my ups and downs and comfort in embrace. Cleanse and straighten Your will within me to contentment desire without. Everything I ever earn is Yours without a doubt. Strong assurance locks me in.

Jesus

Be my firm conviction of truth, resounding renewals delight. I am all Yours.

TBTJC author of salvation

Amen

AUGUST 27

PrayStill

John 6:56
Those who eat my flesh and drink my blood abide in me, and I in them.

Scripture Prayer: Communion

Lord Host of Peace,
Creator of the new covenant of sacrifice in love. The Pascal Lamb of Passover sacrifice for the sins of the world. Your magnificence rules invitations to glory's Heavenly kingdom. Creator and ruler of fleshly earth abiding in redemption.
Holy, mighty and permeating in permanence is Your name, Jesus.
Precious saving Jesus
Permeate abide and imbibe my body to my soul. Reside and fill this fleshly vessel with Your Holy Spirit reigning in graceful hover surround.

Selah

Fill my body with your Holy Spirit transforming.
I taste and see. I see and believe. I believe, and I feel your still calm essence presenting.
I hear you bid me and heed your calling. I touch numb surround. Incensed in incense filling air surround cleansing dust in arising.
Sensing conviction in Your nourishing confidence I am overflowing filled beyond containment. Pass through and make new and reflect all back to You. You are in me. You own me. I'm Yours.
TBTHT 3 in 1 reigning in showering delight.
Amen

AUGUST 28

PrayStill

Job 6:14
Those who withhold kindness from a friend forsake the fear of the Almighty.

Scripture Prayer: Kindness

Lord of love and mercy
Master of situations. Creator of gentle, soft and loving words spoken over in healing. Soothing balm of the hearts hearing calm. Father of peace and assurance. You are masterful.

Hear my prayer, oh Lord
Loosen the stronghold of fear replenish my faithfulness in You. Adjust my thoughts and inclinations invitation to the kind loving touch of your voice in my beckoning soul. Take me to your calm. Release all the fear and worry. Take the trouble and pain. Heal me again. Remove away the anxious anxiety and apprehensions. Agonize no more.

Selah Vie

Calm my soul
Still my thoughts
Relax me to your embrace
Hold me to rest

Selah Way

Powerfully absorb my angst. You Lord take it all away. You are mighty and strong and I am weak and needy.

You fill me with your calm to melting numb. Kindle kind serene waves of peace and make me freshly new. Meditate the peace surrounding. Speak still to my soul and rest my heart's content. All is clear and easy. Peaceful is my soul pulse.

TBTHS

Amen

AUGUST 29

PrayStill

Job 7:19
Will you not look away from me a while, let me alone until I swallow my spittle?

Scripture Prayer: Redemption

Lord God all-knowing ever-present powerful creator, richly kind in mercy and forgiveness. Eager Holy Spirit, convictor of truth and intention, present in surround. Jesus, Lord, friend and brother substitution for flaws and sins, the beautiful essence in creation following.

Pour it all out. Lord let me pour it all out to You. You have it all anyway. It is all yours. Even what I think is mine is Yours. Even what I do not know and will discover is all Yours. The comfort of this embrace is awesome. The conviction of this embrace convicts my dis grace. Great and graceful and grateful is my souls' spirit.

Take me all and shake me small and break me to my cry out. Render me in senselessness and turn me back around. Place my feet upon Thy rock a firm foundation footing. Hold my heart and gaze my eyes to graze upon Your glory. The song I sing, the life I live, are prayers lived for Your story.

Great are You Lord
It's your breath
Amen

AUGUST 30

PrayStill

Psalm 18:2
My God my rock in whom I put my trust, my shield, the horn of my salvation, and my refuge; you are worthy of praise.

Scripture Prayer: Beholden

Lord God of power and might, of strength and life, the sure footed rock of salvation. Cornerstone of ages; Foundation and bulwark never failing. Protective castle mansion of all glories overwhelming. All that is, is Yours Lord Jesus.
Jesus
Lord of creation you surround me. My comfort in protection astounds my soul to peace. Past my understanding is Your grace filled pastures of peace in deep. In the eye of the storm, You are my rest, my reprieve, my revive and my strength. You embrace me.
Rest
Confidence and assurance, you place reigning in my heart. I am comfortably Inescapable of Your awesome love filling.
True trust in You never fails. You are always there to catch me when I wane away to fear. You subside me and deride my misconception. You awaken my unknown fears to your beautiful excitement. All the glory is Yours, Lord Jesus.
You magnify my soul. My heart leaps in joy to your surround.
All the days long my mouth lips proclaim You are my rock and my salvation. Whom then shall I fear? My fear with You, Lord of generations, is all love conquering.
Amen
TBTJC

AUGUST 31

PrayStill

John 8:45
But because I tell the truth, you do not believe me.

Scripture Prayer: Discernment

Jesus, Son of God
Saving Shepherd of true truth and light. Revealing Master of all hidden secrets, lies and deceits. Persistent lover and welcomer of souls. Retriever of souls to God's Kingdom with convicting and convincing persuasion.
Mighty Counselor
Let my true yes in You, be yes.
Let my true no to lies, be no.
Open my eyes to the ever-living loving light of the Father Divine. Fill and saturate my being.
You are welcome here.
Devein my wander to unknown deception. Take away my flaws, sins, and indexes of defects. Step me over the stones of unrighteousness to safety. Focus my path to your garden.
Son of God, King of kings, You have Your way in me. Son of God and Son of man, my grace I find in Thee. Lord of lord and word of truth the living Christ in me. Hold me close and hold me tight and never let me flee.
Blessed be the name of the Lord. He is worthy to be praise and adore......x infinity
TBTJC
Amen

SEPTEMBER 1

PrayStill

Job 10:4
Do you have eyes of flesh? Do you see as humans see?

Scripture Prayer: Despair

Father all knowing,
All powerful and everywhere, maker and judge of all things. Provider of grace and mercy for both wheat and tares. Sanctuary refuge in the angst of the days. The magnificent ocean of love that absorbs all the tears of the world. From east to west are the cries of lies heard before time began.

Holy Lord Spirit
You repair my despair. I cry out to you in inconsolable tears of exhaustion. My soul is stuck feeling on one thing. My soul pain is recursive and does not go away. The spectrum of darkness upon me takes my breath away. Waves of pounding whitewash thunder in my ears screaming. I cannot hold back the tears. Pour me out to empty.
You take and have it all. You gave it all and I give it all back to your magnificent glory. Your potent knowing is everywhere I go.
Pause
Rest
Breath
Selah
Mamma Abba guardian,
Protector of my soul. Life giver to my heart. You sinew my life's fleshly desires. You mold and make my skin anew and take away the sin.

In with You, and You in me, You calm my breath's desire. You take me to that place You make and turn my tears to fire.

In warm embrace You show Your face to make me be at one. You delight in me 'til I delight in You and all my ways are true

TBTHS three in one

SEPTEMBER 2

PrayStill

Psalm 15:5-7
He has sworn to do no wrong and does not take back his word. He does not give his money in hope of gain, nor does he take a bribe against the innocent. Whoever does these things shall never be overthrown.

Scripture Prayer: Solidify

Lord of truth,
Creator of the economy of love. Tender of the truth and author of the gift of giving. Maker of all things judge of all people. Owner of all accountability and keeper of all flaw debts. Mighty King indeed.
Jesus Lord God
Merciful and true collector of debt. I make my amends and you wash me clean and show me where to go next. You lift up my countenance and walk my stance back to you, to learn more of your wisdoms unveiling.
King of kings, Lord of lords, you make me tried and true. You hold me up you shake me out You take my worth in hand. You teach me love and give me Hope and set my eyes above. My motives melt to Your pure hold to give, in all for love. The time and gifts are in uplifts since all is Yours to give.
TBTJC

SEPTEMBER 3

PrayStill

Matthew 6:24
No one can serve two masters; for a slave will either hate the one and love the other or be devoted to one and despise the other. You cannot serve God and wealth.

Scripture Prayer: All in All

Master Lord, Creator, Jesus
True source or love truth and harmony. Attractive foundation firmly receiving allegiance and bonding. Strong jealous lover of souls insistent on focus and surrender submission. Highly Alpha exhalation reigns in Your mighty and powerful Kingdom love calling.

Counselor Jesus
Friend and advocate, you mend and weave your binding mortar to my soul. You guide and protect each step and motive. You reconcile me. You clarify my yes and convict my no. You discern my being to truth light. Precious is your hand on my shoulder. Intimate is your whisper in my ear. Eternal is your I AM residing.

My self-will riotous living allows reference to discern Your truth. The burn of idling on the false idols sears memory lessons for rightful living. Gentle kind and merciful are the callings to the one true Lord God Jesus, pleasantly drawing near.
Maste,r King of everything delighting in my ways. One true Lord, of this I sing, You straighten my astray. I light delight insight within, only to Your love. The love I have for other things is misdirected fear. When I come surrender all, to You I will draw near.
TBTHT 3in1

SEPTEMBER 4

PrayStill

Psalm 26:11
As for me, I will live with integrity; redeem me, O Lord and have pity on me.

Scripture Prayer: Declare

Divine Lord Jesus
Humble son of the ever-living almighty ruler of all the universes and the smallest molecules. Beautiful savior savoring love eternal to the willing wailing hearts and souls desperately crying for the gift of redemption. Open is Your way.

Jesus Spirit
God of my days, let my waking and sleeping words, and everything in between be, I love You with all my heart soul mind and strength. Fill my in-between wandering thoughts right back to You. Weave and integrate me into You. Be my intimate confidante designing each moment. Heal my steps aligning.

God of joy, most moist in renewal, showering the mercy seat forgiveness. The more I love You, the more You breathe through to the breakthrough of surrender to Your ways. Your Word I breath in and imbibe without sin is the true way to spend all my days.
Jesus, guide the reins of my heart.
TBTJC Lord of all

SEPTEMBER 5

PrayStill

Job 14:16

Scripture Prayer: Calling

Lord of beckoning,
Master of key lock desire for meaning. Greatest Holy Spirit of truth, redirecting the desperate cries of longing. The whole earth cries out and sings, signing Your invitation to save. Nature glorifies You and we adorn Your precious glories.

Jesus God Lord
You personally invite me to be with you all the moments of my life. When I sleep and when I am not aware you are with me. My protector in love that watches without slumber nor sleep. My moment of life is your preordained instant.

Show me Your ways and grow me Your praise so I may know and praise You. Lift up my countenance, as a gift for your recompense, trade in my sorrow for laughter. Replace all my sin so in You I begin to bring forth the love weave You Master.
TBTHS calling
Amen

SEPTEMBER 6

PrayStill

Psalm 37:7-9

Be still before the Lord and wait patiently for him. Do not fret yourself over the one who prospers, the one who succeeds in evil schemes. Refrain from anger, leave rage alone; do not fret yourself; it leads only to evil.

Scripture Prayer: Peace

Father in Heaven,
Purveying tender of the realm of heavens castles. Surround in the glory of colors and calm. In your courts are the worshipful desires of souls praising your name. Majesty and honor and peace line every presence in exultation exalting.

Father on earth, Jesus
Take my circumstance to dust. Remove my surround and strip me to my soul. Your peaceful place of glory remains. It is yours alone this place of heaven on earth you plant and grow in my life field.
My refuge in the storm. My peace in the turmoil. My strong delivering conviction. Your whispering silence voice in me.

Father Spirit,
Creator of this place of peace take my sins from west to east. Still my soul to Your recline, incline my heart to hear divine. Relax my body clear my thoughts focus all mind to clear. Empty me as You draw near. Breathe Your WORD to conquer fear. Erase from me my thoughts astray, replace in me Your gracious Way.
TBTMAP Mamma Abba Parent

SEPTEMBER 7

PrayStill

Job 19:25
For I know that my Redeemer lives, and that at the last he will stand upon the earth.

Scripture Prayer: Rock

Lord of mercy and grace, author of ever living generations of faith. Creator and judge of all things. Visible Lord Jesus shining in the eyes of compassion adorning, Garment of healing touching mercy graces, Maintaining sustaining salvation of the world.

Lord of life,
Speak words of life to my soul. Harden my resolve and cast my fleshen fear aside. Resuscitate my breath in your word. Breathe me in your scent of fresh dew. Sparkle the tingles of the tips of my tongue and the taste lips of your scent. In-rhythm my heart to Yours. Come be my life blood redeemer. I am out of me. You fill me beyond full satience. Lay Your hands on me.

Cele-brate rest Selah

Lord foundation bright creation standing tall above. My redeemer awesome retriever, returning all for love. Each mercy new day starts to Your way pathways set divine. Knowing You and allowing New, to put my faith in You. Trust forever the love deliverer in repose unending. Eternal hope of ages past and ages yet to come. Precious Lord redeeming master key lock to my soul in mending.
TBTJC

SEPTEMBER 8

PrayStill

Acts 13:32-33
And we bring you the good news that what God promised to our ancestors he has fulfilled for us, their children, by raising Jesus; as also it is written in the second psalm, "You are my Son; today I have begotten you."

Scripture Prayer: Reign

Forever God.
Alpha Omega beginning end and middle. Generational weaver of life truth life. Masterful creator and presenter of time. Loving guiding hand of understanding. Ever present are Your Ways.

Lord Jesus
You are unique precious and intimate to my life soul and love. Inescapably you know my every inner being pieces. You make me whole. Holy is your way in presentation.
Reveal to me more and more and more and more. You never give up you are always there. Only you provide for my needs. Nothing else can satisfy or come before. Your reins on my heart guide my east and west. Straight in the straits is your narrow path.

Spirit of ages,
You are the generations You are the inspirations You make me lay down in Your pasture. You reign over nations you own all creation, you give life redeeming its value. You sit at the table and make us enable to share and attract to the graceful. In You and with You and alway beside you revealing the stages of ages.
TBTHS Jesus God
Amen

SEPTEMBER 9

PrayStill

Proverbs 22:1
A good name is to be chosen rather than great riches, and favor is better than silver or gold.

Scripture Prayer: Delight

Lord of power and might.
Unending source of eternal life. Masterful maker of Heaven and earth and all the channels in between. Sweet and endearing for all who seek refuge in the storms of life. Fresh and renewing is the Lord

Jesus Lord
Graceful delighting Lord
Merciful and kind in kindling how you own me. I am inescapably Yours. You delight in me and You call my name. Your many names, I cry out, and You respond. You, Lord of all names, respond to all the names I call You. Blessed holy and pure is everything about your receiving listening loving channel to my heart.

Jesus
A thousand names I call you. I always hear reply. You give my life the flavors to taste and see your skies. You love my many names, encourage me be free. You take me as I am, I look to You to be. This love you shower upon is plentiful and pure, the grace you give flows through and through and teaches how to live
TBTJC

SEPTEMBER 10

PrayStill

John 10:27
My sheep hear my voice. I know them, and they follow me.

Scripture Prayer: Beloved

Lord Jesus
God of whisper divine. Song of saints and rock of ages. Roll of oceans thunder. Masterful allure to all you call, hearing every word. Many are the forms of attraction that draw Heavenly spirits from afar. Attractive attraction attracts the receiving.

Holy Spirit
Masterfully present, divine in presence, presenting presents divine. I hear Your voice in the raging silence alone. The calm of your voice quells the quenching valley. I feel your surround. You have my sense around. There is the calling of your sweet sweet name. Taste and see the sea of flavors showering my senses delight. Touch me make me overtake me all my parts can hear you.

God of true light shining,
There is no place to hide. You are the flavors of faith. Some hear you loud some hear you clear some never no your name. Some listen now some hear the truth of your intimate call within. You call the name of all with ears to hear the open-minded faith. Set aside and let me ride and trust in your great name. I believe, I receive, In you I rest in You. You are always new. Of you there is always more.
TBT God Lord Jesus delight.

SEPTEMBER 11

PrayStill

John 10:31
The Jews took up stones again to stone him.

Scripture Prayer: Release

Lord God
Image creator of many human designs. Masterful maker of all there is seen and unseen. Motivator of Angels and Miracles, Masterful healer persuading teacher Beautiful Savior and ever-present loving power of knowledge. Reign the reins of showering rains that wash the earth.

Friend Jesus
Why do I persecute you? Help me to love deeply instead.
Direct all my anger back to God. Take and release my fearful indignation. You are so mighty and strong and all absorbent. You take away the danger angers of the world. I can safely direct it all to God.
Direct my soul to drop the rocks of bite back. Open the hands of blind scratching sands of throwing resentments. Unleash the chains to boulders and concrete of stubborn refusal. Free me to investigate forgiveness. Make my contempt no more....
I give it all to you. You can have it, You are strong mighty and the creator of unending universes. I am barely a grain of sand registered yet You hear my hurt cry and love me back to kindness.
In an instant of release, You remove my pain and make it focused good kindness. You heal the hurt and kindle kindness. You take away the prideful fears of hearts in pain and render the calm. You change my heart Oh Lord. My curse is dismissed into loving praise.

You face and embrace and replace me for You.

Fill this place with calm unending. Silence and still my soul. Reckon and render quite quietly, peace about this vessel and hush my heart to slow. Pour graceful showers of warm calming assurance and clean out all discord. Make my home heart Yours and make me lie down, these pastures green are Yours Lord. I'm free.

TBTG

SEPTEMBER 12

PrayStill

Job 30:3
Through want and hard hunger they gnaw the dry and desolate ground.

Scripture Prayer: Desire

Lord of all,
Beautiful master, lovely protector, lover of souls in wander. Wonder of unknowing revealing and showing and creator of desires within. Cool cool water in a parched land, warm blue sunshine on the ocean drowning. Infinite is the calling.

Holy Spirit
You meet me where I am. You never let me go. You hold and have your way with me. I think I am alone, and you are right here at my side. You guide and draw me home. Beautiful is your touch on my heart inclining.

Selah

Jesus God
My dust strength is in you. I gnaw and gnash no more. You retrieve me from the clay mire sinking in my desire. Fresh Dew, You renew me and give me verdant life. You sustain my life blood water to delight. Fresh air breezes my lift in flight to your womb of life. I am revealed healed and sealed. You have me all.
TBTHS 3in1

SEPTEMBER 13

PrayStill

Job 31:21-23
If I have raised my hand against the orphan, because I saw I had supporters at the gate; then let my shoulder blade fall from my shoulder, and let my arm be broken from its socket. For I was in terror of calamity from God and I could not have faced his majesty.

Scripture Prayer: Resolve

Lord God
Master of solutions. Honest true and genuine lover of all. Welcoming host of nations and individuals at preordained levels of love. Creative author of forgiving graces of salvation. Powerful and strong is the lifting of the weak and the humbling of the haughty.

Jesus God
You fill my weakness with confidence. My Joy's are Your Joys in return. You keep my glory as Your glory. Guide my heart to compassionate giving. Fill me with your abounding love overflowing. Pour out the goodness You shower to floods of calm still silence. Dismiss away the flaws of the day.

Hovering Spirit
Watchful protector of truth. Speak life through me and guide me to thee. Turn my gaze to you. In your presence is the essence of the new in new. Overwhelm and satisfy my desire from within. You motivate and captivate and make us one from two. Reside in my revive alive in You Lord
TBTJC

SEPTEMBER 14

PrayStill

Philippians 2:5-7a
Let the same mind be in you that was in Christ Jesus who, though he was in the form of God did not regard equality with God as something to be exploited, but emptied himself, taking the form of a slave, being born in human likeness.

Scripture Prayer: Subserviency

God Jesus
Most powerful most knowing most present. King of judgement, Master of mercy. Ever loving Creator of all weak and small, all strong and tall, wise to all the wandering souls, heading to Your kingdom gates.

Holy Spirit
Timelessly waiting,
Breath of life living alive. Transporter of the here and now unending. Transcendent are the beautiful blessing and distinguishing touches that arrive from nowhere knowing, except from You Lord.

Your precious WORD weaves without the beyond bonds of time and space. The dimensions of Holinesses breaks open the dimension of time and space. Floating fields of Heavenly embrace are forever breaking through.

Peace in Selah

Lord of the beyond above un endings. Born of God born of man, in in-between eternals. You are the End of space, the end of time, the beginning in eternals. Vernal pastures of dancing Angel seeds are tranquil waxing waves lapping in love adorning.

Possession posing, Angels hosting, divinely place inside, point to you the continual new the life after life Creator.

TBTJC

SEPTEMBER 15

PrayStill

Job 38:1-4
Then the Lord answered Job out of the whirlwind: "Who is this that darkens counsel by words without knowledge? Gird up your loins like a man, I will question you, and you shall declare to me. Where were you when I laid the foundation of the earth? Tell me, if you have understanding."

Scripture Prayer: Reverence

Masterful Lord
God of all that is seen and unseen. Advocate and author of truth. Creator of the beauty of the earth singing out praises. Designer and architect of all creation moments reflecting back to Heavenly realms. God of all gods and King of all kings.

Vibrant WORD of life Spirit
Speak life in moments of suddenly. Aware and waken my weary wander to Your way
By design you authored me. By design you set me free. In my kingdom I find no thing. I return to Thee. Again, and again I am set free. Over and over you reveal to me. You are Lord of all. You are love of all. You are the only everything I need. Instill my still surrender to have me, all in all.

Jesus son of God
Fleshen image of God on earth. Esteem my soul heart desire to receive Your love back in the light of life. Humble my pride to the reckoning of Your awesome powers reigning. Beckon my inflections of Your life reflection all to You in surrender. Genuine my heart to motivate my starts to startling surprises of faith
You are the I am, the Lord of all.
TBTHT 3IN1

SEPTEMBER 16

PrayStill

Proverbs 1:20-21
Wisdom cries out in the street; in the squares she raises her voice. At the busiest corner she cries out; at the entrance of the city gates she speaks.

Scripture Prayer: Insight

AbbaMamma
Lord of learning right from wrong. Convicting spirit of love redirecting. Beautiful convincing conviction of truth. Revealing life giver instilling discernment. Persuading teacher of faith in the living WORD of the Lord God Jesus

Lord Spirit alive,
Masterful wisdom weaver discerning true motives, true intentions, true desires. No secrets are hid.

Fall fresh insight wisdom and discernment into the tides of life. Reveal the unraveling of falsehoods. See right through the flaw and sin to shine light bright upon it. Melt the wash of dust to the ground and renew the knowing of truth. Wise are the ways of God's WORD speaking

Jesus Lord
Open my eyes, reveal Your prize, the healing of wisdom renewing. Learn me the truth of faith in You, remove my fear of change to You, make everything I do be for You. In You through You with You by my side we walk in new.

Statues of wisdom towering delight. Mountains of insight hover over night. Tides of discernment wash away fear doubt. Trust and obey abide in the Good Lord master of truth sight.

TBTHS 3in1
Amen

SEPTEMBER 17

PrayStill

Psalm 56:10
In God the Lord whose word I praise, in God I trust and will not be afraid, for what can mortals do to me?

Scripture Prayer: Truth

Lord of light,
Unchanging God always present, always loving, forever knowing. Great is Your peace promise surpassing. Faith Hope and Trust are the angelic invitations drawing to the mighty flowing pastures of renewal. Your proof reveals in the daily remember of your forever embrace. WORD of truth Speaks courageous life.
You Lord always have and hold me in assurance.

Jesus
Author of truth in salvation trusting. You always are truth. Footsteps in the changing sands of life show my confidence that you carry me. I am weak and needy and exhausted.
You Lord lift revive and inspire me to full knowing. You are The Life giving, trust building, faith instilling, hope implanting, ever loving Son of the most highest God. I believe, and I trust you. If I should fail, you grab my fall in saving graces.

Lord God
Truth unshakeable make me unbreakable, I am trusting in you. I confide in Your confidence. You know me. You assure my soul in the future peace You bestow. You were always with me, You are here now, You will be my future. All my Faith Trust is in You. Faith always

showing, always growing, place my heart at rest. Peaceful calm proceeds in me. Lord of life preceding.

TBTJC

SEPTEMBER 18

PrayStill

John 12:9-11
When the great crowd of the Jews learned that he was there, they came not only because of Jesus but also to see Lazarus, whom he had raised from the dead. So the chief priests planned to put Lazarus to death as well, since it was on account of him that many of the Jews were deserting and were believing in Jesus.

Scripture Prayer: Give Life

God of Breath WORD of life,
Beautiful inspiring God of creation. Life growing force eternal. Owner and redeemer of souls. Masterful author of days. Gorgeous designer of love weaving extravagance. Nourishing banquet feast inviting Host of nations generations. God of all

Jesus Lord
Restorative healer and friend. Humble advocate of beautiful sustaining life. Powerful refining teacher of truth. You know me intimately. You have my conviction abiding. You love me more in revealing. You seal my heart. I am Yours.

Holy Spirit
This place vessel welcomes You. Fill refining fire in surrounding warm gentle love. Wash away the fear. Convict the prideful selfish motive. Rest me in Your place of peace beyond my comprehension. Satisfy my soul. Your loving on me enlivens my resolving faith. FAITH, Forever Always In Thy Hands.
TBTHT 3in1
Amen

SEPTEMBER 19

PrayStill

John 12:24
Very truly, I tell you, unless a grain of wheat falls into the earth and dies, it remains just a single grain; but if it dies, it bears much fruit.

Scripture Prayer: Genesis

Life giving Lord
Eternal love blossom of life sustaining nutrients. Bread water air and light of creation. Foundation of diamond rocks reflecting colors throughout. Beautiful redeeming master of Heaven and earth. Jesus

Spirit Lord
Grow shoots of Heaven into now from eternity past and eternity future. The roots of eternal creation grow into today pushing away the dusty mire. Heaven on earth weaves into the holy pathways of gorgeousness. Overwhelming is the call of life creation among the blind and dead to the WORD alive.

Good God
Seed of wheat seed of grapes seed of mustard seeds of faith. Crack my shell and seep right in, and spark my shoots to dig right in. Grow me up and show me love and reach me to the light above. Dry me out with winds about the cool warm breeze of Your way. Standing on the rock of faith the firmament foundation.
TBTJC Lord and life giver eternal.

SEPTEMBER 20

PrayStill

John 12:31-32
Now is the judgment of this world; now the ruler of this world will be driven out. And I, when I am lifted up from the earth, will draw all people to myself.

Scripture Prayer: Victory

Lord Jesus
Forever always consistently the same. Ruler of truth, light love and victory reigning. Masterful transforming Presence adorning. Beautiful inviting Savior of all. Rescuing love that is always in all ways overpowering the falsifying falsity flaws under foot.

God of creation eternal,
Architect of the suddenly now. The moment of light, truth speaks to every corner of the fallen in Your Great Name proclaiming victory unending and mending. Powerful Master, Healer, Jesus with balms of grace, mercy and love that silences the darkness to submission.

Lord God of light,
Father almighty, Maker of Heaven and earth.
Lord of all, great and small designer of grace in all. Master reigning forever deigning, designing every here right now. Conquering love from Heaven above, the true and unending discover. Mercifully altering, life giving salting, flavorful redeeming Lord. Your battle is won and never undone, All victory is yours unending. Draw near.
TBTG TBTHS TBTJC

SEPTEMBER 21

PrayStill

Matthew 9:11-13
When the Pharisees saw this, they said to his disciples, "Why does your teacher eat with tax collectors and sinners?" But when he heard this, he said, "Those who are well have no need of a physician, but those who are sick. Go and learn what this means, 'I desire mercy, not sacrifice.' For I have come to call not the righteous but sinners."

Scripture Prayer: Confess

Lord Healer
Mercifully reaching out in touches of beauty mending. Weaving doctor of all recoveries. God of wholeness inviting holiness healing. Spirit of transforming newness hovering. Creator of healthy vessels holding Holy essence eternal. Lord saving balm of the world.

Jesus Lord
You heal me. You mend my brokenness. I am restored to stronger greater than before. I confess and admit and am free of the pain. You Lord take away my flaws sins and shame. My guilt is no more. Your healing presence washes clean my essence. You revive me to life breath alive.
Spirit Redeemer,

Turn me over inside out. Cleanse your beauty in throughout. Tincture drops of oil healing, seeping in anointing sealing. Balming Peace beyond all passing calming mending everlasting. Faith of love instills me longer, makes me one to come out stronger.
Healing tables divine in purpose take and make my healing all Yours. Jesus, healing, loving on me walks right through me.
TBTG

SEPTEMBER 22

PrayStill

Acts 17:18
Also some Epicurean and Stoic philosophers debated with [Paul]. Some said, "What does this babbler want to say?" Others said, "He seems to be a proclaimer of foreign divinities." (This was because he was telling the good news about Jesus and the resurrection.)

Scripture Prayer: Divinity

God divine,
Ultimate default God of the world. Creator of all things under You that all point back to You. The immortal living God that develops ties that never lies and perpetually supplies. The truthful grace persuader of hard-headed hearts stubborn souls and resistant bodies afraid to surrender to the eternal Way.

Jesus God
Hold my hand Lord. Take me away through the field. Distract and hold my focus to You. Let me drop all my misgiving idols of fear and pride and things. Relinquish my free soul back to your loving realms of loving forgiveness. Clarify my resolve to ask seek and know Your gentle knock on my wanderful heart. Rev up and remove my idle in idols to the light speed of loves light life.

Spirit Persuader,
Lord of all convincing. Hovering in surround lifting up from down, alluring is the sound of Your sweet Heaven chorus. Insistent is the seed revealing one true need and rooted in the firm foundation. Reach me for the light entrance in my delight forever held in Your salvation.
TBTHT 3in1 4evR

SEPTEMBER 23

PrayStill

James 4:1
Those conflicts and disputes among you, where do they come from? Do they not come from your cravings that are at war within you?

Scripture Prayer: Resolve

Spirit of peace,

Prince of human harmonies waving over oceans of peacefulness. Lord of all inner thought feeling, and emotion reflected outward. God of souls, revealing truth in light. Masterful author of motive, truth, intentions, and desire. Revealer of all things hidden.

Jesus Advocate,
Speak to my heart in truth resolve. Align and correct me to my new paths of freedom. Persuade me in gentle nudge of encouragement, solving all my woes. Heal and sustain my resolve for more of You and less of me. Breath out my angst fears and agonizing conflict to expelling. Fill in my breath with your sweet truth of intention.

God of stillness,
Claim my willingness set my truth foundation. light my fire to Your desire, emblazon my creation. Wipe me clean and wash me new, refine and pure my thoughts. My conscious sees convicted pleas that mercy's hand redeems. Your contact in me, removes sin from me, transforms me to be clean.
Thank You, Lord Jesus.
TBTJC

SEPTEMBER 24

PrayStill

Luke 3:9
Even now the ax is lying at the root of the trees; every tree therefore that does not bear good fruit is cut down and thrown into the fire.

Scripture Prayer: Declutter

Lord of renewal
Growing fruitful abundance in flavorful fields of harvest. Abounding is the banquet of angels feasting on the resounding chorus praises. Beautiful tables of nourishing colorful soul food unending.

Jesus refiner
Masterful maker of plentiful. You prune the vine for healthy life. You take away the sin and strife. You set the refining fire of gold dross. Only flourishing blossoms remain. Recycling flames kindle the renewing warmth of Your WORD.
Selah peace

God of creation
The whole earth cries out to you. The seas mountains trees and sands reflect Your awesome glories. The world proclaims Your beauty in fields of trees waving in the spirit wind consuming.
Lord prune me where I should not grow. Burn away the dust below. Lord make in me a fruitful harvest.
TBTG

SEPTEMBER 25

PrayStill

Luke 3:21-22
Now when all the people were baptized, and when Jesus also had been baptized and was praying, the Heaven was opened, and the Holy Spirit descended upon him in bodily form like a dove. And a voice came from Heaven, "You are my Son, the Beloved; with you I am well pleased."

Scripture Prayer: Incarnate

Lord of Heavenly presence hovering in suspended ascension descending. Showering streams of loving kindness pervasive. Warmth in the world, inviting submission to surrender to the will of God. Fainting in the arms of holiness.

Lord of lightning, moments of thundering grace's bestowing stillness in the grace in the world. Diving doves, before times' first and last transforming. Love life, living love. Peace of lapping warmth waves flow through in winds of change. Capture in the essence of truth life.

Lord of the elements of the earthen souls, mixing air and water to life in word present in the pulse of heartbeats. Still my soul to receive the Spirit life. Streaming rivers, oceans flow right through, altering to new. Sudden light beams rolling, crack right to the soul transfixing.

Rushing waters in lashing lids opening focusing eyes delighting. Clearing visions in redemption, scales falling from me. Pull me through in made brand new and push in gentle massage. Standing strong with arms out long gazing love's first loving. First in new, first in last, first in now abiding.

Selah breath

Breathe in Thee. Thirst no more at Heaven's door, hunger only for Thee.

TBTHS

SEPTEMBER 26

PrayStill

Psalm 82:2
How long will you judge unjustly and show favor to the wicked?

Scripture Prayer: Jealous

Lord of all,
Maker of the washing rains that fall on all. Giver of the light that breaks the night in two. Gracious is the gift bestowed to all the peoples of all the lands. Merciful are Your welcoming hands.
Jesus
Take away my comparing jealousies envies resentments and comparisons. You are just and mighty to all in your perfect time. You take away the sins of the world. Faithfully great is your invitation.
Holy Spirit of life,
Take away the strife. Fulfill my judging filled justice claiming heart, to see and acknowledge all the grace's bestowed upon me. Not them. Focus my gratitude in blessing to my side of the street. Enjoy me to this overflowing grace and mercy. Blind me to my usurping justice eyes condemning.
Your plan is perfect, my plan suspect. You give life ultimate respect. Take my heart and deeply inspect. Where I am ungrateful and where love I reject. Overwhelm my reception make Your light reflect.
TBTHT 3in1
WORD UP Rap up WORD up SPEAK LIGHT

Trinity God,
In you is connection protection,
With you is inspection injection,
Without you is deflection rejection.
Lord Jesus
Grow me to your perfection reflection.
Jesus is Resurrection.
I love you.
Amen

SEPTEMBER 27

PrayStill

Psalm 116:8
I will walk in the presence of the Lord in the land of the living

Scripture Prayer: Save

Lord Savior,

Salve of wounds that bind. Freeing Lord of light. Sparkle of eyes, praise of lips, sweet sweet-sounding delight. Touch of caressing waves of wind warming breeze to Your meandering way. So, so good are all your days, lifted up in praises.

God of submission.
You free my will to explore and know the depths of Your creation. The only solace here on earth is in your saving grace. Pervasive is the love You shower. Renew and review me, always for your inviting welcome to your WORD alive.
Peace in lasting life sustain.
Tabernacle Home of never alone alive with joys forever unending.
Jesus Cup of Salvation,
Seek and find me, always behind me watching my every move. Comfort and solace feeling Your embrace, protecting my soul's renew. Walk right inside me and always abide me and never let me go. More closely, more often my heart will Thee soften, and ply all my yearnings to Thee. The strife of this life is with me no longer. Only in You am I stronger.
TBTJGS Jesus God Spirit

SEPTEMBER 28

PrayStill

Acts 19:23
About that time a great disturbance broke out concerning the Way.

Scripture Prayer: Idols

God of light life and wisdom.
You are the way the truth the life and the light. All other ways are idols. The emphatic pride that defends idols to the end is the UN-way, the UN-truth, the UN-life. Lord Jesus of true light, darkness cannot hide. Jesus speaks true WORD, speaks light life and truth.

Jesus Lord of Peace,
How precious is Your name sifting Life through the silent whispers of conviction. At the end of exhausting screams that vehemently defend idols of false comfort, the only breath is in.

The only breath in is the way of Jesus. Fill our lungs with truth, Lord Jesus .

Holy Spirit of conviction. Turn and mold my inflections to Your great name. Give me WORD of stateful inspection. Give me strength for idol rejection. Turn my desires to your correction. Lord reign in me. Let me see the only place to be is with Thee.
JESUS the way, in You I stay and never sway. Weigh my wait for Your way straight. Speak in me Your way all consuming.
TBTJC

SEPTEMBER 29

PrayStill

Genesis 28:12-13

And [Jacob] dreamed that there was a ladder set up on the earth, the top of it reaching to Heaven; and the angels of God were ascending and descending on it. And the Lord stood beside him and said, "I am the Lord the God of Abraham your father and the God of Isaac; the land on which you lie I will give to you and to your offspring."

Scripture Prayer: Awesome

Lord God of predestination, guiding path, revealing steps in guided journey. Anointed is the WAY already determined. Teacher of the send and receive communion of angel saints. Glorious is the light leading direction.

Jesus overcomer

You have my whole heart. You wrestle my faith into shape. I cling to the rungs of Your ladder. The cornerstone anointing showers down messenger angels. Honor and glory and wisdom and power are granted in instances beaming. Faith and persistence and abiding return uplifting. Channel pathway to constant constellations.

Holy Spirit reigning,

Crystal clear water sheets flowing sparkle vividly. Misty dew moisture rising empties all to you. Angel armies shower Your will in surrounding chariots raising. Forever always never letting go.

You take me from my flesh and raise me up a fresh. You wrestle out my stubborn stone bones. Guide me in waiting to your contemplating all my old ways are new. Your land increasing surpasses my dreaming the whole life in You abounding. Warm anointing, fragrant oiling, showering me to You.

TBTG Almighty

SEPTEMBER 30

PrayStill

James 5:19-20 *My brothers and sisters, if anyone among you wanders from the truth and is brought back by another, you should know that whoever brings back a sinner from wandering will save the sinner's soul from death and will cover a multitude of sins.*

Scripture Prayer: Commission

Great Lord
Persistent spirit indwelling. Loving welcoming Father of all prodigals. Harvesting banquet host convincing to wander no more. Hear not the call of the flowing thief's lies. Rejoice and remain at the banquet table safe in beautiful haven fields of joy. Go and sin no more.

Jesus redeemer,
Masterful persuader of convicting decisions to persist and persevere in You. Great is Your faithfulness, powerful is your attraction. You interrupt distraction to focus back to You. Your plow never turns. The desire passion burns. Hope on with mercy forgiveness.

Spirit of commission
You own each submission decision. You foster remission back to Your glory. The doctor of incision that cuts away sins mission replacing all for glory.
Envision the calling, persistence installing, remain in this place all sustaining.

Lord
Fill this place with your grace overflowing. Strengthen this station to bring about nations to wander back into your platform. Capture enrapture and place in the pasture the hearts that wander no more.
TBTG welcoming

OCTOBER 1

PrayStill

Acts 20:24
But I do not count my life of any value to myself, if only I may finish my course and the ministry that I received from the Lord Jesus to testify to the good news of God's grace.

Scripture Prayer: Piety

Jesus
Loving hand of direction. Beautiful convincing advocate of peace and love. Author of mercy and forgiveness, grace and favor. Key to my heart lock. Guardian of my soul. Shield of certain assurance suspending my life in You Lord.
Holy Presence,
Come fill this vessel mending with all of You. Empty me of me and reflect glories deepening back to You. Overwhelm my soul pouring out. Uncontainable breaking forth, Your WORD is alive.
Breath life, speak love, flow works in your great name. Living WORD is thriving.
Guardian God of the Garden
Till my soul in fervent desire for your stable. Seat me at your blessing table. Make me proclaim, forever naming You as the mighty Jehovah Jireh. Bring me to Your peace pastures. Restore my will to Your able. Ever is Your loving present force lovable.
All Thanks Be To God, Jesus, Helper
Amen

OCTOBER 2

PrayStill

Psalm 97:7
Confounded be all who worship carved images and delight in false gods! Bow down before him, all you gods.

Scripture Prayer: True

Lord of light,
True God of gods. Throne in Heaven glorious surrounding.
True light of light. Fire lightning illuminate paths to Your kingdom. Holy Holy Holy is the sound. Clear is the light of colors reflecting crystal clear sounds of harmonies rejoicing softly. Sweet effervescent taste warms enticing.
Say La...
Spirit of truth
The test is yours. You win every time. Let my fear doubt and insecurities be brought to Your test. Lifting up truth the scale dust falls. Fear trembles away like melting wax when shining in the light. Patience waits on genuine revealing.
Selah
Jesus
Way, truth, light. Life creator, Life giver, Guardian shield, implicit protector. Loving you conquers evil. The battle already won. At one with me is your decree that darkness flee from shining. Test in this. Check for truth, test in the Holy Holy Holy. Know the way is here to stay, today and ever after.
Selah brate
TBTHT 3in1 revealing

OCTOBER 3

PrayStill

Luke 5:29-32
Then Levi gave a great banquet for him in his house; and there was a large crowd of tax collectors and others sitting at the table with them. The Pharisees and their scribes were complaining to his disciples, saying, "Why do you eat and drink with tax collectors and sinners?" Jesus answered, "Those who are well have no need of a physician, but those who are sick; I have come to call not the righteous but sinners to repentance."

Scripture Prayer: Mercy

Heavenly God
Beautiful power of great goodness and mercy. Graceful Host of beautiful banquet blessings abounding. Nurturing Jehovah Jireh feasting on glories abounding. Ever forever for good. Great is your overwhelming pursuing presence.
Highest Lord Jesus
Have mercy on us. Lamb of God forgive us and take away sin. Cleanse the thoughts of our minds. Guide strait to Your Way the steps to take and the words to say. Redeem souls to Your passionate compassion for love unconditional. Let the truth of intentions be guarded in rod and staff protecting.
Spirit Ruach providing,
Calm to the hand of mercy. Flow wave breezes of forgiveness and empathy right through to peace places prevailing. Take away the pride that dies at the cross of humble transference. Make strong Your fruitful atonement. Through with and in Your powerful will prevailing.
TBTHT God Spirit Jesus

OCTOBER 4

PrayStill

Hosea 6:6
For I desire steadfast love and not sacrifice, the knowledge of God rather than burnt offerings.

Scripture Prayer: Intimacy

Gracious lover of my soul Jesus
True right and beautiful are Your ways. You have Your way within me and I am at peace. You shower reigning graces throughout my soul. I am nourishing from You. You take the void and make it all love. I am melted to You. Rest me in Your loving arms Jesus.
Father ABBA MOMMA parent,
You go before me. You comfort my way. You are already there. To the left You protect me to the right You select me, You make me straight to You. Delight me to the stars You name, realm in your Heavens. Eyes in Your skies You carry my steps guiding on earth.
Sudden Spirit visiting,
Come be welcome here. Waiting and longing for Your graceful presence surround. Wrestle this vessel to the ground of Your inviting. Enticing is your persistence in my conviction. Breath of life in rest, protector in my slumber. Saturate my soul to dripping dance.
Say La, Selah brate, Selah
Into me, you see
Intimacy
TBTLJ.. Lord Jesus

OCTOBER 5

PrayStill

Luke 6:26
Woe to you when all speak well of you, for that is what their ancestors did to the false prophets.

Scripture Prayer: Praises

Glorious God
Great name worthy of honor and praises. Beautiful Creator, masterful architect of all things great and small. Powerfully presenting the glories beyond description. You alone are God almighty.
Breath of life,
Convector of my soul. Affirmer of my need for acceptance inclusion and accolades in welcoming. Motivating life circulation of souls desiring. May all praises reflect to only You. Keep my confidence in you alone. Make the sweet effervescent incense elevate to you gates of thanks giving. Precious is Your adornment in Heaven.
Jesus life giver,
Holy and blameless are You. Teacher of just the right genuine encouraging words of the world. Present in me the reflecting channels of uplifting to refer all back to You. Protect watch after and guide my words to be Your intention. All praise to you Lord of life. Let us lift each other to Your pleasant pasture grazing on Your Heavenly Kingdom praises.
TBTG

OCTOBER 6

PrayStill

Luke 6:27-28
But I say to you that listen, love your enemies, do good to those who hate you, bless those who curse you, pray for those who abuse you.

Scripture Prayer: Strength

Pure Lord of love divine,
Dismissive of the darkness in a gentle loving way. The hurt pain falls to the ground in dust. Master of the turning hate to grace. Powerful to own remove and recycle any negative energy. Remove me from me to let the onslaught pass right through.
Jesus God
Be between this vessel and the waves of curses and abuse and disrespect. Return back only love. love dismiss this hate to the ground. Overflowing banks of forgiveness pour out before the accuser even presents.
Lord you own the arrows and flames. You are powerful to forgiving reflection of life light shields pouring outward love.
You, Lord Jesus, deflect the hurts of the word to deflate.
You are mighty persuader of love overpowering.
Selah
Forgive x 77
Holy Spirit come,
Angel bumpers quarantine and quiet the echo of the arrows. I do not own these things. They are not mine. Deaf ears can hear the pain in the soundless silence answer. The evil spewed is not renewed, so falls dead to the ground. Smile and grin, love always wins, the cry from within is departing. Love rules away hate to the loving state. Blessings shower the curses fate. Prayer converts the accuser abuser.
Lord you reign in smiles. Amen

OCTOBER 7

PrayStill

Mark 10:14b-15
Let the little children come to me; do not stop them; for it is to such as these that the kingdom of God belongs. Truly I tell you, whoever does not receive the kingdom of God as a little child will never enter it.

Scripture Prayer: Infancy

God provider
Invisible comforter adorning womb of faith weaver. Surround of love lights all taking care. Watching over in hovering without slumber or sleep. Precious wing embrace. Angel army tending in protection. Fortress rock and armor of faith and assurance. God guide guarding greatly.
Spirit of faithful grace
Always guiding protector drawing near. You Lord watch over and guide and protect. You are the autopilot trusted chauffeur captain. I believe I believe I believe You never let go. Trust implicit Your preceding marches through the valley in surrounding light. Precious is your presence.
Lord God Jesus
My faith You cleanse and make strong. Exercise my faith muscles to quell my unbelief. Melt away my flesh fears on Your holy plateaus of innocence. Take away the scars of the world to purify and refine pure faith back to You. You own my past You are my future, YOU fill my right now. I am Yours, protected watched over and owned. You are the giving grace gift of hope.
TBTG

OCTOBER 8

PrayStill

Psalm 106:3
Happy are those who act with justice and always do what is right!

Scripture Prayer: Relent

God of mercy compassion and grace. Strong mighty and powerful are your ways. You let the wandering stop and the saving start. Covenant grace lets the Justice relent to merciful compassionate grace. The cry is heard.

Spirit of love everlasting, thankful praises raising lips of inspiration. In my nothingness you lent me life. You gave life back again even in my dismissiveness to Your gift. You lent me life again to see and know Your beauty. You relent my grief in Your relentlessness for my soul.

Your merciful justice redeems me and quiets my iniquities. Your mercy is true and just. Bend me back and melt me back to You.

Jesus friend of sinners,

Always in all ways, You do right for me. Let me shower adorn and raise all back for You. Hide my faults no more. Seek me out and shake me out and cleanse my soul some more. You are so good to me. Let me abide in you. Persist unrelenting at my heart and mind and guard me. Let me glory in You.

Praise God.

OCTOBER 9

PrayStill

Luke 7:14-15
Then he came forward and touched the bier, and the bearers stood still. And he said, "Young man, I say to you, rise!" The dead man sat up and began to speak, and Jesus gave him to his mother.

Scripture Prayer: Life Giver

God
Breath of life. Heartbeat of the world. Blood and water of the flowing goodness showering the earth. light of life illuminating back to Heaven. Sustaining grace of the life abounding in creation. Power divine.
Spirit
Surrounding protective correcting shield. Victory giver. Persistent in love conquering. Insistent in life renewing. Resistant to wander and doubt. Renewing assurance of life unending resurrects to belief in eternal. God angels purpose author ruling all.
Jesus
10,000 such tears wash the sting of the bier bearers burial away. Son of God, life giver. Whisperer of names. Creator of lightning life in sudden shock to life. Awaken restore and renew to the way. Lover of life souls yearning for purpose and meaning. Ultimate authority of redemption and continual rebirth. Life maker alive in sleep awakening.
Praise God lasting forever

OCTOBER 10

PrayStill

Psalm 130:4
I wait for the Lord; my soul waits for him; in his word is my hope.

Scripture Prayer: Receive Calm

Spirit God Jesus
Three in one. Capturing peaceful Lord of rest in feast on divine word alive. Place of peace presenting surrender to empty. Receiver of exhaling breaths of cries in unspoken emotions. Receptacle of healing redemption breathing in. Word divine alive.

Spirit speaking,
Entranced and advanced in romance with Your communion. With you and in you surround Your reunion. Evacuate me to birth in you. You erase and wipe clean the smudge of sin. Weaned of the wild within me I am child to You.
Talk to me Lord I watch and wait. Multiple perspectives of Your words divide parallel ways of how you love me. Images of Your graceful love present.
Restful envision.
Jesus lover of my soul,
On peace as it is in Heaven. I hold no breath basking in the light of Your WORD. my soul pants for You, Lord. Your name in my breath fills my soul. Your words on my lips heal me. Your spirit surround enjoys my patience for you. The weight of the waiting for you is in the desiring. I know you were, are, and will be with me. Perfect communion is in Your here and now.
Forever grateful,
Amen

OCTOBER 11

PrayStill

1 Peter 1:8

Scripture Prayer: Fruits

Lord of lords

Hope of nations. Desire of good and faithful servants. Overwhelming conviction of converting souls turning to Glory. Masterful revealer to truth abiding in the hearts and minds of the yearning.

King of kings,

Brilliance shines away all the dust of the earth. Words of the WAY silence doubt. Worship of The WORD reigns over idols. Light of the world divides the day in sparkling crystal waves. Light through the lids, through the clear water reflecting pure white.

God of gods,

Jesus King, glorious forever, eternal everlasting presence. Silent invisible is the power of Your sweet persuasion calling all to God. Awesome mighty and all powerful are You.

Precious is Your name, Jesus

TBTG

OCTOBER 12

PrayStill

Luke 8:8

"Some fell into good soil, and when it grew, it produced a hundredfold." As [Jesus] said this, he called out, "Let anyone with ears to hear listen!"

Scripture Prayer: Abundance

God overflowing,
Creation revealing in bounty. Author of the way, truth, light. Fallow rich and fervent are the forces of great and good. Nourishing beyond any need or want or desire are fields of plenty. Unending lifeline sending in presenting.
Christ all knowing,
Lord of all growth. Fervent is Your WORD working wonderful. Beautiful are the never ending Joys flowing continuously. Growth life lifting forever sifting refining the folds to You. Your kingdom exploding with countless blessings abounding. Capture and sustain the beauty.
Spirit expansion,
Lord creator of growth and change. Magnifier of light untamed. Wild shoots and roots wrap hold of You in expansion beyond sight or belief. Awesome in possible are Your holy ways unstoppable. Grow my soul to Your unendings.
TBTHT 3in1

OCTOBER 13

PrayStill

Psalm 144:3-4
O Lord what are we that you should care for us? Mere mortals that you should think of us? We are like a puff of wind; our days are like a passing shadow.

Scripture Prayer: Lament

God Lord

Precious sign and signature of Heaven awakening grace alive. Mountains reach for Glory pressing to earth. Celestial Angels hover in waiting for moments in folding streams to rivers of renewal.
Lord Jesus
Walking to the river of crystal-clear reflection shines the illumines piercing darkness divide. Conquering Son of God reigning glory. Washing pure delight by keeping all in sight. Making what is right what will be.
Jesus God
Author of full Alpha Omega. Full circle in eternal beginnings and endings. Forever is your gracious loving presence in the light. Shine bright on the hearts hearing your vision of truth renewing grace convictions.
TBTG

OCTOBER 14

PrayStill

Romans 12:2
Do not conform to the pattern of this world, but be transformed by the renewing of your mind. Then you will be able to test and approve what God's will is—his good, pleasing and perfect will.

Scripture Prayer: Discover

Lord
Revealing veils, enlightening pathways, crackling light ways.
True and right tested revealing. Beautiful refine shines.

Jesus
It is all yours. I give it back to you. Water falls off, dust drowns down. Loose garments reveal the pure empty vessel.

Spirit
Divine force within. Divine flow about. Revealing truth around. Appealing truth changing to light. Right revealing truth reigns.
TBTHT

OCTOBER 15

PrayStill

2 Samuel 7:22
How great you are, Sovereign LORD! There is no one like you, and there is no God but you, as we have heard with our own ears.

Scripture Prayer: Beautiful

Spirit of beauty

Reign shower-shows of delight across the skies. Paint colors in brilliance that glorify magnificent rooms of glory. Fill space and time with infinite presence. Harmony in waves washing laps in peace.

God of creation,
Powerful voice echoing truth. Sole providing redeemer. Only you alone are. Blessings honor and glory flow to and from your precious gates inviting.

Jesus
The sound of Heaven is Your precious name. All bow down you Lord. All confess your name is Holy. You alone are God from the beginning. All praise glory laud and honor are echoing sweet, sweet sounds.
TBTJC

OCTOBER 16

PrayStill

Psalm 19:14
May these words of my mouth and this meditation of my heart be pleasing in your sight, LORD, my Rock and my Redeemer.

Scripture Prayer: Pause

LORD,
Masterful seed of life speaking WORD truth. Genuine binder for word and intentions. Words and deeds fall together in fields of submission to true light glories.

Abba Mamma,
Guardian of lips secure in perspectives to your beautiful creation. Silence the noise of the confusion. Make true the reflection back to you. Pause and rest to rehear. Guide and protect the steps through the mist ascending and descending. Keep diligence in pursuit of WORD.

Jesus
Words without, words within, Walking talking love begins. Truth in step and truth in Voice. Angels speak through us in choice, the glory chorus raising praise. Sing resounding echo days. Forever LORD forever praise.
TBTG

OCTOBER 17

PrayStill

Psalm 25:14-15
The LORD confides in those who fear him; he makes his covenant known to them. My eyes are ever on the LORD, for only he will release my feet from the snare.

Scripture Prayer: Focus

Lord of freedoms abounding through You. Whom shall I fear? You are my light and my salvation. All other falls to the floor in dust. Beautiful are your clear pathways to soul conviction. Goodness mercy and love fill your chambers. Confiding covenant seals lean in.

God of True light,
Shine crystal clear in the foggy mist of dust unstirring. Beam the pathways of truth direction to your glory filled chambers. Focus fear in holiness surrender. Less of me is more of You. Dismiss my petty anxious. Take away my meager upset. Clear my blocked pathways to your content. Be in my surround conviction trusting.

Jesus Lord
Take my stride let me abide and know your loving welcome. Fill this place with Your graceful face harkening to my soul. Lift my countenance from snares impotence to your unending peace. Live and reign over my pain disdains and lead me to your glories.
TBTJC

OCTOBER 18

PrayStill

Psalm 119:11
I have hidden your word in my heart that I might not sin against you.

Scripture Prayer: Gift

Lord revealing
God of destinations surpassing. Beautiful saving redeemer. Anticipation of ages. Delight and desire of hopeful promises. Prelusive yearning of truth.
God supreme,
Pursuit of the best, lays in Your house. One moment of your grace lasts a lifetime. You are the craving of perfection. You are the gift present. You are every bit of all I need. Continuously revealing is your glory
Jesus
Just a drop of your sweet desire delivers oceans of reward. A seed of your word grows forests of shelter. A smile of your countenance spreads fire wild dancing.
An inclination of your precept's guards desire rightly to You. You save me from my tendency to fall. I hold guard and revere You knitted in my heart. Your chamber abides in me pure. Awaken me to slumber not nor sleep in your Word guarding.
TBTJC

OCTOBER 19

PrayStill

Psalm 37:4
Take delight in the Lord and he will give you the desires of your heart

Scripture Prayer: Joyousness

God Glory,
Pleasurable treasure beyond all measures, maker of Heaven and earth. Lord you reign in every gain and every smile reflects you. Only in you are my ways true to the powerful grace overwhelming. Magnificent significance forever giving pertinence, the author of divine direction.

Ruach of Life,
Giver of succulent Joy's flooding in. Surrounding warmth and light of delight. Hovering love hold protecting in embrace hold, fulfilling all desire. Breath of True life that wipes away strife and contents my contentment delight.

Jesus
Friend of ages eternal. Alive and walking in well please. Happy with me because of my plea to guide and design in the rightful. Narrow and straight is the walk to the gate to the left or the right I will not go.
TBTHT 3in1

OCTOBER 20

PrayStill

Psalm 51:12
Restore unto me the joy of thy salvation; and uphold me with thy free spirit.

Scripture Prayer: Heal

God Lord
Creation groans into existence. Alive are the stretch marks of growing. Callous are the scars scared of iniquities' injustices. Stronger is the Lord than all the failings of man. Humble and meek are the righteous patients patently waiting. True are Your recovery redemptions.

Spirit healer,
Talk and voice are sharing your victory over ailing elements. Your balm psalm anoints healing in the community of faith resounding. Hear our prayer. Your song is soothing. Reclaim the Glory. Restore peace within. The pain gives to set right.

Jesus Life Giver,
Comforter of ages and nations. Open my hidden unknown wounds gathered in innocent ignorance. Restore renew and repair the thoughts words and deeds of imperfection. Thyne be the Glory risen conquering King.
Jesus, I draw near to Thee to have your loving WORD in me. Whisper my sword to suddenly, my foe ashames away.
TBTJG Jesus God

O C T O B E R 2 1

PrayStill

Philippians 4:8
Finally, brothers and sisters, whatever is true, whatever is noble, whatever is right, whatever is pure, whatever is lovely, whatever is admirable—if anything is excellent or praiseworthy—think about such things.

Scripture Prayer: Beautiful

Spirit Glorious,
All honor is Yours in fruits of love, joy, and peace. Enduring is Your goodness, and kindness in faithfulness, You, Lord, are gentleness persuading to holiness. You are the persistence in pure truth abiding. All praise rises up to You. The song of silence resounding.
Jesus God Spirit
Adornment praise and worship reign around You. You are good, well pleased and holy in essence. Sweet sounding is Your name above all names. Touch of warmth in gentle kindness. Assurance of the salve of creation healings. Friend above friends encouraging is Your embrace.
Mamma Abba Parent God
Noble admirable in powerful force. Selah
Red yellow blue are three in Your vivid collages.   Selah
Sweet salt of life and bitter sour to sin are the tastes of light.   Selah
Seven notes of symphonies ring true delight.   Selah
Order of lilies fragrances sparkle Heavenly scent sensations.   Selah
Inspiring is your breath breathing LIFE upon us.
Praise God.
Your Precious Presence is above all senses in the hearts beating for you.
Praise God from whom all blessings flow in excellency.
Amen

OCTOBER 22 (AT 8:08 AM)

PrayStill

Proverbs 22:6
Start children off on the way they should go, and even when they are old they will not turn from it.

Scripture Prayer: Born Again

God Creator,
Seed of truth spurning inside. Author and architect of the genuine key hold inside that unlocks You into me. First love, first impart, first before time begins. Weave my knitting divine nurture adorning (DNA) to enlighten with You.
Spirit youth,
Truth in pure innocence beliefs. You care and nurture and love me in my need. I am nothing and helpless before you. You caretake guardian me. You give eternal watch over me. My comfort, my guide. My everything inside reflecting back to You.
Jesus God
All lineage goes to you. Your divine, holds creation together. Child faith is calling. I believe I believe because of You. You bring me full circle to you. Always new, all ways renew, forever anew with You. Naissance renaissance to you again and again.
TBTG

OCTOBER 23

PrayStill

Psalm 55:22
Cast your burden upon the LORD and He will sustain you; He will never allow the righteous to be shaken.

Scripture Prayer: Lift

God rule of law
Masterful way truth and life of all deeds thoughts and words. Revealing author of truth shining brightly. No secrets are hid. Cleanse clear and reveal the genuine in the facade. Make known the true light of generosity caring and empathy. Love lift enliven the craving of love.

Lord
Hear our prayer. Let it be a sweet, sweet sound in your ear. Magnify and multiply the goodness of our love pouring out for You, to You, through You. You plant in us care and concern for freely giving love. All our heart soul mind and strength are directed in redirection to You.

Jesus
Keep my gaze and steps forward to you. Guide me from the detours of despairing selfishness. Tune my ear to your WORD. Set my sight right to You in bounty. Strengthen my renew. Warm my scent for tender mercy grace and love abiding. Carry me, carry me, so I may carry thee to those who need uplifting. Hands make light, shine upright, pure delight to glory's height.
TBTJC
Amen

OCTOBER 24

PrayStill

1 Peter 5:7
Cast all your anxiety on him because he cares for you.

Scripture Prayer: Release

God Supreme,
Towering truth emits beauty all around. Overcoming in overwhelm is Your goodness. Powerful persuasion of light and justice. Shining light of love beaming into darkness revealing sovereign pure reflection.

Lord of love.
All the dust of the day gravitates away. Wash away the fear burden of the uncertain. Loosen my grip and slip away the doubt. Cast this ship away from the shore of unease. Please me in release of the unknown. Ease away the comfort of complacency in pain. In you, Lord, is no fear, no regret, no remorse, no resign, no reiteration. Revive me to You.

Son of God, friend, Jesus
Loosen my grip in stronghold. Make easy my let go to let You in. Let me gently release and toss away all that is not of You. Cleanse my soul in renewal. Cast down to the ground the false deceiving. Receive me to your release. Calm still my soul to silence listening. Revive me to You.
TBTG

OCTOBER 25

PrayStill

Luke 10:29
But wanting to justify himself, he asked Jesus "And who is my neighbor?"

Scripture Prayer: All

God of all,
Maker and judge of all things. Creator of choices opportunities and revealings. Powerful truth signing justification of all intentions. Most merciful and gracious redeemer to the way, truth and life light. All Powerful, All present, All knowing Lord.

Spirit of love,
All creation is yours. All love is yours. All forgiveness mercy and truth are Yours. Take away the sin between me and my enemies. Remove out the unease disease of prideful judgement persecution and resentment. Instill in me love compassion and forgiveness for all encounters. Grateful gracefulness bestows abounding graces to trample away the enemy.

Jesus
Walk me to the river of love in to action. Inspire giving forgiving. Emblazon lightning living through mercy seat forgiveness. Make the love I have for You be the love given freely to my rival. Value the peace passing all understanding giving and returning through you. Substitute You in the place of my foe so I may right channel peace.
Through, with, in Christ Jesus.
Amen

OCTOBER 26

PrayStill

Luke 6:27

Scripture Prayer: Agape

God love,
Pure love, pure delight, pure joy. Powerful towering overcoming force of goodness. Beautiful saving lover of all. Divine unending never changing lover of just and unjust. You reign over the fields of delight. The joy font abounds unending.

Spirit love,
Lord of understanding... ...Take away my confusion,
Lord of Belief......Take away my doubt,
Lord of Peace......Take away my turmoil,
Lord of Joy......Take away my pain,
Lord of Inspiration......Take away my desperation,
Lord of love......Take away my loneliness.

Jesus love,
Help me to continue......To love
Help me to continue......To do good
Help me to continue......To bless
Help me to continue......To pray.
Help me to continue......To You my Savior

Show me the way to Your sanctuary of peace. Remove me from my tent of wordless worldly turmoil. Assuage my angst and anguish in agonizing. Free my discord to Your accord. Alter and transform my unrest to Your renewing peaceful calm assuring grace residing. I am weak and needy. You are my redeemer alive reviving.

TBTJC

OCTOBER 27

PrayStill

Hebrews 4:12
For the word of God is alive and active. Sharper than any double-edged sword, it penetrates even to dividing soul and spirit, joints and marrow; it judges the thoughts and attitudes of the heart.

Scripture Prayer: Speak

God Lord Divine,
First alpha of all love. Seed germinating powerful force of creation. Essence of beauty emanating from beyond understanding. Precious bold and convincing in the way of goodness to and from You.

Spirit Holy Ruach
Breath of life continual. Breath life light invading to my soul and spirit. Divide out my dust. Persevere my feel right and make my thinking wholly from You. Be my new pneuma. Inspire my desire to do Your will insights.

Lord Holy Jesus
Word alive in me you thrive. Take me to Your changing graces. Judge my heart's desire and make my mercy deserving. You heal and esteem my soul for Your mercy and grace receiving. Lord above all lords. King above all kings, mighty everlasting love of loves.
TBTHT

PrayStill

1 Peter 4:8 Above all, love each other deeply, because love covers over a multitude of sins.
Scripture Prayer: Fervent

God Caring,
Charity of nations. Beneficial love generator inspiring in giving. Motivating master of forever forgiveness healing any ailing woes. Foundational root of love branching into every form of beautiful interaction. Loving God of loving people designing love from the heart.
Spirit Caring,
Carry me, carry me, make me at one. Fill my heart with love.
Heal me, heal me, let my sins be gone. Forgive my heart in love.
Hear me, hear me cleanse my heart's desire. Wash me clean again.
Cover me, cover me, help me love a friend. Make me whole again.
Be my ardent fever of desire.
Jesus Caring,
Anointing altering well of hope. Teacher of truth in love. Beautiful savior mandating forgiveness and giving. Charity my character to brotherly love unending. Let me lift, in life speaking. Let me joy, in love giving. Let me cheerful in grace abounding.
Amen
TBTJG

OCTOBER 29

PrayStill

Roman's 12:1
Therefore, I urge you, brothers and sisters, in view of God's mercy, to offer your bodies as a living sacrifice, holy and pleasing to God—this is your true and proper worship.

Scripture Prayer: Offering

God Yahweh,
First and last, circle of life throughout. Continuous Deity, merciful unchanging Lord of beauty. Pleasing parent of children in need. Mamma Abba provider Lord of protection. Genesis of love instilling silence.

Lord God of Life.
You are vibrant waves of gifts uplifting. Make match and transform my motives to and for Your joy. I learn I cannot earn. Your free grace gift. Let me offer all You give, to lift the gift in love. Let me offer free in joy Your glory love results. God, I offer me to thee.

Jesus God
Brother, friend, advocate, and healer. You drag my errant earthen vessel from the mire of sins. You are my patient advocate inspiring me to surrender all to You. Your way, Your hand embracing, lifts and cleans my soul. Renew a holy offering in me with faith eyes up to You.
TBTHT 3N1

OCTOBER 30

PrayStill

Psalm 47:6-7
Sing praises to God sing praises; sing praises to our King, sing praises. For God is King of all the earth; sing praises with all your skill.

Scripture Prayer: Exaltation

Lord God
Song of centuries, Rock of ages, Rhythm of nations. All people praise in voice and song acclaiming. The Glory of the Lord chants the power of the praise. The echo of the joy resounding rings true light waves brightly sounding. Sing to the King alive.

Lord Spirit
Sing my soul to Heaven. Beat my rhythm to your drum. Fill my lungs with joy rejoicing. Exalt my breath in exultation. Synchronize my beat to dance and rhythm feat. The hum of my soul sings Your name. Lift my eyes and arms to you in dance. Pour my soul into your Heavenly chorus.

Lord Jesus
You speak your verse to me in tune. I learn Your WORD up from the song sung in my soul. The echoes of the Spirit rings teachings to my heart. You come to me in melody. You parallel in my harmony. You make my whole body resonate to You. You are the song I long for. All praise honor and glory be Yours.
TBTHS

OCTOBER 31

PrayStill

Ecclesiasticus 28:17
The blow of a whip raises a welt, but a blow of the tongue crushes the bones.

Scripture Prayer: Wise Words

God King,
Lord of life, Breath of love, Word of worship. Vibrant waves of words uplifting speak life vigor from all creation. Wind of love weaves to the tune of ears hearing. light speaks truth in love conquering.

Spirit King,
True word of True life of True Joy. Shower Your breath surrounding. Fill the lungs with goodness speaking. Dance tongues to delight in Your Holy name. Flavor sweet succulent praise uprising glories. Guard the lips to uplift only.

Jesus King,
Offering transforming. Be my thoughts words and deeds acceptable. Present your presence in replies. Let the roaring lion prowl and devour itself in dust speaking foment in torment. You Lord Jesus are perfect love, speaking perfect truth, bringing bones to dancing life. Filter me to pure receive and speak Your joyous life speaking.
TBTHT 3in1

NOVEMBER 1

PrayStill

Wisdom 3:1
But the souls of the righteous are in the hand of God and no torment will ever touch them.

Scripture Prayer: Saints

Lord God in all good newness. Daily refreshing starter, opening to holy growth. Pure and perfect home, attracting goodness and purpose. Lord of dedicating persevering obedience in adherence to the conviction of souls and hearts living all for You, precious Savior of love eternal.

Lord Spirit of transform, dedicating conviction of confidence in Christ Jesus. Powerful jealous and relentless pursuer of whole love. Abiding attractive magnet to holy holiness. Beautiful bold and bountiful embracing all who humbly ask seek and knock for truth. Shield guard and protected impenetrable Your light shining in us.

Lord Jesus

Lover of souls and walker of the way. Your easy yoke welcomes true straight and easy surrender to simplicity. My burdens melt away in your presence. Keep my gaze forward at the new mind, full of grace, mercy and love deeply grabbing hold. Praise your name eternally. You are holiest holy saint of saints abiding.

Amen

NOVEMBER 2

PrayStill

Proverbs 22:4
By humility and the fear of the Lord are riches, and honour, and life.

Scripture Prayer: Wisdom

Father God
Maker and judge of all things. Forever name in revere through ages by the humble. Master of all things surrounding. King of kings Lord of lords, love of life. There is no other who reigns sovereign. You are the wholly holy and mighty divine designer of all that is seen and unseen.
Spirit Nurturing Lord
My dust hume breathes to life in Your Spirit inspiring. You form and lift me from the mire of life. You mold me to Your desire. You obtain and train my liking to Your way of truthful freedom. In You is perpetual creation new. You humor my prideful ego to right size. You submit me in obedience to your Holiness. I melt to the ground in refinement and submission. I am signed resigned and marked as Yours.
Son Human Jesus
Oh how you know my woes. None can compare to Yours. You show how love divine grows through sacrifice and obedience and tender loving persuasion. You are my Lord who reigns in me through me with me around me and on behalf of me. Wisdom and royalty are in Your robe. Yoke in Your humble steps is easy with You as my Master.
Raise and praise God from whom all blessings flow.
Amen

NOVEMBER 3

PrayStill

Luke 12:34
For where your treasure is, there your heart will be also.

Scripture Prayer: Touch

Joyful God
Granting guaranteeing graceful joy giver. Delight of lights shining in hearts hearing. Happy welcoming and generous author of uplifting. Channeling master of waves of raising joyous noises to Heaven. Instill in me your calm joy.
Spirit smiling
Receive me to peaceful love of contentment. Shower and adorn my now moments with the warm and calm succulence beyond my knowing. Suddenly illumine Your reflex truth that my heart treasures You and Your treasure is in my heart. I am satisfied true to you.
Jesus Rejoicing
Hear our prayer. Let us hear Your continuous good and well pleasing child prayer fall fresh all over. Help us to seek and find the glimmering gems that generate joy. Let us bask and seal in Your graceful glory light of Selah.
Amen

NOVEMBER 4

PrayStill

Ruth 1:16
But Ruth said, "Do not press me to leave you or to turn back from following you! Where you go, I will go; where you lodge I will lodge; your people shall be my people, and your God my God."

Scripture Prayer: Promise

God Provider,
Creator of cell formation and growth. Knitting tapestry designer of bones in the womb. Masterful ruler fulfilling preordained steps and circumstances. Refuge of ages seeking home in Heaven's havens.
Spirit Insider,
Obedience follows You in full circle with You right behind. Where I go You are there. Where I stay You care. You adopt me and follow me first. I follow You, You set me free. You are my strong provider invite.
Jesus Inviter,
You are the WORD alive in old and new law, present everywhere, pointing to God. Comfort in all generations. Persuasion of inclinations. masterful restoration of wanting to be with You. I go to You. There is always more of You. You seek me out first always in all ways.
TBTG

NOVEMBER 5

PrayStill

Psalm 139:14
I praise you because I am fearfully and wonderfully made; your works are wonderful, I know that full well.

Scripture Prayer: Servitude

Lord God Creator,
Knitting Weaver of the key to life. Planting Spirit of the ways back to Heavenly kingdoms. Open are the gates to Glory rising shining and luring in attractive sweetness to places where love is right and well. Just a glimpse of knowing a drop of your glory now overwhelms and sustains.
Lord Spirit Joy,
In obedience to your precepts is no fear of the world. Fear in You, Lord of Joy, brings freedom of life. My trust in you is fearless to the world. My esteem is in knowing you created me as Yours in flavors of wonder and designs of fulfillment. My life is Your song singing praise. You know my days and ways.
Lord Jesus Savior,
Surround me in my escape. You touch my wonderful marveling. You own my moments of sand escaping. You are my healer, sealer and revealer of truth in my imprint. I give you all of me, it is Yours to begin with. Let Your will be my life prayer.
TBTHT 3N1

NOVEMBER 6

PrayStill

Psalm 62:1
For God alone my soul in silence waits; from him comes my salvation.

Scripture Prayer: Pacem

Glorious God
Colorful creator shining misty beams flowing through all darkness. Sparkling Spirit of divine pureness brighter than the eyes can feel. Radiant reins draw and steer the crystal spectrum rains of colors reigning on creation. Brilliance revealing are beams of truth light.
Waiting Spirit
Rest my soul in you. Place me in peace beside the breath of calm. Slow my heart and mind. Erase away the thought of the day and let me be all for You. Melt my body, calm my soul. Tune me to your still calm peace. Silence listening draws near.
Selah x infinity
Smiling Jesus
Affirm me in the firmament of Your Heavenly pastures. Receive away my transgressors to the pit. Lift my countenance to the renewing midst where grace meets mercy and peace beyond all understandings goes and comes from me. Fill me with Your well with my soul.
TBTJC

NOVEMBER 7

PrayStill

Matthew 6:3
But when you give to the needy, do not let your left hand know what your right hand is doing.

Scripture Prayer: Laud

Heavenly Provider
Abba Mamma Protector worthy of all acclaim and Glory. Root of the goodness living and adorning all upward in fragrances dancing in delight and fresh. Harmony sounds brilliance in the glory and praise that are always pointing to Your marvelous creations.
Channeling Spirit
None can usurp Your inherency of praises. Even the boastful in themselves are humbled. Every estimable glory comes and goes amazing to You in reflection. Long life, riches and honor are placed at Your altar. You sign and seal them all. In silence is affirmation of Your glory. Let not Your authorship be taken.
Jesus life giver,
All giving is in Your bounty. You remove my bow of pride and arrows of supplanting. Oh, how I long for praise glory and affirmation of all the good I think I do. I want others to envy me. Take away my pride inside to let all the praises raise up to you. Let me be a reflection to you. Take the swords of my fear and insecurity and turn them to plowshares of glory headed straight to You. May I not look back at me.
TBTJC Savior, Praise God!

NOVEMBER 8

PrayStill

1 Corinthians 12:4
There are different kinds of gifts, but the same Spirit distributes them.

Scripture Prayer: Body

Lord God
Breath of life breathing life into each vessel. Masterful designer of multitudes of gifts and treasures manifest in each human unique. Corporal common binder of sameness of masses in each life living. Purposeful combiner of gifts miraculous into the temporal body uplifting.
Lord Spirit
How awesome and brilliant is the way you build relation. You fall fresh in new mercies to bind and thrive community. You fill and renew to You all the glories that come from us welcoming you in. You first welcome us. You grow us in endless varieties of colors, flavors, smells, tinglings, harmonies and sensations. Rest is in the overwhelming.
Lord Jesus
God of flesh. Speaking light into darkness. Speaking life into nations. You personally sign and affirm the believing body. Every gift given to each is a cheerful gift returning to Your body. Let us lift the least. We imbibe Your creation and emit your Glories. You reign in the Heaven gift you plant in each soul reflecting to You.
TBTHT 3N1

NOVEMBER 9

PrayStill

Proverbs 27:17
As iron sharpens iron, so one person sharpens another.

Scripture Prayer: Foundation

Powerful God
Rock and Redeemer, Master and Revealer. Constant and pure are the bulwarks surrounding Kingdoms of glory. Sower and reaper and ruler of outcomes. Generation and nation maker. Masterful mighty and unbending. Truth, light and hope are Your selah bastions.

Watchful Spirit
You taper all focusing love and protection. Keen points align to straight and narrow edges. You watch out for me you protect me and lift me up. You take all my true earthy ways and use them for Your Glory. You cleft away my earthly errant wander woes. I am in transform and renew. You surround me with guarding angels working through your humble servants to guide my inside. Rebuke and reward are Yours.

Knowing Jesus
You have my breath before exhaling. My thoughts and words you see. My heart's delight is in Your sight you take my cries from me. You hone my home to make Your own my focus turns with Thee. The place I go I do not know you watch and tend to me. I am corrected in your palace fields. Thy rod and thy staff they comfort and direct me.
Selah
TBTJC

NOVEMBER 10

PrayStill

Hebrews 11:1
Now faith is assurance of things hoped for, a conviction of things not seen.

Scripture Prayer: Heaven

Glorious God
Kingdom creator, whispering wisdom of WORDs building up powerful places, steps breathing to the beat of the WORD. Mighty powerful and persistent force in attractive desire for unseen revealing of majesty honor and reverence. Holy Holy Holy is the name God above all names.
Majestic Spirit
Vibrancy in brilliance numbs and sustains in Your presence. You make knowing in revealing the next right thing. The next Kingdom move ideal, the next move to You. You are the WORD way truth that illuminates direction to guide and follow in peace. Comforter of all who acquiesce to Your desiring call. Inescapable is Your relentlessness.
Praiseworthy Jesus
Take my hand, walk me through this foreign land. Be my guide to steps inside and show me how to go through. The confidence of you drawing nigh sets my fear aside. I hear Your voice and am not lost, to You is straight divide. Over around under beside the way is true to You. I go where I cannot see knowing we are two.
TBTJC Precious Savior

NOVEMBER 11

PrayStill

Matthew 28:18,19
All authority in Heaven and on earth has been given to me. Therefore go and make disciples of all nations, baptizing them in the name of the Father and of the Son and of the Holy Spirit.

Scripture Prayer: Inviting

God
Mamma Abba, Creator of Heaven and earth. Mighty Savior of nations. Wild cleansing master of salvation. Altering altar of good transforming. Cleanse the thoughts words and desires of our hearts. Wash away the sin of the world in the light of Your truth. Make us bow and worship and lie down to your authority.
Holy Spirit
Flowing, Speaking life renewing. give us doves of hope, diving love upon us. Well pleasing are we to You. Take us to your many rooms of many colors well pleasing. Wash us in mikveh and send us out into the world. Embolden our proclaim. lengthen our sustain, hold us in remain, make it all your gain.
Jesus
Walking love, Powerful accompaniment of angels. Archangels clear the pathways of wheat and chaff, sheep and goats, gold and dross. Make the names in Your life book claim with the souls of those abiding. The gift we receive in trust and believe is the gift we keep giving in trinity. The gift that you give we open and live and offer others as You give.
Thanks be to the Holy Trinity weaving through nations.
Amen

NOVEMBER 12

PrayStill

1 John 3:1
See what great love the Father has lavished on us, that we should be called children of God! And that is what we are! The reason the world does not know us is that it did not know him.

Scripture Prayer: Storage

God love,
Abundant forgiving and greatly protective. Forever watching over with never slumber never sleep. Guardian lifter and deliverer of souls and raising Spirits of life. Nothing separates the love place deep in hearts welcoming the joy seeing love in others.

Spirit Life,
Giver of goodness sparking love infectious. Pure delight and commitment is the presence of Your knowing love. Showering rivers of adornment wash in new waves of philia love without words. Unspoken is the knowing. Your love is in the showing. Your presence is surrounding obedience.

Jesus Knowing,
Master of my desiring free will. I am child with Teacher of my right and wrong, my ups and downs, my voice resound. How comforting is the joyous grace and mercy pouring in my full cup. My overflow cup vessel is giving to show the childlike faith I remain in. I inherit adoption to the womb of Your kingdom life!
TBTG Lavishing father.

NOVEMBER 13

PrayStill

Colossians 3:16
Let the message of Christ dwell among you richly as you teach and admonish one another with all wisdom through psalms, hymns, and songs from the Spirit singing to God with gratitude in your hearts.

Scripture Prayer: Communion

God in presence,
Powerful, masterful creator of moments of praise and worship instilling in the soul of the prayerful. Beautiful God of peace and calm bringing bindings between believing and worshipful WORDs alive in Christ surrounding. Holy Wisdom is Your Name above all names.

Spirit in connection,
Hands holding, eyes closing trusting flows of worship. Lapping waves of HOLY harmonies hovering all around. Shower adorn and lift the sparking Spirits of truth that show sweet sounds in delight. Precious is your name singing in vibrant unison. Melodies and harmonies placed by angels resonate through us to echoes in Heaven.

Jesus in God
Jesu, Messiah, Savior. Teacher and friend director. You right me when I'm wrong. You comfort when I long. You are my one and true long song. True praise be in your name. Your angels speak acclaim. Your friends, protect and guide me to the end. You are present when we speak Your name in praises.
TBTHT 3N1

NOVEMBER 14

PrayStill

2 Corinthians 12:9
But he said to me, "My grace is sufficient for you, for my power is made perfect in weakness." Therefore, I will boast all the more gladly about my weaknesses, so that Christ's power may rest on me.

Scripture Prayer: Tears

Lord God
Pure truth, pure love, pure hope, pure light pure desire. Straight and narrow and unbending. Perfect are the ways of the Lord. Rightful and just is the robe of God glory. A tiny glimpse of God humbling holiness is worthy for a lifetime. Awesome brilliance is eternally glistening.

Holy Spirit
You sift and glean the truth. Your thrashing floor splits away the dust. You are strong and able to dismiss away the fear. You crucify my pride and I am left empty. Selfish me no more. My center turns to you. My rest is in knowing you can handle all my woes. You are healer, masterfully strong and exchanging all my bad for good.

Christ Jesus
You are mighty and strong, and I am weak and needy. With you is life. With me there is pain and anguish and agonizing. My defects and woes overwhelm me. Who am I really fearing. Where else can I turn? My redeeming joy is in knowing Your key of love unlocks and releases me to freedom in Your presence. You transform my grief to grace. You mold my mire to mercy. Your perfect love lifts my longing to plateaus of resting calm in peace abiding.
TBTJC Son of God and man.

NOVEMBER 15

PrayStill

1 Chronicles 29:13
Now therefore, our God we thank thee, and praise thy glorious name.

Scripture Prayer: Name

Father God
Voice of creation. Beautiful sounding love supplanting all in peace. Magnanimous name of eternity sung out in incense rising. The name of mighty reverence. The name above all names. The author of hearts and souls resounding praise.

Mother Spirit
All glory laud and honor bubble out for You. These beautiful gems and scents and flavors vibrate up to Your tabernacle of graces, loves and mercies. Adorning sounds relish in in exultation in the breath beating pulses of Glory. Consecrating words form rejoicing rivers in meander. Always back to You. Always all for You. Exalting is excitement for enticing.

Son of God Jesus
All things come from on high. All things are prospered in abundance back through You. The sound of Your name, Jesus, on my lips, melts my soul to submitting pastures of pathways and fields. Complete is my wholeness in the embrace of your magnificent name, Jesus. Fill me with your radiant obedience.
TBT LORD CHRIST

NOVEMBER 16

PrayStill

James 1:19-20
You must understand this, my beloved: let everyone be quick to listen, slow to speak, slow to anger; for your anger does not produce God's righteousness.

Scripture Prayer: Hearing

Lord God
Immutable, unchangeable, forever glorious King of all creation. True revealer Lord of all that is good and all that can be good. Good God, Creator of time and life and space and justice. Holy Holy Holy and magnificent is the Creation Chamber. Adorning principalities flourish from every aspect. Emanating beams of imminence flow forever.
Holy Spirit

Convict my soul to Your placid. Reign me into Your field supining. Strengthen and channel all fear and lashing out to be deflected to the pit. Reflect away the incoming fiery darts. They are not mine. I did not create them. They are easily dismissed. Teach guide and protect my thoughts words and deeds to channel outward for your Glory. Take away the fearful anger of unacceptance. Dismiss away my unrestful uneasy distress. Barometer my thought of curses mumbling to Your directed energy to change for goodness. You are mighty strong and absorbent. I am easy and free to give all unease to You.
Christ Jesus

Let my hearing be understanding. Let my understanding be true. Overflow my understanding in repeating parallels of perspectives alive in light and light in burden. Relax release and renew my soul heart and mind spirit. Help me to receive Your precious peace passing surpassing and impassing my flesh life abiding. Seal my lips with coals transforming. Make my desire to speak only in Your glory. Emotion my balance in your embrace. All is well with my soul.

TBTHS conviction of truth.

NOVEMBER 17

PrayStill

Psalms 27:1
The Lord is my light and my salvation; whom shall I fear? the Lord is the strength of my life; of whom shall I be afraid?

Scripture Prayer: Aware

Glorious God
Redeeming Rock and Firm Foundation. Buttress holding fortresses of strength against all earthen gravities. Only the light is left in and around the tabernacle tents of righteousness. Strength and light reflect everything good and assuring. The enemy is lost and NOT found. Only Angels of pure bright light fill the sanctuary. Pure goodness pours reigning out immaculate.

Loving Lord Spirit of light,
I know my fears are my weakness. My darkness creeps in. You save me with Your warning light. The fear of loss, gain, or change I offer up to You. My fear of being judged by peering peers is set right knowing You. I answer just to You. My fears of idols of perfections breaking, are made perfect handed up to the altar. I flaw in my wandering worry of outcomes. Make me worthy to be free. I fear my mistakes causing remorse regret and reservation. My renewal is in reverent release of all of this inside fear to you. My worries, doubts and fears are exchanging for Assurance conviction and Faith. My fear is no more in the light of your love. You are transforming light.

Selah

Justifying Jesus

My fears of illness death and dying You know more than anything. You walk right through death dark stings. You take away the sins of the world. The gravity of the valley and the shadows cannot retain you. Lord God, Jesus, grant me strength to relinquish and replace my earthly fleshly fears with reverent abiding faithful fear in your obedience. I humble my fear away to you. You catch and carry my distress away. You place me in laydown up to faithful abiding fields.

TBTHT Faith of nations.

NOVEMBER 18

PrayStill

Psalm 3:3
But you, Lord are a shield around me, my glory, the One who lifts my head high.

Scripture Prayer: Arise

God of Heaven,
High above all kingdoms. Utmost authority. True WORD of Life and protector of ways. Law of justice watching over. Life giving Jehovah instilling floods of light colors tingling in calm and warming numb. Joyful souls are overwhelmed.

Spirit of Redemption,
Invisible forces of love uplift and sift my soul. I am dead without you. You are my lifeline lighting. You enlighten and lift my heart to beat for You. You raise my eyes to see like You. You feed my feeling senses to elevation. I am free from the mire and free to be with You always. Keep me above myself. Let me dwell in your glorious presence.

Jesus Rescuer,
Compassionate binding warrior of setting things High and Right. Your hand pulls me from the ditch half dead. I cannot help myself. You lift me to heal me in High fallow soils in Heavenly plains. You set me true and right. My foes are in defeat. You keep protection in advance. You settle my account for all my tomorrows. I lift my eyes to knowing You never let me go. You are masterful redeemer of souls.
TBTJC Lord God Savior

NOVEMBER 19

PrayStill

James 2:17
So faith by itself, if it has no works, is dead.

Scripture Prayer: Motive

Father God
Showering grace and mercy from Heavens to earthly havens. Faithful is the ever flowing always present supply of riches. Grateful in graces and moving in mercies are the towers of the great tabernacle of choirs singing words fed by angels. Attraction to the light and sound and sensations are the receivers of faith flowing faith always in all ways. Heavenly works prevail.

Holy Spirit
Great is Your faithfulness. Let my faith be spoken into life by You. Turn my assurances into Your desiring actions. Alert and ready me always to intercede and welcome on Your behalf. Your guiding watchful ways spark works of joyful noises and happenstance. Willingly the offerings flow back to the Glory Throne resounding Joy's echoes. Faithful works are flowing faithfully in works back to You.

Jesus Revealer,
You know my intent. You see my repent. You find me and set me on my way. Let my works from inside me be from You that inspires me, reflecting a beautiful desiring. Take the brag of my rag offering, and my pride aside loosening, to know all of my good works are from You. Let Your Kingdom be my FAITH works motivate. I want to work for The Eternal King of kings in body and Spirit Alive.
TBTJC LORD of lords

NOVEMBER 20

PrayStill

Psalm 100:1
Be joyful in the Lord all you lands; serve the Lord with gladness and come before his presence with a song.

Scripture Prayer: 100

Praise God
From whom all blessings flow. All things bright and beautiful. Praise Him all creatures here below. All things great and small. Praise him amongst the Heavenly hosts. All things wise and wonderful. Praise Father, Son and Holy Ghost. The Lord God made them all.

Holy Spirit come fill this place and be free. Fall fresh in your graceful mercies and guide me to you. I hear and know You are near. The echo directs and reflects me to the light of Your countenance. Draw me near, supplant my fear, and let me stare upon your mist of fresh. You move like waves of dancing flames. My gaze is bound to you.

Selah

Jesus Song
Hear my prayer. Jesus song sing along. All glory laud and honor lifted up on high. Meet me where I am and let me draw on nigh. The whole world sings Your praises. All to your great name. In you I find my comfort, in You, my life, You reign.
TBT God on High

NOVEMBER 21

PrayStill

1 Corinthians 1:4,5
I am always thanking my God for you because He has given you such free and open access to His grace through your union with Jesus the Messiah. In him you have been made extravagantly rich in every way. You have been endowed with a wealth of inspired utterance and the riches that come from your intimate knowledge of him.

Scripture Prayer: Forever Grateful

Lord God
Master of mercies, maker of redemption. Loving God attracting everything. Beautiful in every blessing. Glorious in every giving. Wise in every weaning in waning and waxing. Tender in every touch and careful in every conviction. Blessed be the name of the Lord.

Jesus God
How grateful and thankful and glorious that you live in us. My wealth is in your presence in others. Oh, to see you manifest in many friends. You pour through like no other can explain. Majesty honor glory and riches are the fruits of your inclinations pouring in and through us. Holy is your Name. Rightful are Your gifts. Precious is your abiding.

Spirit God
Blossoming fervent colors and rhythmic sounds the scent of your presence fills and sustains. Taste and see you are good indeed. Beyond the expectation beyond the present knowing. Forever increasing and showing is the breath mist you pulse into life. Lavishly excessive, brightly expressive, powerfully impressive, You make the world smile in joy.
TBTHT 3N1

NOVEMBER 22

PrayStill

Psalm 100:4
Enter his gates with thanksgiving and his courts with praise; give thanks to him and praise his name.

Scripture Prayer: Give

Holy Spirit of Thankfulness
Reign in me. Grace this place with honors in giving. Fill me with love of thankfulness in the small things. Overwhelm me with love in great gratitude of blessings in great things. The gifts are presenting in abounding. Let my actions steep thankfulness in the giving and receiving. May breaths of praises be speaking. May Songs of harmony praise forever.

Jesus Christ Son of man
How grateful for this masterpiece vessel that does millions of things in a glorious day. In my sleep I am healed in my rest you are revealed in my life you give purpose and value. I am taken to places, revealing in graces, how thankful I am for You. Designs to give praise through each of Your days. Singing glory to Your name in Your way.

God of Giving,
Living light shining on all the beauty of creation. Creator of moments of thankful. Loving owner of celestial Heavens beyond all comprehension. Loving giver of Holy love in individual signing personally given freely. Showering reigning, light sustaining always remaining, Heavenly God, Father, Son.
TBTHT 3IN1

NOVEMBER 23

PrayStill

James 5:7
Be patient, therefore, beloved, until the coming of the Lord. The farmer waits for the precious crop from the earth, being patient with it until it receives the early and the late rains.

Scripture Prayer: Instill

Restful Spirit
Many moments are Yours. Take me from my angst and deliver me to your peaceful place. Fill me with hope and encouragement. Let my idle time in the want of my idols of accomplishment pleasure and self-seeking be set aside. Move me out of the way to fill Your way in me. My slowdown of me is Your increase in surround me. In you I want for nothing else. Nobis Pacem.

Lord Jesus
Make my vessel soil fallow ground for Your WORD's rebirthing. Define and refine Your WORD in me to growing desires suckling for more of Your WORD. The peace of the pace of revealing is in Your moments. All the preparation falls into place at Your sudden revealing. Resign me to the continuing awareness of Your design. Nobis Pacem.

AbbaMamma God
Firmament of Heaven's foundation. Gardens of growth and nurturing flow from the plateaus of faithfulness. Great and glorious are the courts of nutrients filling to blossom the vessels of humbling love in waiting. The peace is in the patience waiting. Nobis Pacem. TBTG Heavenly designer

NOVEMBER 24

PrayStill

John 8:12 When Jesus spoke again to the people, he said, "I am the light of the world. Whoever follows me will never walk in darkness, but will have the light of life."

Scripture Prayer: Saving Light

Jesus Lord
Clear vision of truth. In the pitch-black mire of darkness there is no hope. Help and save me. Take my darkness away. Your lightning strikes my soul to life. My direction is to You. Basking in Your glory light is the joy of knowing. You are the hope and the way and the truth and the light. Darkness falls to dust.

Holy Spirit
Blessing in the presence of Your glow. Fill and feed the light of the WORD. Let my foolishness be perishing to dust. Let my power reside in Your powerful beams of the cross saving and protecting me from prides gasp of darkness. Lift in light the truth victorious.

Lord God
Immutable ageless transcending Spirit. Master of space and time and truth and light. Focus of the eternal WAY of ages. Gravitating standard above and beyond all compare. Ideal of ages removing earthly desires for Heavenly rewards.
TBTJC Light of the world.

NOVEMBER 25

PrayStill

1 Corinthians 6:19

Scripture Prayer: Surrender

Great God
Breath of life. Beautiful beat in the rhythm of life. Formation of life and light and all that is so. Days of creation lavishly design and give life to all that has breath. Let every breath be praise to you. God creation lifts God exalting on high. Mighty is the breath of Your name on life.

Holy Spirit
In and around, in surround from the ground, is your inescapable watchful way. I am filled with your presence, the true godly essence that holds me through out every day. Conviction infection is built in protection that guides and returns me from stray. The love You imbibe me sets me to beside me so You can fill me and stay.

Lord Jesus
Temple of God in pristine. How awesome that You sacrifice all for everyone willing from beginning to end. Generations of nations cry out for your redemption. Only through You am I personally offered forgiveness and healing. Lord Jesus, King above all kings, speak to my still listening heart and take all of me away. You heal my every moment. You fill me with your goodness and mercies. You make me complete.
TBTHT 3N1

NOVEMBER 26

PrayStill

Luke 18:16
But Jesus called for them and said, "Let the little children come to me, and do not stop them; for it is to such as these that the kingdom of God belongs."

Scripture Prayer: Nurture

Father in Heaven,
Present and protecting the faithful children of earth. Holy Mighty and Loving is the WAY of Heaven on earth. Watching over the Israel in each of us, Never tarrying never sleeping never dismissing. Always present, always focusing, always welcoming. No power formed against can ever prevail. Child Faith reigns Holy.

Lord Jesus
Rising conquering Son.
Protector of youthful faith. In You is the key to childlike faith stronger than any other force. You never let go You always feed and nurture the new. You always welcome my trust and belief in all ways. With you watching over is peace in palaces of protection. Fill this believing heart in persisting youthful faith.

Spirit Jireh,
Fresh and restoring are your mercies every day. Every moment you take me to the place of assurance that comforts my soul. I am weak and needy. You are loving and protecting. You watch for my protection. In you there is no foe. I rest and return in Your inheritance.
TBTHT 3N1 Sing a new song

NOVEMBER 27

PrayStill

Jeremiah 33:3 Call to me and I will answer you and tell you great and unsearchable things you do not know.

Scripture Prayer: Enduring

Righteous God
Saving branches of limitless knowledge pours out. Forever revealings sustain new teachings. More and more and more is always showing in understandings. Teachable learning gives way to verdant pastures of peace beyond knowing.

Holy Spirit
Falling fresh falling new raising up in all to You. Word divine weaves into life and brings to light the new sunrise. Show me your ways I do not understand. Teach me Your truth. Come to my heart. Come to my mind. Convict my soul to Your voice I incline.

Jesus God
You find me in my ignorance you accept me in my shame. You meet me where I am and take me in your reign. Over me you give me everything I need. With you there is no question. With you there is no need. You fulfill my desires and understandings. You are teacher divine. I cry out! Your servant is listening. Help me with my unhearing.
TBTJC Lord God of riches in righteousness

NOVEMBER 28

PrayStill

Colossians 3:23

Scripture Prayer: Alpha

Father in Heaven,
Maker and judge of all things reigning on the just and unjust. Reverence and sincerity line Your cloak and chambers. Special divine and alluring is the ways of words placing on hearts lips and souls of creation knowing.

Nurturing Spirit
Gusting winds work Your ways of love. love is in the work for You. Seeking knowing and loving You above all else is raising rising Heavenly praises. Harmony waves of reward lift lofts of elevation praise.

Jesus King,
Eternal son of man and God. Always alive, always the truth always the light. Dress me in your colorful clothes of kind and gentle and humble and patient. Working in your coat of many colors is inheritance today. Shine brilliance divine in all hearts.
TBTJC Always Present

NOVEMBER 29

PrayStill

Romans 10:10
For it is with your heart that you believe and are justified, and it is with your mouth that you profess your faith and are saved.

Scripture Prayer: Conviction

Lord God
Smiling sunrise over all who hear and abide. Patiently waiting for yes. Always welcoming, forever inviting, preciously accepting. Lord above all other desires.

Holiest Spirit of life,
Insisting is your WAY in me. Your justice measures my steps. Your righteousness rules my height. Fill this place with more of You. Let your presence be forever on my lips.

Jesus Savior
You are my Lord and Savior.
May the words of my mouth the thoughts of my mind and the inclinations of my heart be always acceptable in thy sight my strength and my redeemer. You are justice feet and holy lines alive. You know me before I ever do. My confident conviction is in you.
TBTG forevermore adorning

NOVEMBER 30

PrayStill

Luke 6:37
Do not judge, and you will not be judged. Do not condemn, and you will not be condemned. Forgive, and you will be forgiven.

Scripture Prayer: Circle

Father God
Love and rest and instruction from above. Masterful teacher revealing. Creator and owner of all that is. Always knowing desires intentions and motivations.

Blessing Spirit
Reflect back my thoughts and feelings. Bring me to the place of peace. Erase away my unease for the day that roots me away from You. Let me know and process away the pride stool I climb on. Take away my judge condemn and resent so I may accept love and forgive.

Jesus Christ,
Lord of my strength and rest. Before I think of another let me be right with You. You make me ok so I can be ok to others. Only in you is this true. By myself alone I want to be greater than. With you I can serve in love forgiveness truth and understanding.
TBTHT 3N1

DECEMBER 1

PrayStill

Romans 8:37
No, in all these things we are more than conquerors through him who loved us.

Scripture Prayer: Victory

God of life,
Eternal ever living ever loving solution. Master designer of life through with and in all things. Everlasting is the holy signature that clears away decay. Groans turn to grand songs of glory.

Living Spirit
You show the veil in flesh is perishing for all to see. In You, life conquers death. The groans of these bones come alive in song rejoicing. You Lord are the preordained destiny, the victor of sheepish pain and fear and doubt and worry. Nothing comes between to separate Your love life eternal.

Lord Jesus
Successful victor conquering rising Son. Son of man healing, Son of God revealing. Maker of Heaven and earth. Beautiful appealing, the heart You sign in sealing, this home in you is worth? Forever in eternity, white glory in divinity, affinity for all proclaiming souls.
TBTG Eternal

DECEMBER 2

PrayStill

Jeremiah 33:14-15
The days are surely coming, says the Lord when I will fulfill the promise I made to the house of Israel and the house of Judah. In those days and at that time I will cause a righteous Branch to spring up for David; and he shall execute justice and righteousness in the land.

Scripture Prayer: Adventure

Lord God
Preordained King of kings, saving grace through faith. Lord of lords blessing earth. Eternal WORD alive in life. Face of forever planted in the fields of riches and glory. Loving abiding WORD speaking True life.

Spirit of Creation,
Masterful is the foretelling story of your love forever present. Seeking Your wisdom reveals truth already there. Always preparing to continue You magnify Your everything in all things. Countless and inescapable is Your truth.

Jesus Awaiting,
Open arms in preparation of glory, right, true and just. Preparing heir of inheritance awesome and powerful. Beautiful is Your loving way. All things come of Thee all things return to Thee. Blessed be the name of the Lord. Forever here to love and adore.
TBTG Author of Salvation

DECEMBER 3

PrayStill

Nahum 1:7
The Lord is good, a refuge in times of trouble. He cares for those who trust in him.

Scripture Prayer: Hope

Heavenly Father
King of justice, peace and patience. Redemption to those repenting. Shield of rock and fortress of right. Patient and persistent for acquiescence. The essence of goodness prevailing reflecting all glory and honor and truth.

Spirit of Fire,
Consuming presence, forever whispering in the silence of dancing flames. You counsel in might. Your love extinguishes all my fear. You bring to full circle and fall into place the keys that unlock to freedom. You lighten my deafening darkness away. You bring me back to Jesus son of God.

Jesus Lord
Let me draw near to you and believe and never thirst or hunger. Convict my soul to rely in You. Help me to do good and godly. Give my faith in you conviction beyond my understanding. Let my heart mantra always pulse for you.
Jesus, Prince of peace, You take away the fears of the world. Merciful mighty and true are You.
TBTG Divine

DECEMBER 4

PrayStill

1 Corinthians 13:2
If I have the gift of prophecy and can fathom all mysteries and all knowledge, and if I have a faith that can move mountains, but do not have love, I am nothing.

Scripture Prayer: Author

Heavenly God
Nurturing parent. God eternal in evolving love. Continually revealing, never concealing. God of anticipation awakenings. Worthy of all the foundations of love praise.

Holy Spirit
Motivate my intention. Let it be Your invention. Take away my pride I hide in. Weave WORDs of showering love. Honor respect and dignity flow freely from Your altar. You intercede in love's grace pastures to melt away the crystal ice.

Lord Jesus
In everything I am learning You teach me right and wrong. You place the pieces of intent upon my soul. The treasure gifts are Yours. Let me revere how Your love magnifies thirst in warming light.
TBTG Divine Almighty.

DECEMBER 5

PrayStill

Isaiah 2:4b
They shall beat their swords into plowshares, and their spears into pruning hooks; nation shall not lift up sword against nation, neither shall they learn war any more.

Scripture Prayer: Victory

Awesome God
Loving conquering Father of peace. Highest in exaltation is the name of The Lord above all names. Nothing can overcome or prevail against the law of love. Masterful designer reigning freedom.

Holy Spirit
Settling peaceful silence is in the lullaby of love that quells to calm. You take my struggle and battle to exhaustion surrender. In the calm the enemy is gone. You reign supreme in preordaining victory counsel.

Lord Jesus
You take away the prideful sin of the world. You call me friend and make me friend. My Rock my Shield my Salvation. The healing and weaving relation of peaceful nations abiding in the Lord of all victory.
TBTJC prince of peace

DECEMBER 6

PrayStill

Isaiah 2:17
The haughtiness of people shall be humbled, and the pride of everyone shall be brought low; and the Lord alone will be exalted on that day.

Scripture Prayer: Advent-tageous

Smiling God
Genuine genius of Joy. Masterful maker of merriment and laughter. Sole source of soul food. Grandest gifting God of glory. Reverence and righteousness fill Heaven and earthly courts.

Jesus With us
Root of Jesse, spurning equal justice. Solstice of light, maker of right, designating truth in the WORD. Delight in the way, truth and mercy obey, Your face in flesh assure US. The intimacy of God in us, is with us and for us and over us, loving is LORD Jesus.

Powerful spirit of love
Uncontainable and forever sustainable your Ways fill harkening hearts. Content always arriving in making life thriving for fountains of glory and joy. The turn and repent in the Son that is sent, the powerful meek humbling noise.
TBTHS powerful boldness inviting.

D E C E M B E R   7

PrayStill

Psalm 22:28-29
To him alone all who sleep in the earth bow down in worship; all who go down to the dust fall before him. My soul shall live for him; my descendants shall serve him; they shall be known as the Lord's forever.

Scripture Prayer: WORDs

God light,
Beacon of life eternal. Sole proving soul redeemer. Gate of entry and exit. Keeper eternal of all that is. Magnifier of mercy saving the desperate seeking solstice. Solution of Sacrifice that heals all that ails. Beautiful savior WORD in light alive.

Spirit Anticipate,
I come to... in the darkness... I am alone... Fear and doubt and worry surround me.. Tears melt from my eyes... I need You Lord... now more than ever. The storm rages...
Selah – breath Silence, Spirit light,
I sense your presence... I hear your voice. I sense your touch... Your key in me warms me to light... You revive me... Swords of your WORD principle cut away the darkness...
Selah - brate
You rescue me... You lift me from my mire and resuscitate... There is hope... There is light. there is breadth in Your breath of life...Your calm still pasture warms my melting heart... Innate is Your key in my soul.

Jesus light,
Selah - bration. Precious Saving grace in nation generation...Song of songs.

You clean the dust in bowing down. Take this life in turn around. Set me free and set me right. My hope in you is all that's right. You make my night return to light. Never let me go... Darkness sees the light and light cuts in through dark. From dark I see the lightness. Light sees not into dark.

TBTJC Light of the world

DECEMBER 8

PrayStill

Proverbs 13:6
Righteousness guards the person of integrity, but wickedness overthrows the sinner.

Scripture Prayer: Shields

God Protector,
Lover of souls, giver of freedom, gifter of free will to choose. Reigning ruler of righteousness. Parent of protection guarding love and mercy. Welcoming Deity of following faithful believers.

Spirit Revealer,
Show me where I slide, show me where I slip. Show me how to live, surely guard my lips. Let Your seed inside me grow to shadows on the tares, let the love light shine and wipe away the fears. Across the cross to die, You overthrow my sin. Your diadem You wear, forever always wins.

Jesus Redeemer,
Walk me away from wickedness. Correct all my mistakes. Take me to the place of peace where...
guards drop, and worry stops, and freedom reigns my soul.
Guide me, carry me, take me away, a closer walk with You, with me You always stay.
TBTHT 3in1

DECEMBER 9

PrayStill

Proverbs 5:21
For your ways are in full view of the Lord , and he examines all your paths.

Scripture Prayer: Truth

Lord God
Maker and judge of all things. Inescapable author of all that is, all that passes, all that will ever be. Knowledge of True knowledge, purest in refinement. All knowing, all showing, all growing from Thee.

Spirit Revealing,
Lord spirit, you weave my soul to truth. You are showing me my growing groans to where I go astray. In your chamber you show me the WAY. You bridle me before I am born you set me on my way. My sight is blurs in intoxication of the world. I am walking to aloneness.

Jesus Redeemer,
Carry my aloneness away.
I am forgiven. You know my errors you know my misdeeds you love my broken pieces back to peace. You know All secrets. You reveal the reviving truth. Lord Jesus, you know me and show me the wife of my youth.
TBTJC Lord of all

DECEMBER 10

PrayStill

Roman's 13:10
love does no wrong to a neighbor; therefore love is the fulfilling of the law.

Scripture Prayer: Alarm

Father God
Ever living never changing Commander of Law and Prophets, power and justice and honor and glory pour out from the breath of Heaven and glorify all that is. Rightful righteous and true is the loving Rock of ages.

Spirit Divine,
Help me to pray peace, speak silence, and caress calm. Let me give goodness and cheerfulness. Let me honor with praise and respect. Let my soul submit to you in peace so I can be peaceful to others. Guard the thoughts word and deeds of my moments. Keep my harm alarm watchful over words and ways.

Jesus Friend,
You smile at me in contagion. My ears and eyes rise as my cheeks smile back. Show me and teach me in each occasion to be a kind deliverer. Let me bring brightness. Let Joy reign over. Enlighten my lips to lavish love on others. Make me a bold beacon of your flagrantly flourishing forgiveness. Pastor me in Your pastures of righteousness. To Thine be the glory conquering King Jesus.
TBTHT 3IN1

DECEMBER 11

PrayStill

Jeremiah 29:13
You will seek me and find me, when you seek me with all your heart.

Scripture Prayer: Courageous Assuring Trust

Master Creating God
Maker of stars in Heaven's expanses. Intimate whisper of souls. Guardian author of relation and understanding. Conviction of innate relation. Light of all.

Beautiful Spirit Divine
Holy and only in thee do I find reprieve. I do love You with all my heart. I do love You with all my soul. I do love You with all my strength. I do love You with all my mind. Complete me where I am falling short. Love my emptiness to joy.

Holy Lord Jesus
Brand Your mark on my heart to always lead me to Your pasture. Carry my soul to freedom. Focus all my thoughts and ways for Your glory. In You alone is my strength. Jesus God Counselor, all of me and my unknowing rests in Thee.
TBTG in Trinity Perfect Peace

DECEMBER 12

PrayStill

Mark 8:34

Scripture Prayer: Supplicant

Holy God
Beautiful alluring and attractive is the Good News calling. Precious ringing Savior tune for anyone listening. Pathway divine and true. Forever increasing in transforming renewal surrender.

Holy Spirit
Maker and judge of all decisions known and unknown. Masterful mosaic of all.
Hearts cry out for you. Minds obsess for You. Souls define in You.
In knowing You the WAY comes true the pleas are humbly beholden. Golden in Your consuming fire is eternal refining.

Holy Jesus
Corporal crowd Creator and Director. Powerful is the enchanting fascination for Your living breathing WORD alive in flesh.
I am empty you are free, all I need is you in me. Take me out and take me in. From me to you this life begins. love alive in You I thrive. Save me from self-will inside.
TBTHT insistent and persistent in surrounding love.

DECEMBER 13

PrayStill

1 John 4:20
If anyone says, "I love God" and hates his brother, he is a liar; for he who does not love his brother whom he has seen cannot love God whom he has not seen.

Scripture Prayer: Hume Man

Loving God
Showering all that is in goodness. Washing all that is in dust. Firm rock foundation of clay propitiation. Overwhelming presence dismissing prideful sin. Author of the abiding, true love.

Loving Jesus
Son of God, delicate as the firstborn day, Jesus. Powerful as the first risen son, Jesus. As powerful as the redemption of all creation, Jesus. Soul abiding, light inciting, lover of believing seekers. Lord of humble healing contrition, Jesus. Divine Brother of love.

Loving Spirit
Humble me to lift the weak. Strengthen me to meet the meek. Esteem me just enough to love elite. In you the relation never sleeps. You love me first, you give me thirst, to love each as You do. The spirit fills and overflows, In You there is pure love.
TBTHT 3in1 showering love.

DECEMBER 14

PrayStill

Matthew 5:16
In the same way, let your light shine before others, so that they may see your good works and give glory to your Father who is in Heaven.

Scripture Prayer: Gifts Reflecting

Great God
Goodness kindness and light with us. Spring star of hope and faith. Beam of Heaven revealing truth within. Magnificent magnifier in the light in the world. Light seed of all the worshiping fruits of the Earth.

Great Jesus
Precious and delicate sparkling ember of the world. You ignite the realm of creation. Overflowing gifts from "with us" pour out freely in worshipful adoration. The gifts you give, to let us live, are reflective back in chorus. The light abounding wraps surrounding knowing You are for us.

Great Spirit
Wonderful warming ray. You show us light and take the night and turn fright into lightness. It passes through right back to You and sets to live in rightness. Light with us is born in trust, the covenant shining brightly.
TBTJC Light of Creation.

DECEMBER 15

PrayStill

Matthew 15:28
Then Jesus answered her, "Woman, great is your faith! Let it be done for you as you wish." And her daughter was healed instantly.

Scripture Prayer: Nobis Pacem.

Lord God of lords,
The peace that places all understanding. The calm surpassing all knowledge. The pure cure still before during and after the white waves tearing. Renewing restoring reawaking God in pastures of delight. All welcoming mighty healer.

Lord Spirit of lords
Remembering surrendering to moments of grace. Tighten and righten my Spirit to you. Remedy my soul. Ease my thinking to unblinking to You. Resolve my angst and anguish agonizing. Badge scars prove miracle Healing marks. In the storm raging is peace remaining, assurance without end. Army angel's watch and tend and mend my broken to You.

Lord Jesus of lords
Peace like a river flows healing balms anointing in the touching of your robe. The imbibing of your WORD brings warming love communion. The abiding in Your ways offers obedient stillness in Heaven sanctuaries. Heal me, free me, take me to your place. Pastor me, reveal in me, the grace upon Your face. My rest is You.
Sing Selah

PEACE
Prepare. ing
Eternity. ing
Accept.   ing
Christ's
Embrace. ing
TBTJC Suddenly Healer Almighty.

DECEMBER 16

PrayStill

Ephesians 6:12
For we do not wrestle against flesh and blood, but against the rulers, against the authorities, against the cosmic powers over this present darkness, against the spiritual forces of evil in the Heavenly places.

Scripture Prayer: Whose Am I

Lord God Almighty
WORD of the Heavens and world, in all of the names and places. Creator of conversion to the ever living, ever loving Lordship. Author of mind renewing holy allegiance. love tending light inclination in masterful persuasion.

Impounding Holy Spirit
Perpetual victor of all my contentions. You always win. You always let me exhaust my will to Your surrender. Precious whole and True is the assuaging to your protective renaming light. I am yours. You lift revive and name me Yours. Inescapable love shields watch over dominions.

Jesus with us,
Make me suited for your palace courts. Dress my deeds words and thoughts to tune to Your light. Let darkness slip away. Assure my faith to know, You never let me go.
Pacem Selah

You are my protection you give me direction you guardian my soul from within. You choose my selections with finite inspection, my rest in Your wrestle, You win. In you is the power to face and to shower and reign victory over sin.

TBTHS guardian of Holy principalities reigning.

TBTJC Strong Standing firmament truth.

TBTG Righteousness, ready in peaceful good news with shields of faith.

TBTHT Ambassadors of freedom.

DECEMBER 17

PrayStill

Isaiah 6:2
Above him stood the seraphim. Each had six wings: with two he covered his face, and with two he covered his feet, and with two he flew.

Scripture Prayer: Seraphim

Lord God
Cross of redemption, Altar of altering, mercy seat of forgiveness. Blessed be the name of the Lord. Holy Holy Holy to Adore. King of kings, Lord of lords, Prince of pleasing peace.

Lord Holy Spirit
Revealer of all truth. My sight and path are yours. You cleanse the thoughts and inspirations of my soul key. You alter and renew me and make me always yours. My eyes are cleansing, my feet are sending, in you is all forgiving. East and West remember no more. Not left or right, my lips secure. White wings wash away.

Jesus Savior,
Son of man, born to earth divine the land. Heaven angels all surround. The barren land to turn around. Hope is born in God in Son, the world redeems the victory won. Angel escort, angel fire, cherubs cleansing pure desire.
TBTJC Lord of lords with us.

DECEMBER 18

PrayStill

Isaiah 26:9
My soul yearns for you in the night; in the morning my spirit longs for you. When your judgments come upon the earth, the people of the world learn righteousness.

Scripture Prayer: Awakening

Lord God Yahweh
Igniter of fires of passion for truth. Song of conscious embrace of the dawn. Beautiful refreshing brilliance of the Day. Glorious author of the celestial canopy creating signature mosaic moments of grace throughout.

Holy Spirit Ruach,
Breathe life and light into my rising. Seep your love embracing into my first thought. Rejoice and sing my voice in praise to The Eternal King that patience abides in. Reveal in awareness all that is and will be. Humble my ear to hear and channel to true and righteous self judgement.

Jesus Peaceful Counselor,
Grace and gratitude surround Your Throne. You take away the sins of the world. Your Church weaves through the world of nations. Help me to hear and abide in the obedience and faith of fathers knowing Your justice prevails. Open my hearts eyes to seek, see and know that all is for Your Glory, Yashua, Jesus with us.
TBTHT 3in1

DECEMBER 19

PrayStill

Romans 1:16
For I am not ashamed of the gospel, because it is the power of God that brings salvation to everyone who believes: first to the Jew, then to the Gentile.

Scripture Prayer: Adorn

Heavenly Father
Heavy blessing of joy to the world. Weight of grace descending for all to see. Glorifying Goodness brightly shining Truth to reveal. Sanctified in pure attractive adoration. Persistent God of all creation.

Heavenly Spirit
Ignite in me the faith contagion that amplifies Your Holiness. Consume my desire to mutually encourage, believing in your powerful redemption. Fall fresh on me to show in confidence the peace, joy and blessing of Your magnificent love interceding. Take selfish worship to selfless praise, and worship!

Heavenly Jesus
Sweetness is the ring in my soul to Your name. Never shame, never dis grace, always Praise and Glory. Adorable beautiful precious NAME eternal is Your Story. Every knee bowing, tongue confessing, raises Your name to holy.
TBTHT 3N1

DECEMBER 20

PrayStill

Matthew 1:21
She will give birth to a son, and you are to give him the name Jesus because he will save his people from their sins."

Scripture Prayer: Emanuel

God with us,
How beautiful the gift of life. How precious the invitation. How glorious the anticipation. How overwhelming the grace and bright calm silence. Blessed is the name of the Lord Jesus.

Holy Spirit with us,
Within, between and surrounding, Your presence presents where grace and mercy meet. The freedom of the joy of life ignites the flames of holy dancing. The rhythms of love abounds in resounding choirs. The harmony chorus praises, glories to the Lord most high.

Jesus with us,
Alpha arriving in angels escort, brilliant divine and captivating. Precious small and tender attraction of ages past and present. Powerful name, strength for the lame, humble servant from on high. Beautiful Savior, redeeming creator, salvation for all drawing nigh.
TBTHT 3in1 Emanuel

DECEMBER 21

PrayStill

1 John 4:9
This is how God showed his love among us: He sent his one and only Son into the world that we might live through him.

Scripture Prayer: Naissance

God in communion,
Thoughtful caring and endearing lover of souls. Rich and luscious in treasure and gifts of glory. Extravagant beyond belief. Forever revealing pieces of more through seeking.

Spirit in communion,
Intimate abiding hovering over patient allure. You reveal awesome. Your love lingers. Your thought energy tarries. You are perpetually waiting for wills to align and transform water into reverent wine. Speak to my soul, peace through Your Spirit.

Spirit of Jesus
Help me to see the infant child of peace in all I encounter. Friend me to your focal point to use gentle delicate and loving ways about all relations. Let the babe in nurture, beholden to the future, be the ambassador of truth and light and life.
TBTJC Door of relations knocking.

DECEMBER 22

PrayStill

John 3:17
For God did not send his Son into the world to condemn the world, but to save the world through him.

Scripture Prayer: Mercy and Grace

God so loving,
God giving everything. Giver of hope and meaning in knowing. Retriever of the believers and grantor of eternal life. Imperishable in eternal glory providing. Freedom and redemption reign overflowing to abounding believers.

Spirit so giving,
Heir inheritance in the pulse and beat breath of life. Counselor of my soul You are. You are my obsession possession. You make my confession regression turn to a freshen progression that answers the question whose am I? Joy giver, life giver author of my soul.

Jesus so redeeming.
Your free grace I cannot earn. Your free mercy I cannot repay. Your redeeming my deserving is the beautiful sweetness in the middle of your loving grace and mercy. The two spices of life that flavor estimable sense in my soul.
TBTG who makes us right

MERCY
My
Errors
Receive
Christ's
Yearnings

GRACE
God's
Riches
At
Christ's
Expense

FAITH
Father
Always
In
Thy
Hands

DECEMBER 23

PrayStill

Isaiah 7:14
Therefore the Lord himself will give you a sign: The virgin will conceive and give birth to a son, and will call him Immanuel.

Scripture Prayer: Miracle Wonder

God Prophecy,
Planter of signs throughout the ages. Grower of belief in the unseen. Harvester of the witnessing beliefs of acquiescing understanding. Little planted inexplicables lead to greater explainable evidences of holy intervention.

Spirit Holiness
Faith is growing, Lord I believe. Lord I receive. Your holy intervention I perceive in my life. You sustain me and remain in me and give me life. I am guarded and protected. I see numerous signs of your unexplainable wonder in living presence. Easy miracle easy relief, home of Heaven inviting belief.

Jesus Purity
Son of God descending pure holiness. Dependent love for those who can believe and conceive your birth, your scars, your eternity. Your Glorious gorgeous greatness gives faith to the doubt. I let out a shout. You turn my world inside out, to the begotten line though Joachim. Holy and blessing is the name of the Son of God with us, Jesus.
TBTHT 3IN1

DECEMBER 24

PrayStill

Luke 2:13

Scripture Prayer: Peace Favor

Heavenly Father
Author of salvation alive in the hope of nations. Beautiful light of life. Way of the world delivering suddenlys to all with receptive senses. Beautiful annunciator. News of renewal in joyful peace and hope.

Holy Spirit
Powerful is Your assurance in hope conviction. You wrestle me to resolve. Immediately my doubts and fears are gone. You rock me to rest in faith of knowing. Strike me in lightning and thunder demarking. Signs from Heaven are signed in my soul key believing.

Jesus Savior
Yashua, Joshua saving nations. Mighty healer sent to overcome the dark shadow valley in chaos and light the way to redemption! Tender mild and calm is the ever present always open welcoming invitation to surrender all to Your gentle delicate infant love.
Rest x 7
Selah - stialisation
TBTJC Awesome Redeemer

DECEMBER 25

PrayStill

Luke 2:11
To you is born this day in the city of David a Savior, who is the Messiah, the Lord.

Scripture Prayer: Alpha Omega

Heavenly God
Miracle of life, the answer to strife, the balm that cures the ailing world. Revelation of Genesis and deliverance in a day. Masterful calm silent force of peace quelling the shadows of unrest. The desperate cries of centuries silence at the sounding Messiah.

Holy Spirit
Breath of life's first cry. The whole world in ages cries out for redemption. The Peace to the unrest, the Calm for the fearful, the love that cures the hate. You are the forgiveness mercy that heals revenge. All in the precious breath of a delicate God as a newborn. The day the sun stops to see the Yashua awesome wonder of God as man from before to after.

Jesus Christ
Savior Messiah. Savoring savior of souls made tender and mild for all the world to see how to care for others. Jesus you have me believing all is for the infant Christ in others. Open my eyes to see know and love the beautiful Messiah you are in everyone.
TBTJC Lord King and Counselor of Peace.

DECEMBER 26

PrayStill

Matthew 4:4
Jesus answered, "It is written: 'Man shall not live on bread alone, but on every word that comes from the mouth of God.'"

Scripture Prayer: Diligence

Father God
Guardian protector of principle deceits. Shield and cure for tempting songs of sins short reward. Magnificent WORD of truth victorious over all distraction from the way. WORD seeing, WORD speaking, WORD applying thoughts and deeds. WORD, the vaccine cure for all thought of wandering stray.

Son, Jesus
Beautiful commander of defeating evil all day long, every day, throughout, with walking in the WORD. Jesus master in victory, rooted in imbibing the holy scriptures in divine comprehension. Jesus focus, Jesus with us, Jesus lead us not astray, Jesus with us, Jesus lead us, Emanuel to stay!

Spirit Holy Ghost,
Sprinkle the letters of God goodness that makes up the conviction of what right and true is. Grant me the ever living, ever loving, everlasting, discerning to know Your way in truth and love and Choice. Appetite my thirst in WORD rather than guttural pleasures. Feast my fast to You.
TBTHT WORD alive

DECEMBER 27

PrayStill

Colossians 1:16
For in him all things were created: things in Heaven and on earth, visible and invisible, whether thrones or powers or rulers or authorities; all things have been created through him and for him.

Scripture Prayer: Son Supreme

Indivisible God
The invisible first creator of time and space. The beautiful author of life eternal. The gorgeous supplier of all that is and will be. Precious, holy and true, forever lasting Lord of all.

Invisible Spirit
Presence of calm in peace and around. You take me in sound and turn me around. I am lost and then found, You are my King.
Master of full circle surrounding astound. You find me in drowning and place my firm ground. I am right side up and upside down. You are my King.

Immortal Jesus
Inventor of all that is. Supernatural and supreme. Heaven and earth are signed in your authorship. You reign almighty. Everything that is, is for and through you the greatest I AM ever.
TBTJC Savoring Savior.

DECEMBER 28

PrayStill

Revelation 21:5a
And the one who was seated on the throne said, "See, I am making all things new."

Scripture Prayer: Alleluia

Praise God
Glory of all things, places and people returning to the creation throne. Beautiful restoration of aging dust. Fresh new and never ending is the Glory Holy Holy Holy. All blessings flow from Thee.

Chant Holy,
Chant Holy Holy Holy divine.
Spirit divine, spirit entwined Spirit of revealing all newness.   Precious in bold forever to hold, inspiring the joy of the ageless. Friend of the meek, humble who seek, in drawing nigh to God with us.

King Jesus
Merciful mighty and True, for every rapture in new. The love of your land, spoken in hand, is delivering old to renew. In you all gain is sustain. Your deliverance has no refrain. The beauty within, is the love you spread out. Heavens calling is all through You.
TBTG Judge of all things

DECEMBER 29

PrayStill

Luke 6:35
But love your enemies, do good to them, and lend to them without expecting to get anything back. Then your reward will be great, and you will be children of the Most High, because he is kind to the ungrateful and wicked.

Scripture Prayer: Triumph

Mamma Abba God
Richest adorning healing love all around. Fire shields that melts away pain fear and anger. Beautiful refinement of pillars of sin dust into ponds of beautiful pastures. Glistening attractive, listening to the sound of contagious choruses of choirs praising the conversion to goodness.

Holy Spirit
Guaranteed anticipation of victory rules the masses. You are uncanny in convincing the wicked to desperation deliverance. No more anger no more fears, no more revenge no more tears. No more cursing, no more rude, no more living attitude. Only in Your light is wrong made right, day cuts through night and wicked washes away.

Lord Jesus
How many cheeks must turn? How much forgive to live? How many extra miles, how many persuading smiles? Let light attraction entertain beautiful child angels. Let love overcome darkness. Let good be good. Let me only see the possibility of redemption in all. Smile all the while and the child of God melts millstones of wrath to ornaments of kindness.
TBTJC Lord of Loving Kindness

DECEMBER 30

PrayStill

1 John 4:15
If anyone acknowledges that Jesus is the Son of God, God lives in them and they in God.

Scripture Prayer: Perfect Abiding!

Lord God
In around, over under, forever with. Sovereign reigning Supreme. Perfect Holy and True Everlasting. Leader of Righteousness, Master Creator! Lover of True Submission. Lord God Almighty, Lord God, King of kings.

Lord Jesus
You make the simple clear, you whisper in my ear, I never am to fear. In me is You, no room for pride. In You is me all in abide. My selfishness slips all away, into your arms I'm born to stay. Welcome in! and welcome stay! never ever let me stray. Shepherd rod blocks my way, shepherd staff returns astray.

Lord Spirit
Even when I am alone, with me is Your call to home. Forever beckon my delight, my faith in You has turned to sight. I know you are my Lord divine you tell me I abide your vine. Breath in me my life to live, in You my life I truly give.
TBTHT 3N1

DECEMBER 31

PrayStill

2 Corinthians 5:17
Therefore, if anyone is in Christ, the new creation has come: The old has gone, the new is here!

Scripture Prayer: Reconcile

Imploring God
Exchanging righteousness for sin to make bad lives good. Cleansing advocate renewing. Altering Eternal love for earthly stewardship. Master tent maker of souls. Home of homes, Dwelling of dwellings, Castles of dominions. Abiding pasture abode.

Surrounding Spirit
Clothe me in your majesty, take away my decay. Renew my robe in Your palace of fine linens and silks and furs. Comfort my soul. Make my life lie down to Your allegiance in my soul. Take me to your place inviting. Set me on your WAY reciting, all to hear and see your truth.

Awesome Jesus
Beautiful exchanging reconciler. Wonderful stand in counselor. You design my value in You. You take away my sins in this world and wash me clean. My tent of life is empty for renew in You. My home is in You alone. My soul is for you to own. Every day awakes anew, the resounding review of the new life in You. Blossom me as your new fruit.
TBTJC Savior Divine

DAILY SCRIPTURES

1-Jan	Psalm 19:14	1-Feb	Colosians. 3:2	1-Mar	Luke 10:3-4
2-Jan	John 6:35-36	2-Feb	John 15:5	2-Mar	Luke 10:33
3-Jan	Proverbs 16:3	3-Feb	Philipians 4:8	3-Mar	Luke 11:2-4
4-Jan	John 14:13	4-Feb	1Peter 1:22	4-Mar	Luke 11:24-26
5-Jan	Psalm 2:13	5-Feb	Isaiah 43:19	5-Mar	Luke 12:6-7
6-Jan	Matthew 2:2	6-Feb	Hebrews 11:6	6-Mar	Luke 12:48b
7-Jan	Matthew 5:6	7-Feb	Psalm 143:10	7-Mar	Luke 13:12
8-Jan	Isaiah 55:6-7	8-Feb	Mathew 7:7	8-Mar	Luke 13:32
9-Jan	1 John 5:14	9-Feb	Philipians 4:6	9-Mar	Luke 14:16-18a
10-Jan	James 1:5	10-Feb	Luke 13:18-19	10-Mar	Luke 14:26, 33
11-Jan	Jeremiah 17:7	11-Feb	Luke 1:3-4	11-Mar	Luke 15:4
12-Jan	Colossians 2:2	12-Feb	Luke 1:59-60	12-Mar	Luke 15:20
13-Jan	Romans 10:17	13-Feb	2 Timothy 1:7	13-Mar	Luke 16:8-9
14-Jan	Lamentations 3:22-23	14-Feb	Hosea 2:15	14-Mar	Luke 16:24
15-Jan	Matthew 11:15	15-Feb	Luke 3:16b	15-Mar	Luke 17:1-2
16-Jan	Matthew 16:	16-Feb	Luke 3:23-24, 38	16-Mar	Luke 17:31-33
17-Jan	James 1:17	17-Feb	Luke 4:13	17-Mar	Luke 18:7-8
18-Jan	Matthew 7:24	18-Feb	Luke 4:18-19	18-Mar	Luke 18:35-38
19-Jan	Colossians 2:7	19-Feb	Luke 5:6	19-Mar	Luke 19:5-6
20-Jan	Genesis 1:27	20-Feb	Luke 5:18-19	20-Mar	Luke 19:39-40
21-Jan	John 15:2	21-Feb	Luke 6:20b, 24	21-Mar	Luke 20:25-26
22-Jan	Hebrews 10:24	22-Feb	Luke 6:31-32	22-Mar	Luke 21:16-19
23-Jan	Ecclesiastes 4:9-10	23-Feb	Luke 7:33-35	23-Mar	Luke 22:3-4
24-Jan	Galatians 5:22-23	24-Feb	Luke 7:38	24-Mar	Luke 22:44-45
25-Jan	Hebrews 4:16	25-Feb	Luke 8:1-3	25-Mar	Luke 22:52b-53
26-Jan	Matthew 18:22	26-Feb	Luke 8:44	26-Mar	Luke 23:10-11
27-Jan	Isaiah 11:6	27-Feb	Luke 9:17	27-Mar	Luke 23:26
28-Jan	Philippians 2:12	28-Feb	Luke 9:28-29	28-Mar	Luke 23:44-46
29-Jan	Mark 9:35	29-Feb	Joshua 10:12	29-Mar	Luke 24:4-5
30-Jan	Psalm 119:66			30-Mar	Luke 24:13-14
31-Jan	Psalm 86:5			31-Mar	Luke 24:40-42

1-Apr	Ephesians 2:10	1-May	Acts 14:27	1-Jun	Matthew 13:33
2-Apr	Acts 3:16	2-May	Acts 15:8-9	2-Jun	Matthew 13:36
3-Apr	John 3:16	3-May	Acts 15:28	3-Jun	1 Samuel 3:1b
4-Apr	Hebrews 11:6	4-May	Acts 15:38	4-Jun	Psalm 44:6
5-Apr	John 14:2	5-May	Acts 16:15	5-Jun	Matthew 13:55
6-Apr	Matthew 6:6	6-May	Acts 16:16-17	6-Jun	Ecclesiastes 3:1
7-Apr	Mark 4:31	7-May	Acts 17:6-7	7-Jun	Matthew 14:20
8-Apr	Acts 4:31	8-May	Acts 17:19-21	8-Jun	Matthew 14:27
9-Apr	1 John 2:15-16	9-May	Acts 18:26	9-Jun	Galatians 3:28
10-Apr	Acts 5:7	10-May	Acts 19:24-25	10-Jun	Genesis 3:9
11-Apr	Acts 5:14-15	11-May	Acts 20:29-30	11-Jun	Acts 11:23
12-Apr	Acts 5:38-39	12-May	Acts 21:12-13	12-Jun	Matthew 15:34
13-Apr	Proverbs 17:9	13-May	Acts 22:6-7	13-Jun	Galatians 5:14
14-Apr	Psalm 145:18	14-May	Acts 23:6	14-Jun	Psalm 74:16
15-Apr	Acts 7:51	15-May	Acts 23:12	15-Jun	Galatians 6:2
16-Apr	Acts 8:1	16-May	Acts 24:5	16-Jun	Matthew 17:4
17-Apr	Acts 8:13	17-May	Acts 25:12	17-Jun	2 Corinthians 5:7
18-Apr	Acts 8:29-30	18-May	Acts 26:24	18-Jun	Matthew 17:20b
19-Apr	Acts 9:18-19	19-May	Acts 27:9-10	19-Jun	Numbers 11:9
20-Apr	Acts 9:39	20-May	Acts 28:24	20-Jun	Matthew 18:7
21-Apr	Acts 10:15	21-May	Matthew 12:22-24	21-Jun	Matthew 18:20
22-Apr	Acts 10:28	22-May	Matthew 12:33-34	22-Jun	Matthew 18:21
23-Apr	Acts 10:46b-47	23-May	Matthew 12:47-48	23-Jun	Psalm 90:17
24-Apr	Acts 11:16-17	24-May	Matthew 13:29-30	24-Jun	Mark 4:38
25-Apr	Acts 11:29-30	25-May	Galatians 5:9	25-Jun	Luke 1:66
26-Apr	Acts 12:7	26-May	Matthew 13:37-39	26-Jun	Matthew 19:26
27-Apr	Acts 12:22-23	27-May	John 3:8	27-Jun	Matthew 20:10
28-Apr	Acts 13:7-8	28-May	Matthew 13:51-52	28-Jun	Matthew 20:26
29-Apr	Acts 13:40-41	29-May	Matthew 13:55-56	29-Jun	Ezekiel 34:11
30-Apr	Acts 14:11-12	30-May	Matthew 14:8	30-Jun	Psalm 33:10
		31-May	Matthew 14:16-17		

1-Jul	Mark 5:36	1-Aug	Judges 3:12	1-Sep	Job 10:4
2-Jul	Matthew 21:12-13	2-Aug	Matthew 27:55	2-Sep	Psalm 15:5-7
3-Jul	Matthew 21:32	3-Aug	Psalm 69:22	3-Sep	Matthew 6:24
4-Jul	Matthew 5:46a	4-Aug	Matthew 28:15	4-Sep	Psalm 26:11
5-Jul	Matthew 22:14	5-Aug	Psalm 51:3	5-Sep	Job 14:16-17
6-Jul	Matthew 22:21b-22	6-Aug	2 Peter 1:13-14	6-Sep	Job 14:16-17
7-Jul	Matthew 22:37-40	7-Aug	Acts 3:6	7-Sep	Job 19:25
8-Jul	Mark 6:4-6a	8-Aug	Acts 3:25	8-Sep	Acts 13:32-33
9-Jul	Matthew 23:11-12	9-Aug	John 1:46	9-Sep	Proverbs 22:1
10-Jul	Matthew 23:23-24	10-Aug	Acts 4:13	10-Sep	John 10:27
11-Jul	Matthew 23:27-28	11-Aug	Psalm 87:6	11-Sep	John 10:31
12-Jul	Psalm 18:17	12-Aug	2 Samuel 18:33	12-Sep	Job 30:3
13-Jul	Psalm 16:7	13-Aug	Psalm 89:1	13-Sep	Job 31:21-23
14-Jul	Matthew 24:36	14-Aug	Judges 13:3	14-Sep	Philippians 2:5-7a
15-Jul	Mark 6:26	15-Aug	Galatians 4:4-5	15-Sep	Job 38:1-4
16-Jul	Matthew 25:3-4	16-Aug	Psalm 105:1	16-Sep	Proverbs 1:20-21
17-Jul	Matthew 25:25	17-Aug	Acts 7:23	17-Sep	Psalm 56:10
18-Jul	Matthew 25:45	18-Aug	John 5:5	18-Sep	John 12:9-11
19-Jul	Matthew 26:6-7	19-Aug	1 Kings 3:9	19-Sep	John 12:24
20-Jul	Romans 12:12-13	20-Aug	Acts 7:59	20-Sep	John 12:31-32
21-Jul	Psalm 30:2-3	21-Aug	Psalm 124:7	21-Sep	Matthew 9:11-13
22-Jul	Mark 6:31a	22-Aug	John 6:13	22-Sep	Acts 17:18
23-Jul	John 20:16-17	23-Aug	Job 1:21	23-Sep	James 4:1
24-Jul	Romans 14:7	24-Aug	Psalm 91:11	24-Sep	Luke 3:9
25-Jul	Matthew 20:26b-28	25-Aug	Job 3:20	25-Sep	Luke 3:21-22
26-Jul	Romans 15:1-2	26-Aug	John 6:64	26-Sep	Psalm 82:2
27-Jul	Psalm 40:1-2	27-Aug	John 6:56	27-Sep	Psalm 116:8
28-Jul	Psalm 139:6-7	28-Aug	Job 6:14	28-Sep	Acts 19:23
29-Jul	John 6:8-9	29-Aug	Job 7:19	29-Sep	Genesis 28:12-13
30-Jul	Matthew 27:24	30-Aug	Psalm 18:2	30-Sep	James 5:19-20
31-Jul	Romans 16:17-18	31-Aug	John 8:45		

1-Oct	Acts 20:24	1-Nov	Wisdom 3:1	1-Dec	Romans 8:37
2-Oct	Psalm 97:7	2-Nov	Proverbs 22:4	2-Dec	Jeremiah 33:14-15
3-Oct	Luke 5:29-	3-Nov	Luke 12:34	3-Dec	Nahum 1:7
4-Oct	Hosea 6:6	4-Nov	Ruth 1:16	4-Dec	1 Corinthians 13:2
5-Oct	Luke 6:26	5-Nov	Psalm 139:14	5-Dec	Isaiah 2:4b
6-Oct	Luke 6:27-28	6-Nov		6-Dec	Isaiah 2:17
7-Oct	Mark 10:14b-15	7-Nov	Matthew 6:3	7-Dec	Psalm 22:28-29
8-Oct	Psalm 106:3	8-Nov	1 Corinthians 12:4	8-Dec	Proverbs 13:6
9-Oct	Luke 7:14-15	9-Nov	Proverbs 27:17	9-Dec	Proverbs 5:21
10-Oct	Psalm 130:4	10-Nov	Hebrews 11:1	10-Dec	Roman's 13:10
11-Oct	1 Peter 1:8-9 NIV	11-Nov	Matthew 28:18,19	11-Dec	Jeremiah 29:13
12-Oct	Luke 8:8	12-Nov	1 John 3:1	12-Dec	Mark 8:34-
13-Oct	Psalm 144:3-4	13-Nov	Colossians 3:16	13-Dec	1 John 4:20
14-Oct	Romans 12:2	14-Nov	2 Corinthians 12:	14-Dec	Matthew 5:16
15-Oct	2 Samuel 7:22	15-Nov	1 Chronicles 29:13	15-Dec	Matthew 15:28
16-Oct	Psalm 19:14	16-Nov	James 1:19-20	16-Dec	Ephesians 6:12
17-Oct	Psalm 25:14-15	17-Nov	Psalms 27:1	17-Dec	Isaiah 6:2
18-Oct	Psalm 119:11	18-Nov	Psalm 3:3	18-Dec	Isaiah 26:9
19-Oct	Psalm 37:4	19-Nov	James 2:17	19-Dec	Romans 1:16
20-Oct	Psalm 51:12	20-Nov	Psalm 100:1	20-Dec	Matthew 1:21
21-Oct	Philippian 4:8	21-Nov	1 Corinthians 1:4,5	21-Dec	1 John 4:9
22-Oct	Proverbs 22:6	22-Nov	Psalm 100:4	22-Dec	John 3:17
23-Oct	Psalm 55:22	23-Nov	James 5:7	23-Dec	Isaiah 7:14
24-Oct	1 Peter 5:7	24-Nov	John 8:12	24-Dec	Luke 2:13-14
25-Oct	Luke 10:29	25-Nov	1 Corinthians 6:19-20	25-Dec	Luke 2:11
26-Oct	Luke 6:27-28	26-Nov	Luke 18:16	26-Dec	Matthew 4:4
27-Oct	Hebrews 4:12	27-Nov	Jeremiah 33:3	27-Dec	Colossians 1:16
28-Oct	1 Peter 4:8	28-Nov	Colossians 3:23-24	28-Dec	Revelation 21:5a
29-Oct	Roman's 12:1	29-Nov	Romans 10:10	29-Dec	Luke 6:35
30-Oct	Psalm 47:6-7	30-Nov	Luke 6:37	30-Dec	1 John 4:15
31-Oct	Ecclesiasticus 28:17			31-Dec	2 Corinthians 5:1